Kazuo Ohno's World

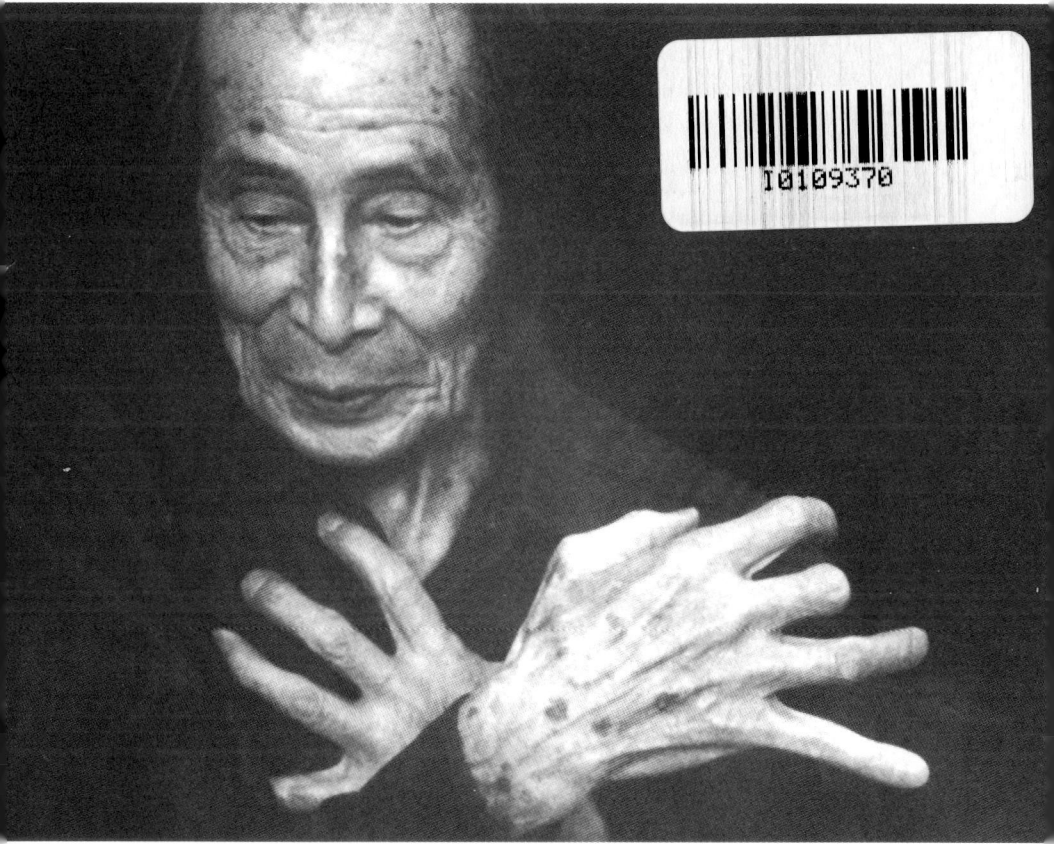

Kazuo Ohno's World from Without and Within

Kazuo Ohno and Yoshito Ohno

Introduction by Toshio Mizohata

Translated by John Barrett

Wesleyan University Press
Middletown, Connecticut

Published by Wesleyan University Press,
Middletown, CT 06459

Food for the Soul (大野一雄 魂の糧,
Tamashii no Kate, ISBN 4-8459-9997-8
C0074) originally published in Japanese
by Film Art Sha, Tokyo, copyright
© 1999 by Kazuo Ohno Dance Studio.

Workshop Words (稽古の言葉, *Keiko no
Kotoba,* ISBN 4-8459-9766-5 C0074)
originally published in Japanese by Film
Art Sha, Tokyo, copyright © 1997 by
Kazuo Ohno Dance Studio.

Library of Congress Cataloging-
in-Publication Data

Kazuo Ohno's world from without and
within / Kazuo Ohno and Yoshito Ohno ;
introduction by Toshio Mizohata ; trans-
lated by John Barrett.
p. cm.
Translated from Tamashii no kate and
Keiko no kotoba.
ISBN 0-8195-6694-2 (pbk. : alk. paper)
I. Åno, Kazuo, 1906– 2. Dancers—
Japan—Biography. 3. Dancing—Japan.
I. Barrett, John, 1958– II. Ohno, Yoshito.
Tamashii no kate. English. III. Ono,
Kazuo, 1906– Keiko no kotoba. English.
GV1785.O56K39 2004
792.8'092—dc22
[B]
2004041948

Supported by the Saison Foundation and
the Japan Foundation

5

(page i)
1. Kazuo Ohno, portrait, Florence,
1999. © Ulli Weiss.

(page iii)
2. Ohno in the workshop studio he
constructed next to his home in
Kamihoshikawa, 1960s. © Ohno
Dance Studio Archives.

(right)
3. Ohno on his way to take a seat in
the auditorium of Madrid's Centro
Cultural de la Villa for *Admiring La
Argentina,* 1987. © Sachiko Takeda.

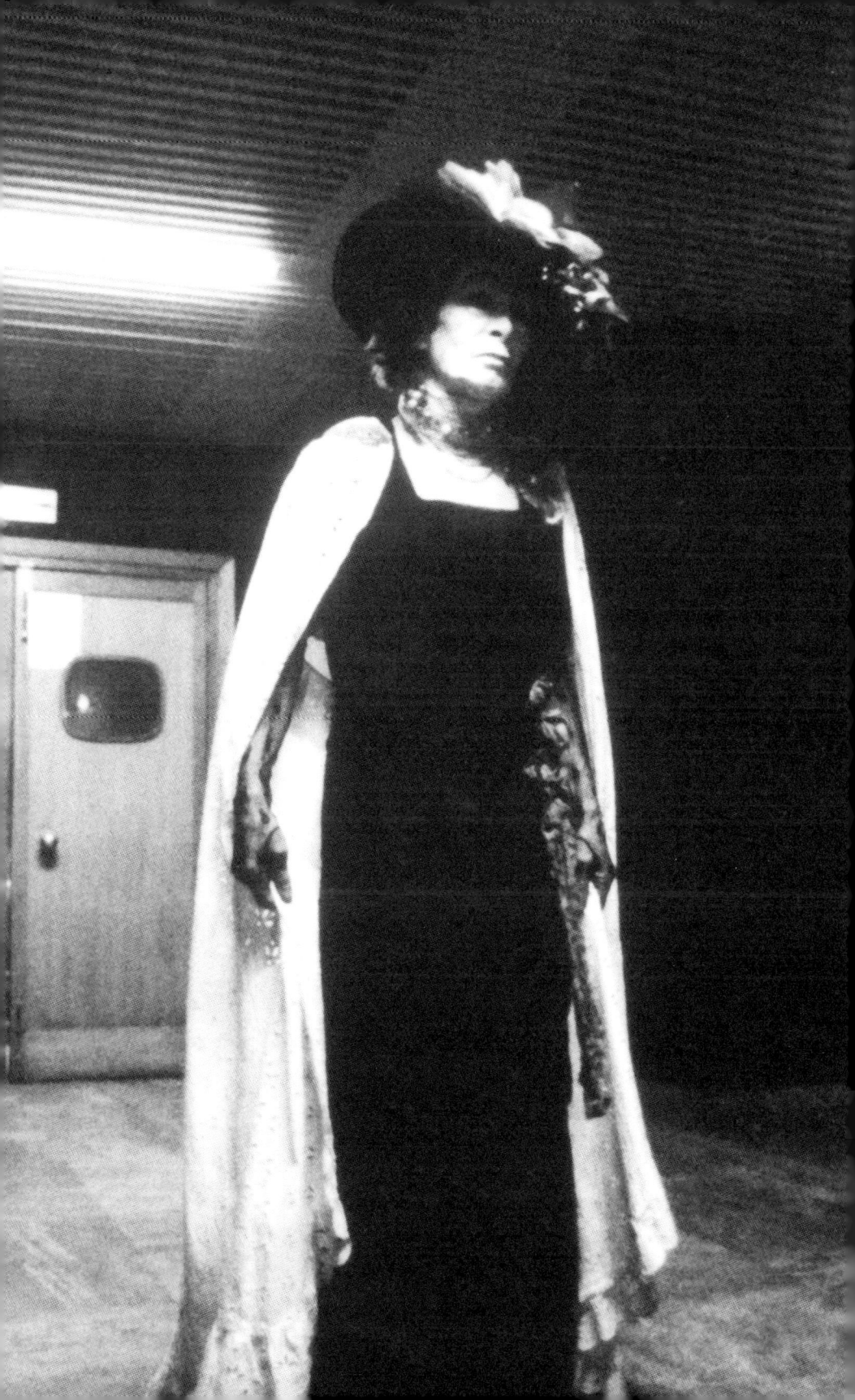

Contents

Contents

Illustrations

Illustrations

———————

Acknowledgments

On behalf of Kazuo and Yoshito Ohno and their manager, Toshio Mizohata, I would like to thank the following photographers for permitting the use of their photographs: Kenichiro Aita, Colomba d'Apolito, Alain Denis, Mitsutoshi Hanaga, Naoya Ikegami, Akira Inoue, Hideaki Ishizaka, Teijiro Kamiyama, Peggy Jarrell Kaplan, Xavier Lambours/Métis Images, Nourit Masson-Sekine, Carlos Menandro, Shin Mikami, Kaname Moriya, Nobutaka Murayama, Takayuki Nakatake, Hiroko Oishi, Tōjun Okamura, Philippe Pelletier, Jan Rüsz, Reiko Sawa, Hiroshi Takada, Sachiko Takeda, Hiroaki Tsukamoto, Jack Udashkin, Ulli Weiss, Haruhisa Yamaguchi, and Munesuke Yamamoto.

On a personal note, I am especially grateful to Toshio Mizohata for his ever present help; his knowledge and encouragement have been invaluable. I would also like to thank the Ohno family and Mina Nakamura Mizohata for their hospitality during my stays in Japan. Knowing that I could always count on the unwavering support of my mother, Rosaleen Barrett; my sisters, Geraldine and Mary; and brother-in-law, Dr. Tae-Hee Yoon lightened the task immeasurably. I would also like to thank Masaki Itoh, Koyo Konishi, Flora Margalit, Carol Martin, the late Yvonne Tenenbaum, and Tom Walker for their insights, comments, and criticisms of the translations. Finally, no words can express my gratitude to Kazuo Ohno. This truly remarkable man is a constant source of inspiration.

John Barrett

Translator's Note

All endnotes have been supplied by the translator, and the authors, Kazuo Ohno and Yoshito Ohno, bear no responsibility whatsoever for them. Photo credits and captions have been translated as in the Japanese editions, except where it was possible to supply additional information concerning the date and/or location where the photographs were taken.

A major problem in translating *Food for the Soul* (as also *Workshop Words*) is the large number of biographical references to both Kazuo Ohno and Tatsumi Hijakata, for which it is assumed that the reader understands the historical context. In a work of this complexity, containing numerous allusions to persons, events, dances, and other things not necessarily familiar even to the average Japanese reader, I thought it essential to add some explanatory or supplementary material in the form of endnotes. These notes often contain information that I hope is of direct relevance to a deeper appreciation of the texts. A certain amount of cross-referencing to *Workshop Words* has been provided in the endnotes to *Food for the Soul*. Otherwise, editorial interference has been kept to a bare minimum. Scarcely any cuts have been made, with the exception of a couple of sentences that seemed obscure in meaning, and several others that were somewhat superfluous in translation. Two chapters have been given different titles than in the originals.

For the transcription of Japanese words into English, I made use of the Heburn system of romanization, the system in widest use today. Japanese vowels are pronounced **a** as in f*a*ther, **e** as in b*e*d, **i** as in mar*i*ne, **o** as in s*o*lo and **u** as in m*u*le.

To be consistent with commonly accepted usage, I made exceptions in the romanization of certain words, notably *butoh,* and Kazuo's family name *Ohno,* where as a rule, a macron should be placed over the letter ō. Also, to avoid confusion, the original English performance titles are written as translated by the Ohno Dance Studio.

Given the fact that Kazuo and Yoshito Ohno, along with many other Japanese dancers mentioned in the book are internationally recognized performing artists, I have not followed the traditional order whereby the family name precedes the first name. Ease and clarity have been aimed at rather than formal consistency.

A word should perhaps be added with regard to the manner in which Yoshito Ohno refers to his father. In the Japanese edition of *Food for the Soul,* he consistently calls him Kazuo, or Kazuo Ohno, except when speaking of his father as head of the household. He never employs the personal pronoun in reference either to his father or to his one-time mentor, Tatsumi Hijikata. In translation, this usage has been modified somewhat for simplicity's sake.

For the convenience of the reader, Toshio Mizohata's postscripts in the originals have been modified slightly so as to serve as introductions in the translations.

Finally, with regard to Kazuo Ohno's spoken words: they have astounding vitality, subtlety, and scope. While invariably simple and colloquial, they nonetheless are extraordinarily rich and poetic, and do not in any way strain for effect. In fact, he unconsciously makes use of sound and word association in the manner in which a dancer of genius uses the body.

Such qualities obviously confront the translator with well nigh insurmountable difficulties, and I am under no illusion whatsoever that full justice has been rendered to the original. The task of adopting one's own native tongue more or less mimetically to a foreign text, particularly one that has been transcribed, is a contradictory one. As a translator, one is inevitably forced into making decisions about what to retain and what to lose. All that I can hope is that I may have offered English readers an approximate idea of the value of this great work.

John Barrett

Part I **Food
for the
Soul**

**Yoshito Ohno
Speaks about
Kazuo Ohno's
Dance, Life,
and Craft**

Introduction

Toshio Mizohata

Several years ago I decided to assemble and catalogue all the photographs Kazuo Ohno had accumulated since the outset of his stage career in the late 1940s. After first numbering each of the four thousand or so slides, stills, and prints, I indexed them under the following headings: name of the photographer, year in which the image was taken, and location and subject matter. As research for this present project got under way, the editors at Film Art Sha and I looked through that database in order to choose apposite images for several chapter headings we had in mind. We subsequently had Yoshito Ohno, Kazuo's son, look through our preliminary selection so as to provide a more penetrating insight into what lay beneath the surface of the favored images. *Food for the Soul*, the fruit of this collaborative effort, juxtaposes edited extracts of Yoshito Ohno's spoken commentary with 129 photographs documenting a career spanning almost six decades, stretching from the immediate aftermath of World War II to the dawn of the twenty-first century. Yoshito Ohno's words underpin these images, creating an authentic description of his father's dance, life, and craft.

Kazuo Ohno's fondness for having his photograph taken partly explains why he possesses more than four thousand slides and prints of himself. In fact, most of them were sent to him directly by photographers. A telling incident occurred back in the 1960s. Once, as Kazuo was rehearsing for an evening's performance, a crowd of photographers bustled their way down to the front row of the auditorium and, with a sudden burst of clicking camera shutters, started to shoot. Inwardly, he was delighted by this unexpected intervention, for it hadn't been in any way stage-managed. When it came to the actual performance, however, Kazuo felt completely let down. He had secretly hoped for a repeat of that impromptu happening, but, as it turned out, not even a single photographer came.

Not only does Kazuo Ohno truly enjoy coming face to face with a camera, he also takes the image-making process seriously. Obviously, many diverse factors contribute towards the quality and impact of a photographic image, but it must be said that it is the dynamic force Kazuo Ohno triggers when facing a camera lens that ultimately determines the imposing results seen in this present book. Whenever a photographer visits the Ohno home to request permission for a photo session, Kazuo, without any ado whatsoever, ushers him into the rehearsal studio located at the rear of the house. He then starts to improvise on the spur of the moment, and, more often than not, continues to dance for the best part of an hour. He has neither need to prepare a costume or accessories beforehand nor to follow any specific choreographic motif. The setting for these impromptu performances might strike one as somewhat unusual, given that the audience is comprised merely of a camera lens and the operator's eye, while the performance itself is born in, and of, the moment. For what reason, then, does Kazuo Ohno dance? This is a pertinent question and can be readily answered in this instance if we consider the nature of Kazuo's rapport with photographers. Kazuo Ohno dances for the photograph. In front of the lens he is a complete natural. The images in this present work capture that reality; the camera eye witnesses the coming to life of *somebody else*.

The photographs chosen for publication are truly outstanding in how they expose his intrinsic character; at times they even seem more forceful than the everyday Kazuo Ohno we know. Long ago people were terrified if confronted with a camera; they were afraid they might lose their lives, or the spirit living inside of them, on having their picture taken. The criteria applied in compiling the photographs for this book reflect a similar bias. Our decisions were not made upon purely aesthetic merit as such but rather for how the images revealed and drew forth Kazuo's interior world. Our intention isn't to present the reader with a glossy photo collection. To navigate us through the depths of Kazuo Ohno's creative output and personality we had Yoshito Ohno—himself an acclaimed butoh performer—help us to decipher these images. With the aid of his commentary, this book attempts to explore his father's inner world by means of an in-depth analysis of the context in which the photographs were taken.

Yoshito Ohno's stage career was launched in 1959 when he participated in his father's fifth modern dance recital, which featured an adaptation of Ernest Hemingway's *The Old Man and the Sea*. In the same year he also danced the role of the young man in Tatsumi Hijikata's *Kinjiki*, whose title likewise was borrowed from a literary work, Yukio Mishima's novel *Forbidden Colours*. This groundbreaking performance was to be the first in a series of avant-garde happenings directed and produced by Hijikata and posthumously referred to as Ankoku butoh performances. Throughout the 1960s Yoshito took part in many of these events until withdrawing from the public eye—for sixteen years—following a solo performance at Tokyo's Kosei Nenkin Hall in 1969. At his father's request he made a comeback in 1985, joining him on stage in *The Dead Sea*, under Hijiikata's direction. This was to mark the beginning of a collaboration between father and son that continues until the present day.

In 1986, following Hijikata's sudden death, Yoshito began directing and producing his father's performances. In addition to assuming the roles of coperformer and director, he also, more importantly, became directly instrumental in the creation of Kazuo's performances. His proximity, in every sense of the word, to the roots of his father's dance undoubtedly facilitates him in this endeavor. The intimate commentary from which this book ultimately evolved is an eyewitness account by Kazuo Ohno's closest observer and critic.

In compiling the photographs we didn't attempt to catalogue them by performance, nor did we arrange them in any sort of chronological order. Instead, we separated them by what struck us directly, dividing them under loose concepts and tentative chapter headings such as *The Eye, Standing, Walls,* and so forth. The result, we hope, offers the reader an opportunity to explore and discover—rather than merely browse through an illustration of—Kazuo Ohno's universe. Several global adjustments were made before finally settling on what we considered to be three fundamental themes: Kazuo Ohno as a dancer, Kazuo in his day-to-day life, and the impact that the Spanish dancer La Argentina had upon him. As the project unfolded, it became increasingly apparent that these three distinct aspects of his life were inseparable when it came to casting light on his creative force as a butoh performer.

Food for the Soul is divided into four chapters: the first and second are based on Yoshito Ohno's analysis of how his father employs various parts of the dancing body and the specific functions they assume in performance; chapter 3 is devoted to certain key aspects of Kazuo's past and family history. The final chapter, which was intended originally as a separate publication, dwells on the making of his magnum opus, *Admiring La Argentina*. Here, Yo-shito Ohno provides a detailed description of the individual scenes and the work process involved in creating that watershed perform-ance staged in November 1977, which signaled Kazuo's return to the stage at the age of seventy-one after an absence of almost ten years.

Admiring La Argentina is performed in two acts, each composed of several distinct though interdependent scenes. The opening half consists of *Divinariane*, a solo dance that Tatsumi Hijikata especially choreographed for Kazuo in 1960, based on the pro-tagonist of Jean Genet's *Notre Dame des Fleurs*. It was revised for the première so as to contain two parts: *Divine's Death*, in which Kazuo symbolically dies instage, and *Rebirth As a Young Girl*. These two tableaux were later called *Death and Rebirth*. The title's explicit reference to death and rebirth summarizes Kazuo's stage career. The next sequence, *Daily Bread*, brings his audience face to face with his everyday reality. *The Marriage of Heaven and Earth* closes the first act on a meditative note. The second half consists of two scenes: *Tango* and *Finale*. Kazuo Ohno has performed this tribute to Antonia Mercé, more popularly known as La Argentina, on some 119 occasions throughout the world since its première in Tokyo in November 1977. The most recent presentation was dur-ing a retrospective series of his works at Yokohama's Teatro Fonte in September 1994. Because this solo performance requires him to dance for more than an hour, and because certain scenes de-mand the use of the entire scenic space, it hasn't been staged since. In answer to the frequently asked question whether Kazuo will again dance *La Argentina*, we fervently hope that he will do so, for we believe that this particular work conveys the very es-sence of a lifetime's work. While its framework may need to be modified, we are nevertheless convinced that Kazuo will one day continue to reincarnate the presence of La Argentina onstage. In-evitably, a performer must transform and reinvent himself over time. From its inception, butoh has been a living art and the es-sence of life is change. This book, we hope, bears witness to the indomitable spirit of change ever present throughout Kazuo Ohno's long career.

Food

for the

Soul

_____

The title *Food for the Soul* was inspired by *Daily Bread*, a scene from *Admiring La Argentina*, in which Kazuo appears on a silent stage, wearing nothing more than a pair of black trunks, his torso naked. He has always been a supportive and spiritual presence in all our lives and with each successive performance he continues offering sustenance to our souls. His dance itself has been nourished by the changes he has gone through in the course of his many lives, by his spiritual evolution as a human being, even by the physical fact of his growing old. Why, one might ask, does Kazuo Ohno continue to dance, or, why did he ever perform in the first place? He does so to remain alive. At seventy-one, he created his seminal work, and now, at ninety-two, he continues to grace the stage. This is no accidental occurrence; this is nothing other than his true nature manifesting itself. Age poses no barrier; Kazuo Ohno will continue to dance even on becoming a centenarian.

Food for the Soul might have well remained unwritten were it not for the generosity of the many remarkable photographers who kindly permitted the use of their work. We are deeply grateful for their cooperation toward the fulfilment of this project. We would like to take this opportunity to apologize to those photographers whose whereabouts we were unable to trace prior to publication. While every effort was made to trace the owners of copyright of photographs printed in this book, it was not always possible to do so. Any such copyright owner should contact the Ohno Dance Studio with regard to this matter. We ask readers to bear in mind that most of the photographs have been in Kazuo Ohno's personal archives for many years, in some cases even decades. Moreover, we were unable to credit those photographers whose photos were unsigned. We are indebted to them as we are to all of you.

Tokyo
12 July 1999

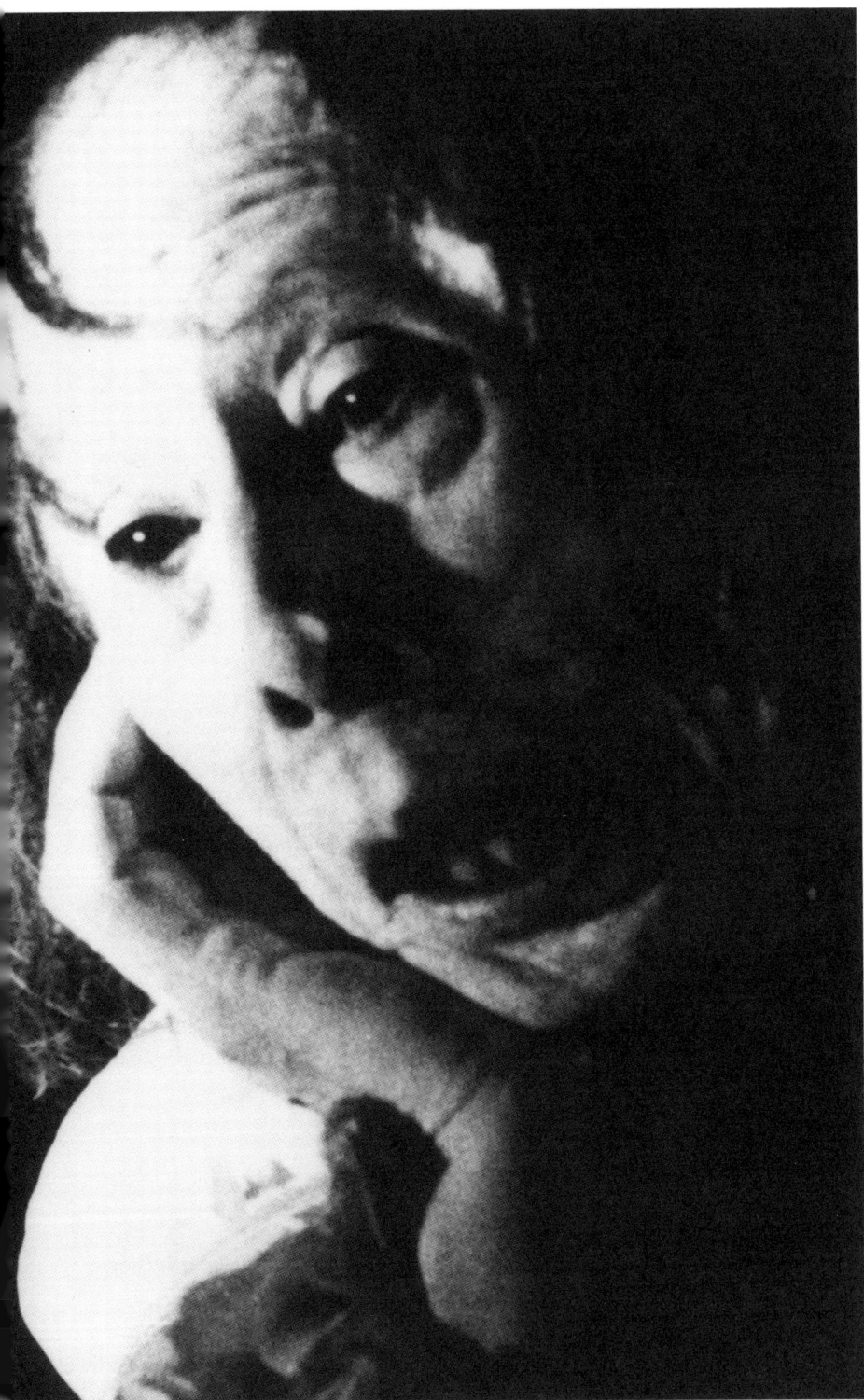

Chapter 1

The Dancing Body

The Face

Kazuo Ohno's facial expression, more than anything else, determines how he comes across to an audience. By observing his expression closely, one can fathom the depths of his movements. His face is simply incapable of masking his true state of mind and body. Speaking as a performer myself, when confronted with an expression as authentic as the one seen in this image (see fig. 4), I become keenly aware of my own limitations. The photographs in this book bear witness to Kazuo's unique working methods, methods that have enabled him to create such compelling facial expressions.

I should first of all mention that Kazuo delves into his creative powers long before setting foot in the workshop studio to prepare the framework for a performance. He does so with pen and paper, by continually writing down his thoughts and reflections. Moreover, he stimulates his imagination by reading poetry and haiku,[1] studying paintings and other visual artists' work during the long gestation period required in his creative process. He always has a black felt marker and regular-sized work journal at hand so that he can jot down any ideas and sketches that flash through his mind (see fig. 5). Based upon a deepened understanding of the poems, writings, and other sources at his disposal, his outpourings gradually lead him to recreate a blueprint of his inner universe on paper. In fact, it is this constant writing and erasing of notes, sketches, and impressions that enables him to embark on a psychological journey into the hinterlands of his inner life and ultimately discover a "new world" in the process. Kazuo has remarked that he's inclined to dream profusely during this very lengthy period of self-exploration.

On lying down to rest, Kazuo isn't altogether sure whether he's

(left)
4. Kazuo Ohno's inimitable expression. *The Dead Sea*, 1985.
© Kenichiro Aita.

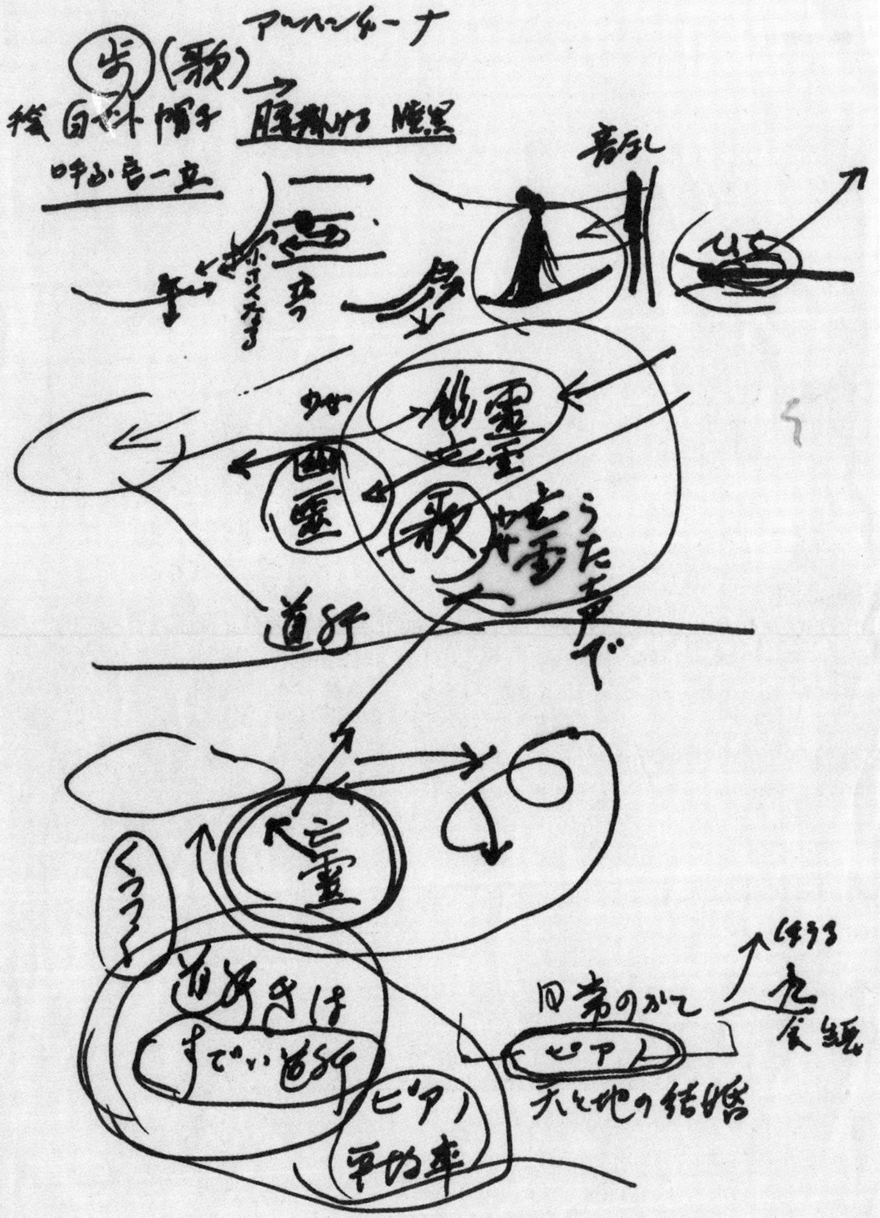

幽霊
歌
うた声で
道行
ピアノ
天と地の結婚

passively dreaming or if he's actively about to plunge into a dream world. In any event, an authentic expression reflecting the depths of his inner world only first becomes visible on his face after he goes beyond what we call "the dreaming phase" in his creative process. The intense facial expressions seen throughout this book would never have risen to the surface had he merely gone into the workshop studio to work on a set choreography. While such a rational and schematic approach might indeed be helpful in establishing a gestural vocabulary, his expressiveness would unquestionably lack both the depth and scope it possesses were he not first to undertake an exploratory voyage through psychic landscapes.

This persistent jotting down, erasing, and revising of notes allows Kazuo to mine the body's many different strata: physical, emotional, and spiritual. Considered in this way, language itself becomes an indispensable tool in creating dance. In practice, he only seriously begins to consider a performance's structure and movement after first probing deeply his subconscious memory with language. It is simply inconceivable that he create a dance without initially "excavating" his body with the written word. In stripping layer after layer of the self, Kazuo taps into the depths of his psyche. The marks of this inward-bound voyage are readily visible. His movements don't consist of a series of consecutive actions in time; they don't simply follow one another in a linear sequence. Instead, one has the impression that he thrusts deeper and deeper into each and every movement and step, as though he were moving within each movement. His performances generate the feeling of being drawn from a great depth in himself. By comparison, when most dancers—and I count myself among them—perform any given movement, it tends to stop dead at a certain point. This explains why my expression often comes across as lacking in something.

Preparation isn't solely confined to writing. While working on the groundwork Kazuo does occasionally step into our workshop studio to improvise. Being sensitive to music, he readily responds on listening to Chopin, Bach, or whatever music is at hand. At this particular point in the process, he's not unduly concerned with establishing a gestural vocabulary or deciding on the structure for the work in progress, but his movements nonetheless gush forth exuberantly like a flower about to burst into bloom. Indeed, his

(left)
5. Work notes for a repeat performance of *Admiring La Argentina*. © Ohno Dance Studio Archives.

1.

The Dancing Body

———

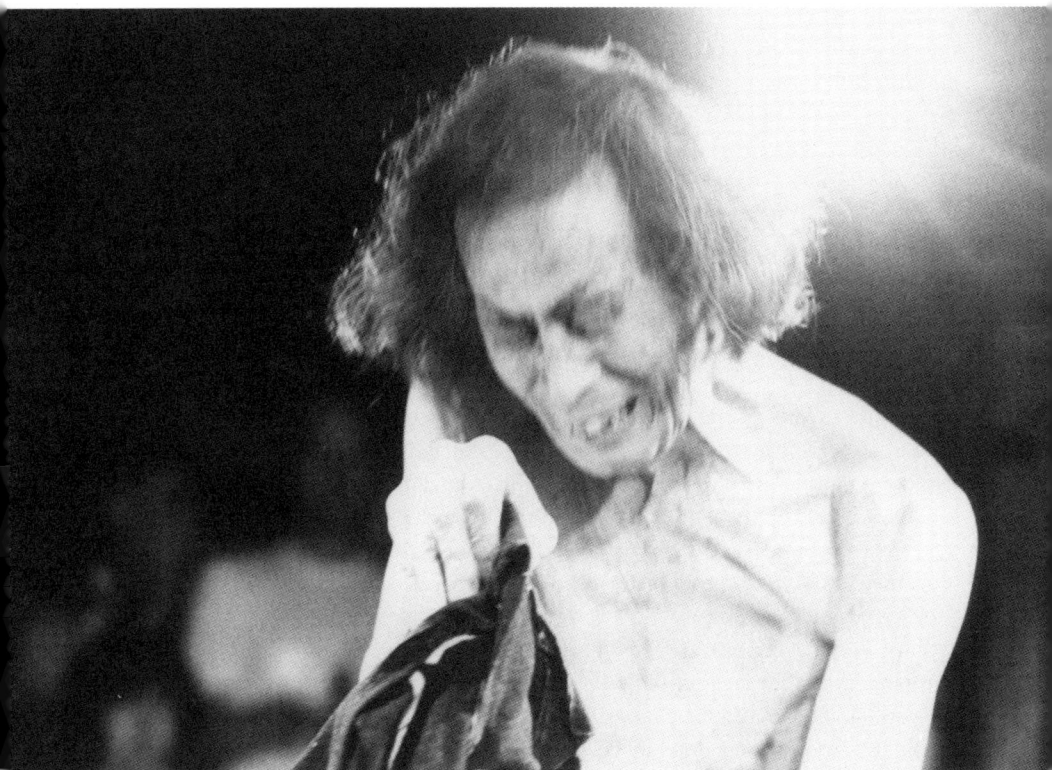

Food for the Soul

dance unfolds spontaneously, without the slightest reticence. One must bear in mind, however, that Kazuo could never respond with the natural ease seen in these impromptu dances were he not first to delve into his subconscious beforehand.

Interestingly, Tatsumi Hijikata[2] would also spend a great deal of time in reflection about how to construct a performance during the very lengthy periods set aside for rehearsals. At the time my father and I worked with him, Hijikata never gave instructions to move in a specific manner, nor for that matter did he criticize or try to correct how we danced. A dancer's movement, as far as Hijikata was concerned, was already deeply ingrained in his or her body ever before he started composing a choreography at rehearsals. If anything, he believed in allowing movement to emerge from the body itself rather than imposing it from the outside. Kazuo's overall approach differs to some extent. He constantly pours over his work notes both at home and in the dressing room;

at times he goes so far as to consult them on exiting to the wings during the course of a performance.

Remark how Kazuo's facial expression in this photo (see fig. 7) is so unlike his habitual one. I can't help feeling that I'm looking at the face of someone not belonging to this world. I simply couldn't imagine my father with such an expression in his ordinary, everyday life. In this shot taken at a performance of *Universal Restaurant*,[3] with Kazuo in traditional formal black attire—we can see a striking example of the shock and fear he feels on being confronted with horror. I've no doubt whatsoever that Kazuo's battlefront experiences during World War II provided him with more than ample insight into the horrors of a living hell. Even now, whenever he looks at the *Jigokuemakizoshi* we have at home—picture scrolls depicting all sorts of infernal torments—he's instinctively moved to voice his deep-felt terror.[4] And yet I can't help thinking at times that the atrocities he witnessed firsthand during the war were far more terrifying.

Through this lengthy exploratory process, another face comes to life: a face so different from his habitual one as to be almost unrecognizable. Onstage, the face doesn't function solely as a means of communicating our everyday sense of astonishment, discomfort, and so forth. Unconsciously, perhaps, it portrays emotions not experienced in this lifetime. I don't think that Kazuo's face would be as expressive were he only to draw on his store of personal encounters with reality. He undoubtedly has also tapped into his dreams, for we are confronted not only with expressions drawn from the recesses of his childhood but also from beyond this life.

Generally speaking, joy and sorrow are considered to be contingent upon each other: joy, as they say, is born of sorrow, and sorrow is the mother of joy. At times, Kazuo's face gives birth to an expressiveness that goes far beyond reflecting the inner strength and gravitas that comes naturally to someone of his age. Figuratively speaking, the face renders visible an authentic self-portrait only if a performer's body and soul reach "crisis" point. However, if a dancer's movements or gestures are not genuinely felt or lived on the inside, and simply correspond to a predetermined facial expression, they are portraying nothing more than a caricatured illustration of our common humanity. They might well succeed in creating an outward illusion, but that is not at all the same thing as digging beneath the surface.

(overleaf)
7. Ohno performs *Universal Restaurant*, Kushiro, 1983. © Nobutaka Murayama.

1.

The Dancing Body

———

8. "An authentic expression only emerges when body and soul reach crisis point." Workshop studio, Kamihoshikawa. © Ohno Dance Studio Archives.

(Right)
9. Ohno opening his mouth. © Ohno Dance Studio Archives.

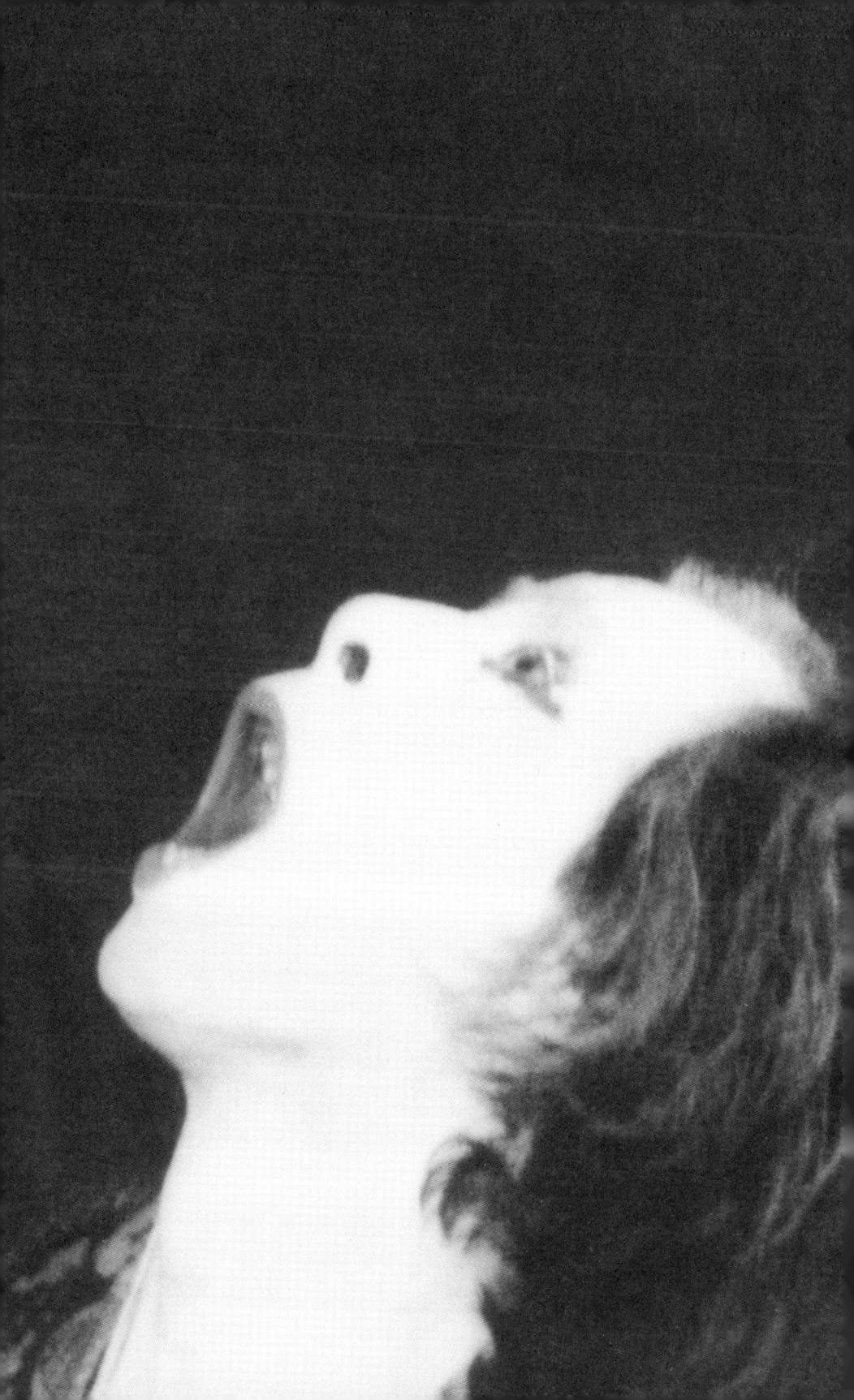

The Mouth, the Voice

Kazuo Ohno uses the mouth's expressive potential to great effect. When opening his mouth wide in a grimace like a madman, Kazuo doesn't—unlike many other performers—do so self-consciously or in a caricatured fashion.

If I, in comparison, spread my lips open in that grotesque manner, my dance becomes far too emotively driven. It strikes the audience as being sentimental and ends up coming across as somewhat gratuitous. Kazuo's use of the mouth, however, isn't in any way calculated; he doesn't strive to impress with simplistic effects. Dancing, let's say, to a piece of music the likes of Elvis Presley's "How Great Thou Art," Kazuo does so with great feeling. In fact, he expresses candidly what he rarely does in his everyday life. His performances have become his way of saying thank you. The stage, in that sense, provides him an opportunity to convey gratitude toward those to whom he feels deeply indebted: his mother, La Argentina, life itself.

Kazuo's fundamental, or what I would call intuitive, approach to live performance[5] doesn't entail that he simply steps out onto the stage and starts improvising on the spur of the moment. There's a lot more to it than that; it's not simply a matter of "anything goes." He doesn't discard an entire life's experiences, or all the knowledge and craft involved in the making of a performance. On one level he remains very conscious of where he is and what he is doing. And yet he attains a level of consciousness that allows him to forget the self. This spontaneous approach frees him from certain strictures—such as rigid choreography—and, what's more, enables him to flow with all that surges forth from his interior life.

Kazuo's dance gives birth to a fluid sequence of spontaneous images; it's as though he's carried on wave after wave of subjective impulses. Prominent among the many landscapes and moods evoked are those he discovers in the recesses of his subconscious memory through his writings. While he's perfectly aware of the fact of that he's onstage, and of the ensuing in-built limitations of a performance's framework, he nonetheless freely interacts with the universe he creates. His creative output exemplifies a working method in which cognitive control is closely allied with an intuitive process. I've often been struck by the fact that it's only when mind and body freely interact that Kazuo truly dances. His dance becomes lifeless as soon as he's caught up in thinking about how to move or is dictated to by habit.

Kazuo rarely, if ever, talks aloud on stage, but just the other day as

Food
for the
Soul

_____

10. "Dance projects the body's voice." *My Mother*, 1981. © Teijiro Kamiyama.

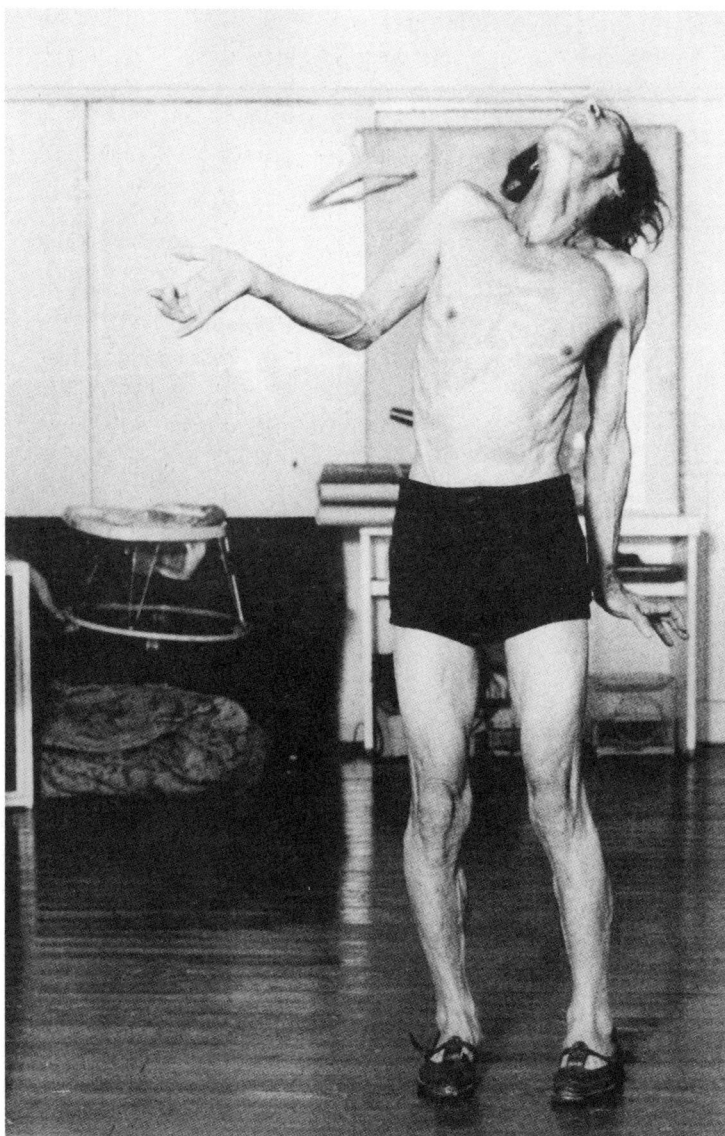

11. "By tightly choking his vocal chords with the back, the body's voice becomes audible." In rehearsal for *Admiring La Argentina*, Kamihoshikawa, 1977. © Tōjun Okamura.

a TV crew were filming him perform *My Mother*,[6] he uttered, in a clearly spoken voice, his mother's parting words to him on her deathbed: "Kazuo, a deep-sea flounder is swimming inside my body. You know, long, long ago it was shaped like a globular fish but over time has been 'flattened' due to the surrounding water pressure on the ocean bottom. When you dance Kazuo, move in such a way that the entire universe rumbles; dance like that flounder does as it jumps forth from the sand on the sea bed."

With these words, Kazuo articulated what he had previously written about on the subject. I was astounded, however, that he would actually repeat onstage the very words his mother spoke on her deathbed. While he might occasionally cry out "Father!" or "Mother!" or some other such exclamation, this was the one and only time I have ever heard him using meaningful words in a performing context. I couldn't get over his unusual behavior, and yet I don't think that he was in the slightest bit conscious of the camera's presence. Seen from the TV viewers' perspective, however, this unexpected verbal outburst might have been enlightening, in that it offered them some insight into his life.

Once, while speaking on the role of voice in dance, the noh specialist Tamotsu Watanabe,[7] made a distinction worthy of note between those dances that embody a voice and those remaining dead silent, like stone. What he had in mind was that dance is the body's voice objectified; it is the body that projects our inner voice. He cited Kazuo's dance as being among those in which the body makes itself heard. Watanabe's comments made me ponder over how voice and body intertwine. Contrary to what one might expect, one cannot hear the body's voice expressing itself in our everyday speaking voice. This photograph offers a telling example of how the body's voice is projected. Kazuo nearly chokes himself by tautening his back to such an extent (see fig. 11). In doing so, he effectively prevents the vocal chords from emitting any audible utterances the moment his emotions are about to rise to the surface and manifest themselves. We're nonetheless left with the impression that we hear his inner voice express itself through another medium, namely, the body itself. Kazuo's "secret" method of enabling one hear this "muted" voice has a forceful impact upon our imagination. We find ourselves perceiving his inner world unravel before our very eyes. Undoubtedly, the art of suggestion is far more evocative than that of straightforward statement.

Most performers are unable to elicit such a strong empathic response from their audience. Kazuo is unrivaled in the way he creates

(overleaf)
12. Ohno in rehearsal for *My Mother*, 1981.© Teijiro Kamiyama.

1.

The Dancing

Body

———

21

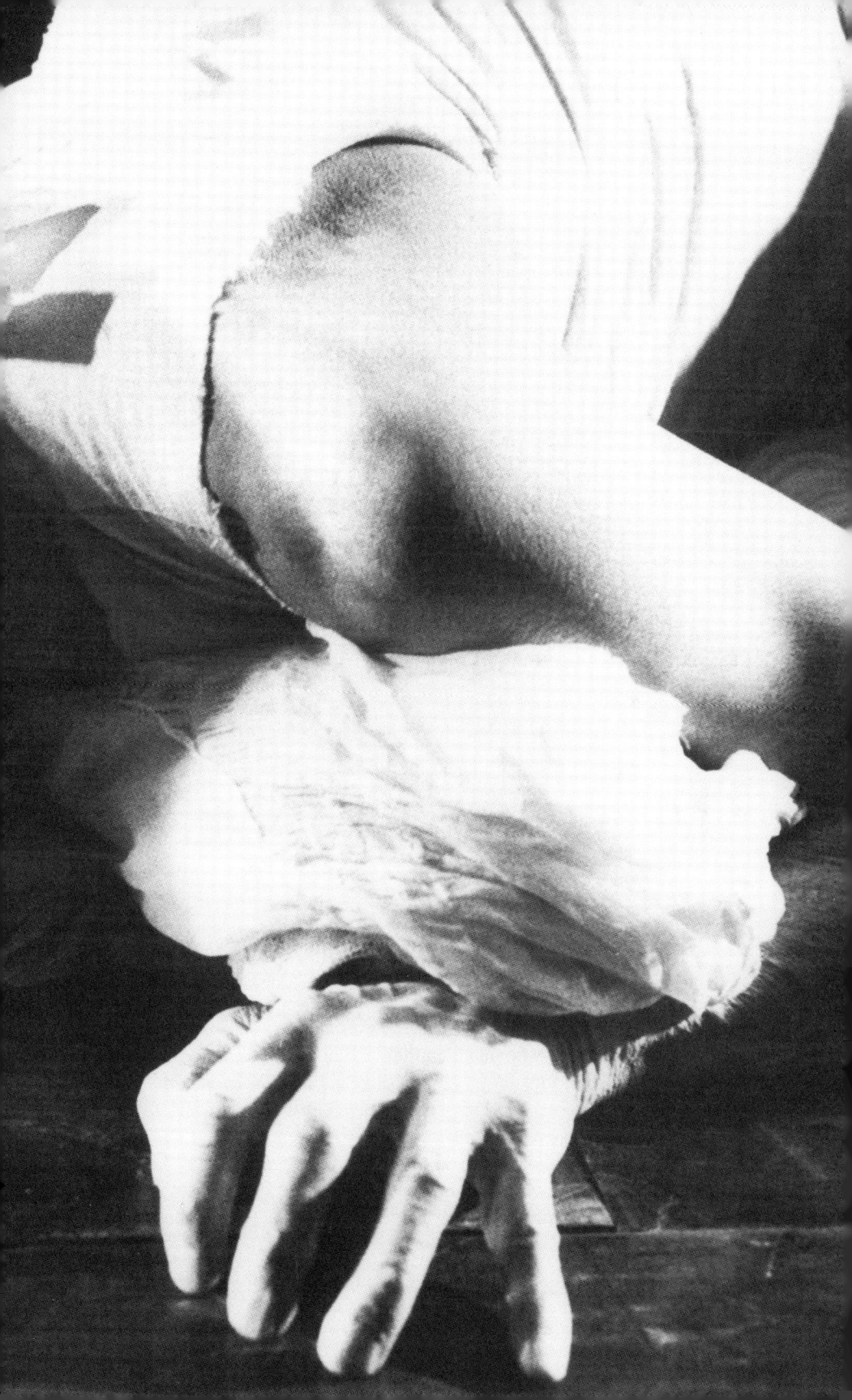

the tension necessary to produce a totally credible illusion of reality on stage. With practice anybody can learn the steps of a folk dance, but becoming a butoh performer demands a lot more than that.

The Eye

We, as performers, need to give careful consideration to how the eye and body interact. It's essential to grasp where exactly the eye is located and how it functions. Moreover, there are things that cannot be seen with the eyes. For a butoh dancer, the entire body must become a receptor organ for light. By this, I mean that the eyes are not our sole visual link with the exterior world. The entire body, from head to foot, is capable of visually assimilating our immediate surroundings. In a performing context, Kazuo's eyes don't, in fact, look *at* things in the conventional sense of looking *out* on one's immediate surroundings; his gaze is also fastened on what is happening inside the body.

At the workshops, Kazuo repeatedly stresses the necessity to start looking with the underside of the foot. He wants us to arrive at a stage where we can see with our feet. The eyes, in his estimation, should be able to migrate throughout the body, thus enabling what one might call a fine tuning of our perception of both outer and inner worlds. Onstage, Kazuo's eyes, while continuing to focus on his surroundings, pass down through the body and cling tightly to the soles of his feet. By attaching themselves to the feet, their gaze becomes more penetrating, for the body itself then begins to respond to external stimuli. Kazuo insists that one shouldn't rely entirely on the eyes to see because their ability to penetrate the visual field—even when making accommodation for focusing on nearby objects—is negligible when compared with the visual acuity of the body. In his own words, "It's impossible for me to dance if I continue to look *at* things in my habitual way." Many years ago he primarily concentrated on the eyes in training sessions.

For me, the learning process is quite the opposite: I first of all need to thoroughly grasp what it means to "see" before working on what Kazuo calls "non-seeing eyes." Once I've clearly understood how the eye functions in the conventional sense of the term, I can then turn my focus on how to make the other parts of the body visually sensitive. This deconstructive process obviously requires a step-by-step preparation. At practice sessions, I might first attempt to sensitize, let's say, the fingertips. Using the palm of the hand as an eyeball, I lie down on the floorboards. I then try to imbue my hands' movements with contrasting qualities such as strength and

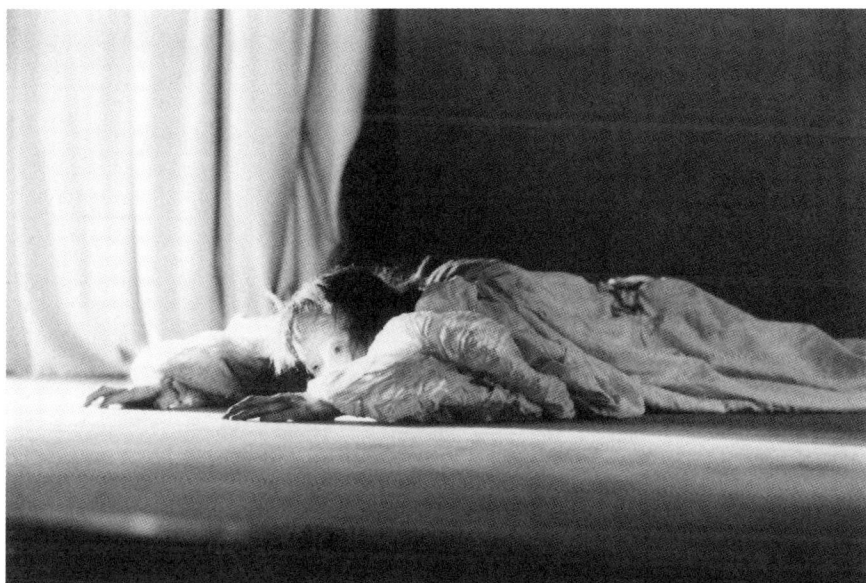

13. Ohno says, "Don't look with the eyes." *The Dead Sea*, 1985. © Ohno Dance Studio Archives.

gentleness. By bringing my eyes down to floor level, I'm ultimately striving to transform the way my feet visually respond to their surroundings. I suppose what I'm trying to say is that I want to the soles of my feet to be able to see. It's impossible for me to walk out onstage without first experiencing that the soles of my feet have been transformed into my eyes. Put another way, my body won't come alive in performance unless my way of interacting with the immediate world undergoes a significant change. Hands have a natural advantage over the feet in this respect because of their innate sensitivity and dexterity.

At rehearsals back in the late 1950s, Kazuo had us experiment with specific images such as "the sun's bigness." He wasn't simply asking us to illustrate the sun's bigness in terms of voluminous movements or large-sized gestures. Rather, he wanted us to try to incorporate the sun itself into our dance. These visualization exercises made us grasp how different parts of the body contained their own solar systems. Not only did we come to the realization of the magnitude and life force present in our hands, but we also discovered that even the gaps between our fingers were capable of embracing an entire universe.

Only through repeated practice of such motifs were we eventually able to grasp what Kazuo had in mind when speaking of "non-

1.

The Dancing Body

———

seeing eyes." To this very day, however, he still insists on lecturing the beginners at the workshops:[8]

"Don't look with your eyes, don't look!"

Although he's certainly right to point out the necessity of learning the art of how to focus one's awareness, I have the impression that his admonitions often confuse his listeners. If anything, they're left somewhat bewildered and end up asking themselves what his instructions mean in concrete terms.

The Ear

Kazuo constantly urges his students not to listen to music with their ears. Instead, he says, "Listen with your whole body and spirit. In doing so, the core of the body, your soul, will open itself up and embrace the music. Your movements will start coming to life as soon as you listen with your body and soul."

As a rule of thumb, we don't consciously select a particular piece or kind of music for our soundtracks. Having being brought up in Hakodate, an important trading port on the south coast of Hokkaido, Kazuo was reared in an environment in which Western culture and music was not entirely unknown. His mother was fond of Western classical music, so from an early age Kazuo had numerous opportunities to listen to Bach, Beethoven, Chopin, and the other classical masters. Music making was always in the background at home, for his mother was also, by all accounts, a fine koto player. Moreover, Kazuo attended a Russian Orthodox Church nursery school. Hakodate, being the seat of American and British consulates and foreign trading companies, prided itself on the many restaurants where Western fare was served. Kazuo often fondly recalls how his mother used to prepare scallop gratin and cook other French dishes for the family.

But to return to the topic: choosing a piece of music or an appropriate sound effect for a performance often requires us to trace all the way back to the experiences Kazuo had before he was born. This exploration allows us to revive that soundtrack long gone astray in his subconscious memory, the soundtrack of his childhood and life in the womb. Kazuo himself has spoken of having heard his mother play *Rokudan,* a well-known traditional piece for koto, while he moved around in the womb. Curiously, his performances trigger a passionate response in many members of the audience. While the public generally do understand what provokes them to cry, the majority of those who shed tears on seeing him dance remark that they're unsure why they react so emotionally.

Food

for the

Soul

___

28

These tears, in my view, are an expression of that unquenchable craving to return to where we, as human beings, originally came from. Listening to music that evokes Kazuo's early years and his existence in his mother's womb is an overwhelming experience for some members of the audience; in fact, many of them are already in tears before they realize what has taken grip of them. If a dancer is genuinely touched by a piece of music or a soundtrack, it has the power to evoke memories and suggest associations in the past. It will, in turn, also stimulate the audience's imagination. A soundtrack compiled by following a rational blueprint doesn't truly move us on a deep level. For that matter, our musical choice cannot be put together in a hackneyed fashion: the essential thing, however, is that dance never be governed by the music, but instead uses the music to render it more expressive.

The Hand

For Kazuo, the back of the hand functions like an eye when dancing to a Viennese waltz or a tango accompaniment. Instead of using his eyes to guide him through the scenic space, he relies on his hands to help him feel his way around. On such occasions, it often seems as though the hand itself turns into some kind of light-sensitive membrane. This phenomenon isn't exclusively restricted to the

15. "Listen to music with your heart and soul." *The Dead Sea*, 1985. © Kenichiro Aita.

1.

The Dancing Body

———

29

(top)
16. Ohno accompanied on guitar by the writer Shichiro Fukazawa, 1978.
© Kaname Moriya.

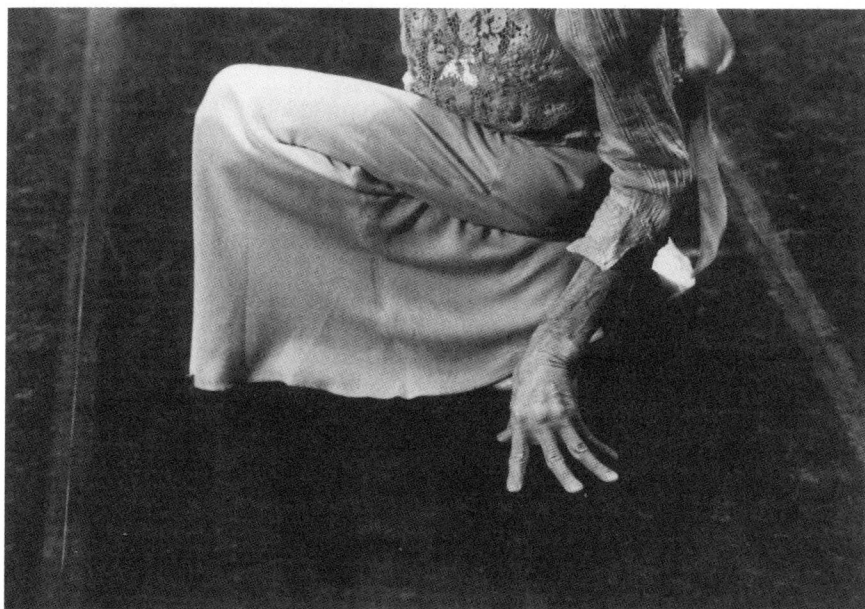

(bottom)
17. "Ohno's hands embody a universe." *Admiring la Argentina,* 1986.
© Kenichiro Aita.

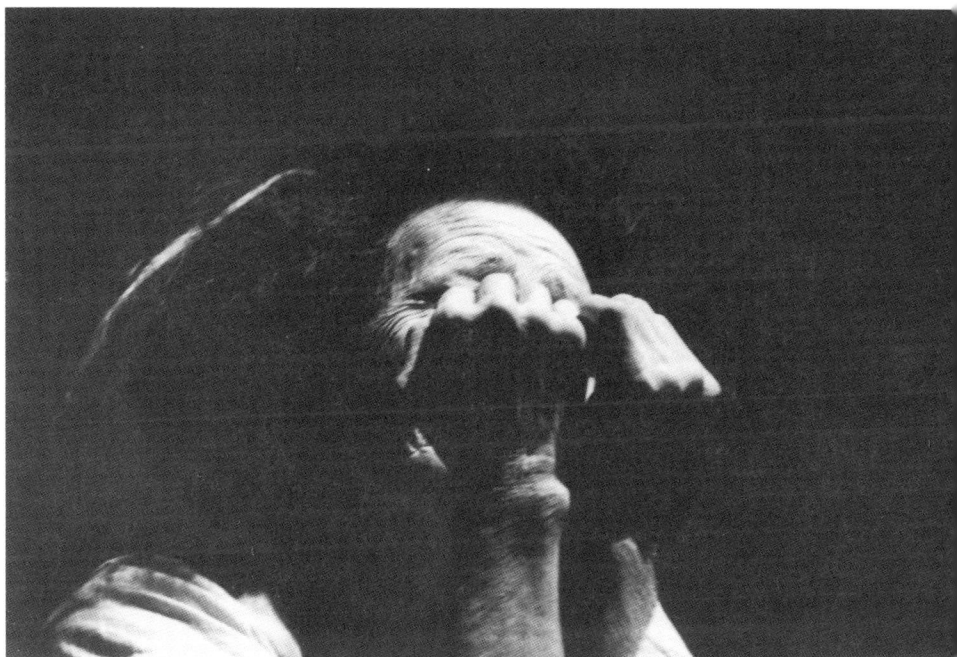

hand. At other times, the elbow, along with various parts of the body, becomes sensitized in a similar manner. This characteristic feature of his dance, whereby the entire body becomes covered with eyes, so to speak, has evolved over many years. In formal dances such as the waltz and tango, where emphasis is placed upon visible movement, Kazuo's gaze isn't focused on his immediate surroundings. Instead, it is the back of the hand and elbow that guide him through space. In fact, one could go so far as to say that at such times the entire body from head to foot functions like an eye.

Another distinctive trait of Kazuo's dance is the way he stares into his interior world. Here, one can observe that his gaze is focused on himself. His own body becomes an object of a piercing gaze (see fig. 18). By raising those tightly clenched fists to face level, he peers deeply into his own eyes. If one considers the feet as being akin to the roots of a plant, then, in like manner, the hands and fingers become buds and leaf-bearing branches. As Kazuo puts it: "Look closely at plants. When in blossom, flowers are petal-laden right to the very tip of their limbs. But take a look at your fingertips: they're lifeless. If your dance is to come to life in the same way a flower blossoms, then be flower-like. Look at trees!

18. Ohno peering into his interior world. *The Dead Sea*, 1985. © Kenichiro Aita.

1.

The Dancing

Body

——

31

From the roots to the tip of their branches, they're vibrantly expressive." This is a common topic at the workshops.[9] He's for ever encouraging the participants: "Make your dance more lifelike. You can grasp what life is all about by simply studying how a tree grows. Look, the trunk of your body is healthy; your feet are firmly planted in the ground. But, don't let your hands fade and wither away; allow your life force flow throughout the body. Though one can't actually see a tree grow, it's still possible to detect that it has grown—even after several days. Life functions in an unostentatious way; it doesn't need to call attention to itself. The audience doesn't need to see you move, but they certainly must be able to sense that you're growing. It makes no difference whatsoever that they cannot see you move. Look at that hand you keep stretching out there: it's no longer the same. While it might appear that it's been doing nothing. it definitely has changed." That makes me think of a haiku by Koi Nagata:[10]

Ah, the Monster!
In the palm of your hand—
The Milky Way.

The poet draws our attention to both the expressive and the brute power inherent in a human hand. Not only does this verse allude to the fact that the hand is the extremity of a limb attached to the trunk of the body, but it would seem also to suggest that the hand is in itself a living entity embodying those ghosts dormant in us. By functioning jointly as an eye and an antenna-like feeler in a performing context, the hand makes it presence felt all the more forcefully.

Speaking as a performer, I'm acutely aware of the uniqueness of Kazuo's hands. They somehow defy comprehension. And yet I can't resist thinking about how one goes about acquiring the sensitivity and presence they manifest. They are so authentic that it's virtually impossible to replicate their movement style. They haven't, however, always manifested the autonomy they now possess: it would be fair to say that it's only in the last ten years or so they've started coming into their own. But, in reality, their extraordinary expressiveness has nothing to do with their actual physical size. If anything, their eloquence is due to those ghosts whom Kazuo incarnates. It has never ceased to amaze me how his hands seem to acquire a life of their own as he improvises onstage. They clearly aren't being driven by his individual strength. Kazuo doesn't choreograph their movements beforehand, nor does he consciously attempt to gesturally express his feelings or ideas. His hands, as I see them, reveal the true character of those ghosts dormant in him.

On that subject, another haiku comes to mind, one in which the poet, Sekitei Hara, touches upon the theme of our latent animal nature.[11]

> What joy I felt
> On coming across a fox's paw
> Amidst clouds of petals.

The fox's unexpected appearance makes the poet reflect on the ephemeral nature of the cherry blossoms' beauty.[12] No matter how we, as human beings, strive to conceal the animal in us, it nonetheless remains an inseparable part of our lives. Doesn't the fox in Hara's verse allude to the dormant ghosts, or animals, in each of us?

Kazuo's enormous hands with those extremely long-jointed fingers are indeed physically remarkable. Needless to say, their very size greatly contributes to the presence he commands onstage. I recall how even Tatsumi Hijikata was envious of them. Kazuo once remarked that a flower is a model of a self-contained universe. This comment exemplifies his belief that a hand embodies a universe covering an expansive space, in which both expanding and contracting forces operate. Also, his hands are truly beautiful to look at. Even the slightest movement they make creates a dance.

In preparing for a performance Kazuo has many different elements to consider—music, costume, lighting, and so forth—but when it comes down to it, what matters most is that his dance takes him beyond himself. In his aesthetic, the basic sentiment governing the spirit of his dance is an insistence that it reach out and touch the audience. Bear in mind that performance, for Kazuo, is not simply the skillful execution of a series of movements or dance steps but rather an occasion on which those ghosts dormant in him come to life. His hands become the dance. They need to go beyond being employed as an expressive tool and instead become instrumental in constructing his personal universe. They were not crafted, it must be said, through years of practice in the studio; they have acquired their lifelike character as a result of all the manual labor he has done over the decades in his capacity

1.

The Dancing

Body

——

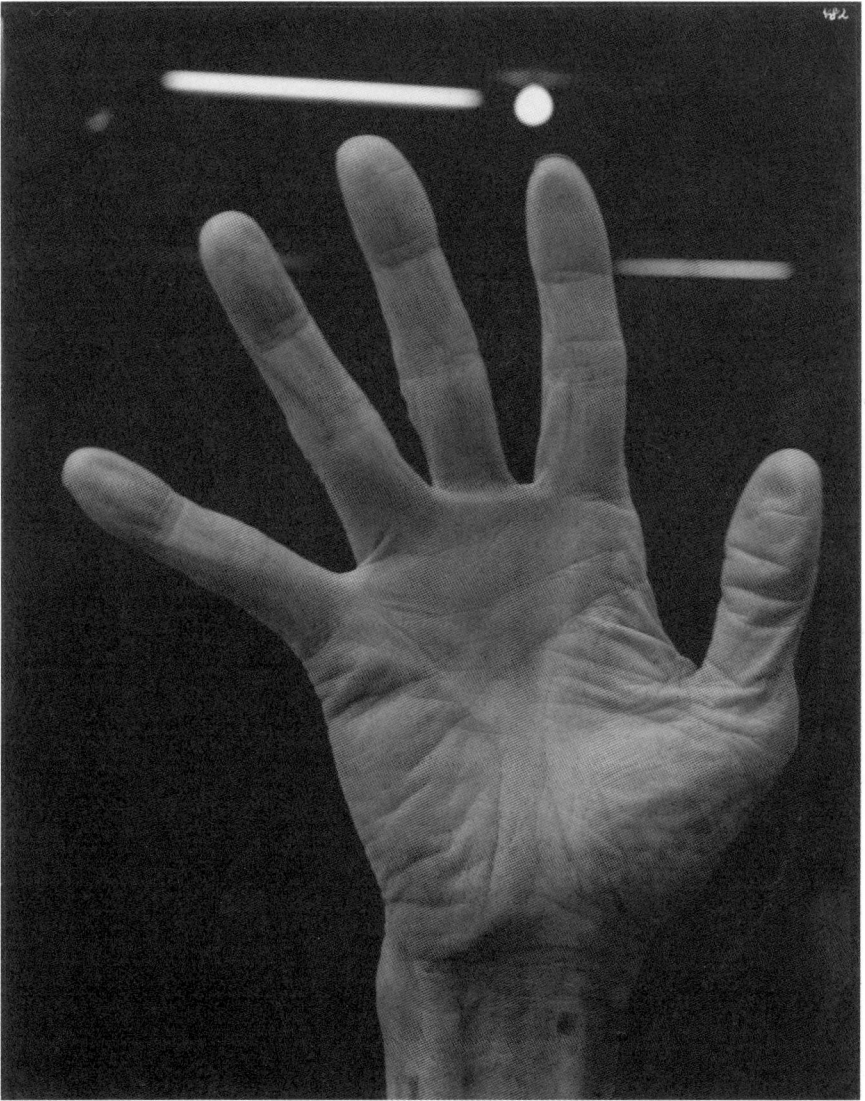

19. Ohno's enormous
hands with deep-
rooted joints, 1999.
© Takayuki
Nakatake.

20. "At that stage, Ohno's hands were still 'young.'" In rehearsal for *Admiring La Argentina*. Workshop studio, Kami-hoshikawa, 1977. © Tōjun Okamura.

as a school caretaker, where repairing drains, mending broken-down boilers, painting walls, and so on were part and parcel of his day-to-day chores.

In this shot (see fig. 20), taken during rehearsals around the time of the première of *Admiring La Argentina* (1977), one can observe how Kazuo hands were still "young," and in an early stage of development.

Why, it is frequently asked, do a butoh performer's hands tend to droop like the branches of a weeping willow? Unlike in mainstream dance, where the predominant tendency is for the hands to reach upward or outward toward the exterior world, Kazuo's bodily language might well strike one as being somewhat introspective. Glancing back over Kazuo's lengthy career, I can readily distinguish the various styles and periods his dance went through by studying his physical vocabulary. For instance, during his modern dance phase at the outset of his stage career, back in the late 1940s, he had a strong tendency to open the body out; his movements were outward and extrovert. Keep in mind that, at that time, he was also an accomplished athlete.

After the first performance with Tatsumi Hijikata in 1959, a radical change occurred. From that point onward, he began reflecting on the question of death. Death, above all else, became the point of

1.

The Dancing

Body

——

departure in his creative process. With this change of focus from the exterior to the interior worlds, from extrovert to introvert, his hands inevitably began reaching into himself.

A fine example of this phenomenon can be seen in the *yūrei* dances, the suite of "Ghost Dances" that we incorporated into *The Dead Sea*.[13] Looking at Kazuo in this photo (see fig. 21) one has the impression that his feet and legs have mysteriously vanished, leaving only those dangling hands as the last remaining vestiges of a human body.

Kazuo's mother used to read him Lacfadio Hearne's ghost stories every evening at bedtime.[14] These stories, and especially her way of telling them, made an enormous impression on him. It's now clear that the effect those supernatural tales had on his imagination ultimately led him to create these *yūrei* dances. In a certain sense, performing these pieces affords him an opportunity to revisit his childhood.

According to Kazuo, listening to his mother tell those ghost stories would often frighten the life out of him. He could never forget her telling a story by Kyouka Izumi,[15] in which a group of people were warned not to turn around and look back on taking their leave. If they dared do so, they would immediately be cast into stone. Under no circumstances, they were cautioned, should they turn around and look. Those who disobeyed were instantly cast into stone and strewn about the place. Apparently, Kazuo's mother would likewise warn her children that if they were naughty and disobeyed her that they, too, would meet a similar fate; she would cast them into stone and throw them along the side of the road. That particular story, he recalls, would send shivers creeping down his spine.

The Back

While viewing the paintings at Masaya Kaburagi's exhibition *The Space between Backs,* Kazuo was forcefully struck by the fact that a person's back, like his or her face, is set apart by its unique character. It then dawned on to him that a dancer's back was in need of eyes. Oddly enough, we often hear how a person's back reveals a lot about their personality, or, for that matter, how somebody has "backbone." Onstage, when turning his back to the audience, Kazuo nonetheless remains facing it (see fig. 22). He is convinced, however, that the back's character, so to speak, wouldn't come across to the public unless he consciously worked at making it felt. Otherwise, as he puts it, "I would end up simply facing the other

1.

The Dancing

Body

_____

37

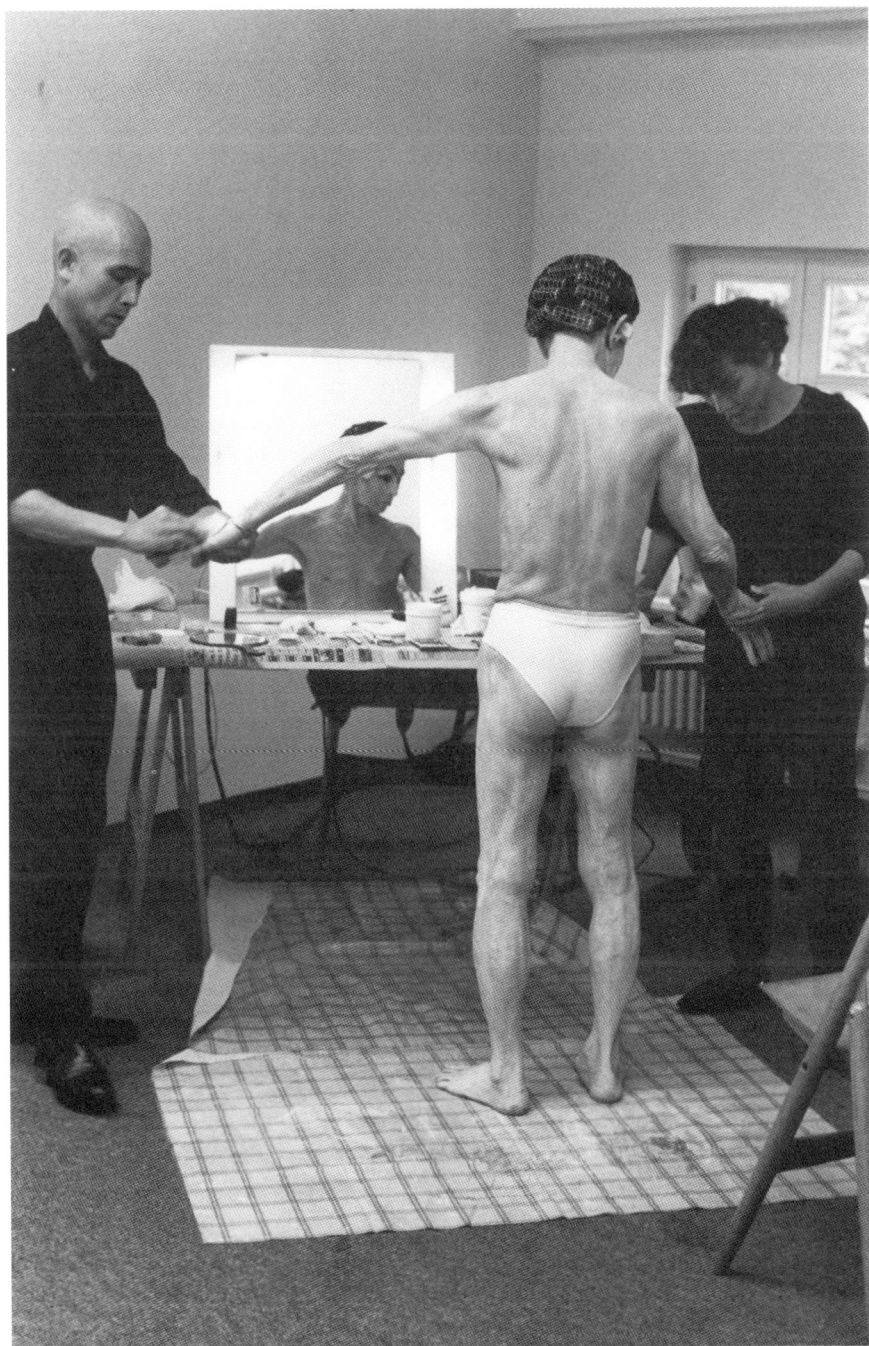

way." Not only does he repeatedly stress the importance for a performer to grant the audience an insight into his inner world, he also emphasizes the necessity for the back to be covered with eyes.

In turning his back to an audience, a performer has got to realize that he's not concealing himself or hiding himself from view. Quite the contrary, he remains fully exposed. In fact, the back plays an integral part in how he creates his dance. But great care needs to be taken so as to engage the audience in this way.

The front of the body ostensibly expresses itself in many ways: a head held high, a chest thrown out, and so forth. The back, it must be said, can be as nuanced as the face in the way it indicates emotion. If anything, I would say that it is even more articulate in the way it communicates. While the eyes are said to reveal more than the mouth, a performer nonetheless needs to work on his back so that it attains great expressiveness.

Kazuo remains conscious of his back even when moving downstage facing the public. The back, in his view, must at all times make its presence felt. We shouldn't disregard it just because we presume that the spectators can't see it directly in front of them. Ultimately, he says, it's up to the performer to construct the image the audience perceives. One shouldn't allow any distinction to be made between the "front" and "back" of the body. Both the back and torso are integral parts of that intimately personal world Kazuo constructs on stage. He deliberately invents this fictional body; it doesn't simply exist and express itself per se. In like manner, he also consciously works on the back's stage presence. Incidentally, Kazuo was once asked where the eyes were located. He replied that the body is so covered with them that it's virtually impossible to count them all.

Food

for the

Soul

———

Chapter 2

Performance

Falling

At the climax of *Divinariane*, the opening sequence in *Admiring La Argentina*, Kazuo lies down on the stage, his head facing the floor.[1] As the scene concludes, darkness envelops this prostrate figure symbolically taking leave of this world. Kazuo again "falls" to the floor in *Daily Bread*, another sequence from the same performance. On this occasion, he suddenly collapses to the ground as though he were falling from one realm into another.

"Falling" constitutes an integral part of Kazuo's gestural vocabulary. On watching him perform this feat, one has the distinct impression that an indissoluble bond beckons him to the dimension that unfolds "below the knees." One senses that a close affinity exists with that lateral space "down there." In falling, he makes the transition from his ordinary, everyday world, where he stands firmly on his feet, to another, "limitless" dimension. The act of falling in itself plays a significant role in the way Kazuo draws the public into his private universe; he has an uncanny ability to draw them into an emotional vortex and thereby open them up to their own inner lives. Unlike in classical and contemporary dance—where movement often tend to surge upward as though resisting gravity—Kazuo is apt to fall earthward when longing to defy gravitational pull. The speed at which he collapses is simply phenomenal—it has to be seen to be believed. He's already hit the floor before one even realizes what's happened. However, these "falls" are completely impromptu; he could never determine beforehand how his body drops to the floor.

Indeed, watching Kazuo "fall," one wonders whether a sharp blade hasn't momentarily pierced through the visible boundaries of the scenic space. On leaving the vertical dimension, he offers the audience a fleeting glimpse of another world, a world we don't nor-

mally come in contact with. Bear in mind that he doesn't accomplish this by merely dropping to his feet. Conventional dance technique could never provide him with a means of falling through the floor. The atmosphere Kazuo evokes onstage doesn't in the slightest hinge on the actual physical location or conditions in which a performance takes place. Rather, it depends on the way in which he draws forth his inner world and renders it perceptible.

Over the years, Kazuo has refined many visual surprises through which he catches the audience off guard. He constantly invents different expressive environments. The impromptu dances that he performs, for instance, when climbing onto the proscenium from the auditorium are a good illustration of his ingenuity, not to mention his sudden entries from and exits into the wings, or his gazing skyward, earthward, and so forth. These extemporaneous moments, however, are quite distinct from the very particular universe he unearths by falling off his feet. One could describe the universe "down there" as some sort of "horizontal plane," or, perhaps, to put it more simply, the "ground." It's remarkable that many dancers—and again I myself am no exception—are completely unable to integrate the floor's full potential as part of the scenic space into our performances. It inevitably acts as a physical barrier to, rather than a continuum of, the stage. I will never forget Kazuo's awesome performance in *Daily Bread,* where, with a minimum of means—a costume consisting of nothing more than a pair of black trunks, utter silence as a musical backdrop, and a bare stage for a prop—he was able to fully incorporate the invisible realm beneath his feet into his performance. Kazuo's head, as can be seen in this shot (see fig. 25), points in a specific direction. Here, death is indicated, for his head clearly points toward the floor. Alternatively, he could turn his head in the opposite direction, so as to designate life. When he stands erect, however, I don't have the impression that the poles of human existence are suggested by his turning the head to the left or to the right, or by pointing it upward or downward. Odd as it may seem, these polarities do become remarkably clear whenever he lies down on the floor. The body itself delineates the boundaries of our mortal existence, of the realms of the visible and invisible. He brings the public face to face with its own destiny by physically substantiating questions concerning the now and the hereafter.[2]

For a performance of *Tendo Chido* at Tokyo's Setagaya Public Theatre in the autumn of 1998 Kazuo chose a pink gown as one of the costumes for the piece.[3] As he emerged on stage under the

24. **"Another world unfolds below knee level."** *My Mother,* Copenhagen, 1982. © Jan Rüsz.

2.

Performance

_____

43

full blaze of the stage lights, I could see from the wings that the gown's color was utterly overpowering; it really was garish. Hoping he might somehow look in my direction, I instantly lay face down on the floor and motioned him to collapse, or at least to somehow fall off his feet. My prompting was in vain because he didn't notice. As a matter of course, we don't establish a set choreography ahead of a performance. Besides, just as we were about to leave for the theater that morning, we had talked about trying on a different costume to the one he had worn on opening night. Why then, one might ask, did I want him to collapse onto the floor wearing that garish pink gown? Let me put it this way: only Kazuo could pull that off. Though it is unlikely that he would fall in such circumstances, it is nonetheless conceivable. One can never predict how he will respond. If I, or anyone else for that matter, fell to the floor in the impromptu manner Kazuo does, my dance would instantly loose its momentum. Getting back on my feet would merely become the execution of the physical motions involved in standing up. I must admit that I'm still unable to incorporate the floor space into my performance. In concrete terms, it remains very much "off bounds," for the moment my body hits

Food

for the

Soul

____

44

the floor my dance no longer flows; it simply ends right at that point.

Kazuo effortlessly demonstrates this ability to "fall into another world" when performing outdoors. He instantly transforms himself into a creature in perfect harmony with its surroundings, his spontaneous reflexes resemble those of an animal or insect interacting naturally with its environment. It would be no exaggeration to say that he becomes completely at one with nature.

Another striking feature of Kazuo's interaction with the world below the knees is the manner he rolls about on the ground. I have never seen anybody, even among those trained in classical ballet, manipulate himself as skillfully as Kazuo does. Upon hitting the ground, his body instantly stiffens on impact and proceeds to roll over and over as if it had transformed itself into a metal bar. For Kazuo, the floor doesn't represent an impenetrable surface; it never acts as a barrier. As he drops to the floor, one has the impression that he's embarking on a limitless free fall, continuing to tumble further and further into the depths of the universe. It's as though one never sees his body hitting the solid surface below him.

26. "The floor opens up to reveal a boundless universe." Workshop studio, Kamihoshikawa. © Ohno Dance Studio Archives.

2.

Performance

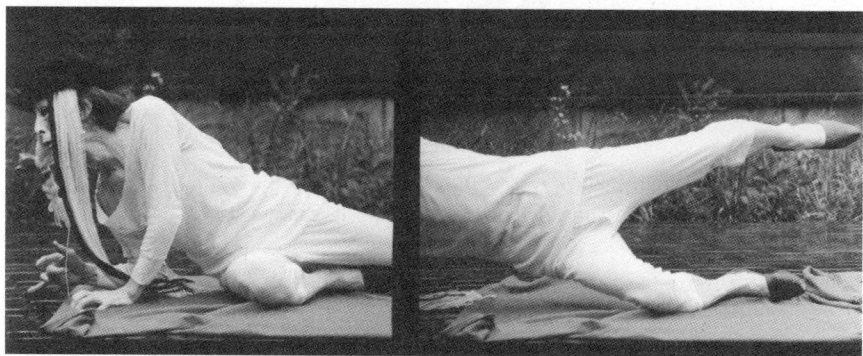

It takes a lot of technical maturity for performers to build a perceptible link between their inherent physicality and their metaphysical outlook on life. Obviously, in using words like "below" or "under" in this context, I don't have in mind our conventional spatial notions of "below" contrasting with "above." It's not simply a matter of somebody physically standing up or lying down. As Kazuo himself puts it somewhat cryptically, "Under us lies a lateral space." By this, he means that dance must awaken us to what lies *beneath* the surface of our everyday lives.

Standing

After falling to the floor in *Daily Bread*, Kazuo rises swiftly to his feet by deftly crossing his right leg over his left. A dancer who lacks formal training would have considerable difficulty executing this movement. Kazuo acquired this and many other technical skills during the six or so years in the mid-1930s when he studied German modern dance under the tutelage of Misako Miya and her husband, Takaya Eguchi.[4] Under their guidance, Kazuo made a determined effort to master the physical skills involved in contemporary dance, persevering until such time that he felt that nothing further was to be gained from such training. Remarkably, to this very day his physical reflexes unconsciously divulge the influences that shaped him during his formative years. Spectators are often astonished to watch Kazuo perform onstage; they are not only taken aback by his phenomenal dexterity but also deeply moved by his spiritual presence.

For Kazuo, dance is at all times an issue of life and death. His performances invariably touch a chord in us and force us to reflect on the meaning and purpose of our lives. As spectators, we become profoundly engaged because his performances confront us with crucial questions about our mortality. He couldn't provoke

29. "Ohno's dance connects us to that which is beneath the surface of our everyday lives." *The Dead Sea.* © Hiroaki Tsukamoto.

2.

Performance

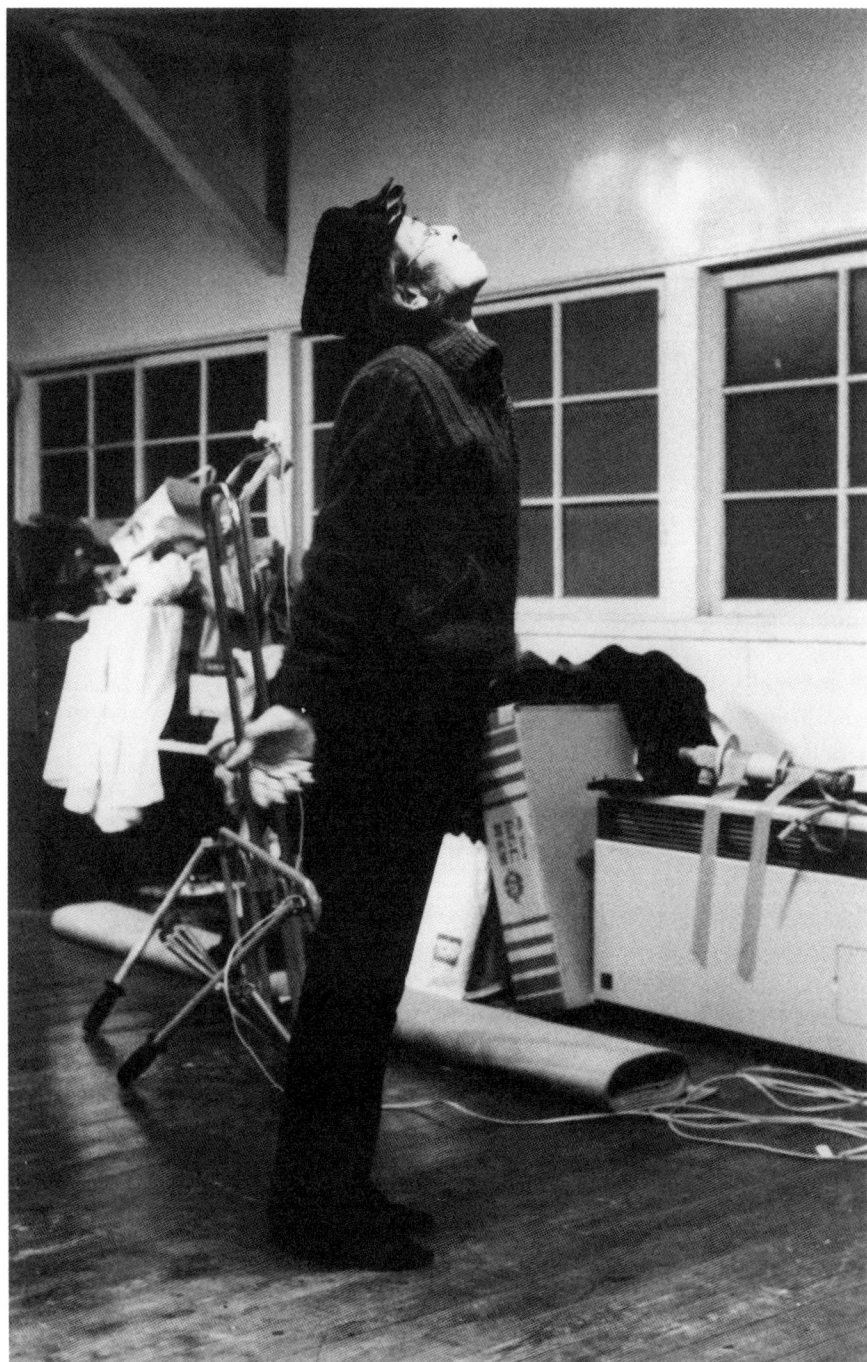

such an emotional jolt merely by crossing his legs skillfully or demonstrating a mastery of conventional techniques. That's not in any way to suggest that his movements are undisciplined, or random in their execution. Suppose, let's say, he crosses one leg over the other—his foot will unfailingly land on the allotted spot. As one can observe in this photo, he demonstrates outright control over his body: His foot lands on precisely on that spot, and not any other (see fig. 31). I was bowled over watching him perform *Daily Bread;* his movements didn't betray the slightest trace of uncertainty. The inimitably singular character of his each and every gesture constantly astounds me. That partly explains why I could never ask him to repeat a gesture or specific movement. Each moment is somehow so intense and perfect in itself that it's impossible for him to replicate it.

In this unusual shot (see fig. 32), we can observe one of those extremely rare occasions in which Kazuo conspicuously raises his leg backward, as though he were posing for a photographer. Regardless of the skill involved, I don't consider dance to be of interest if it merely becomes a platform for him to show off or demonstrate some technical feat.

I was deeply struck by a remark that Tatsumi Hijikata made to me after I dropped to the floor at a training session in his rehearsal studio one day. "You're banging your head against a wall," he said. "Your dance will end right there if you insist on falling to the floor like that. Why not try getting back up on your feet while singing a tune like 'The Steam Locomotive's Whistle Blows on Leaving Shimbashi Station'?"[5] With hindsight, I now realize that he was probably trying to help me understand that I'd never succeed in standing up if I continued thinking about how do it. Singing that popular song might distract me from the task at hand and thus help me become less self-conscious. Obviously, there are many ways in which one can rise to one's feet. If we insist on moving in only one particular manner, then we face a serious risk of finding ourselves in a rut or even of becoming a caricature of ourselves.[6] As performers, we are at every moment confronted with this critical problem. Ultimately, we must find our own individual expression and not simply imitate preestablished forms.

The noted theater critic Masakutsu Gunji[7] once remarked that even "Kazuo Ohno's rising from the floor in itself contains the makings of a complete dance." Though he may be standing immobile, his feet planted firmly in the ground, one can't help feeling that Kazuo's body is being thrust upward through the air, as

30. Ohno in rehearsal at the studio in the 1970s. © Teijiro Kamiyama.

(overleaf)
31. "Ohno's foot lands precisely on that spot." Stage run-through for *Admiring La Argentina*, 1986. © Mitsutoshi Hanaga.

2.

Performance

49

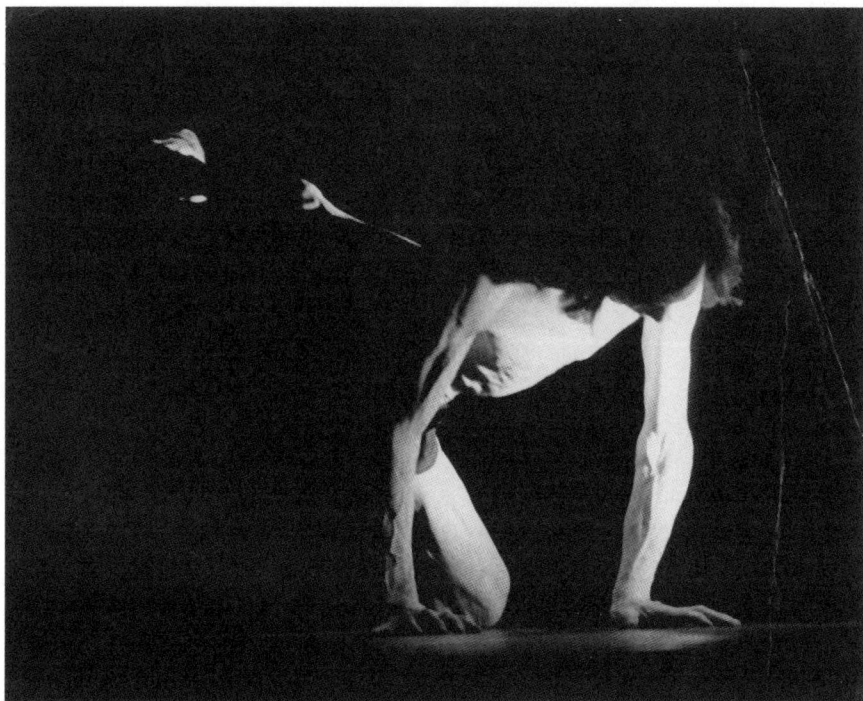

if it were soaring toward the edge of the sky. Curiously, however, his strength remains concentrated in the lower part of the body. The fact he soars up so effortlessly might lead one to believe that he has been thrust by some external force. As he rises, his body, contrary to what one might expect, doesn't propel itself upward; rather, it tugs itself toward the floor. The torso moves up in the air, while the lower body descends in a countermotion in vertical space.

That brings me to a critical question: where is Kazuo Ohno when standing onstage? By this, I don't have in mind the physical spot where his feet touch the floorboards, but rather the "where-abouts," so to speak, of the character or spirit he inhabits. The illusory *height* he attains determines how his inner world is perceived by the public. He might even come across as being much taller and bigger than he is in real life. The audience needs to be able to see the truth of his inner world unfold. That is why he has to constantly reinvent his physical appearance so as to give tangible form to something that by its very nature is invisible. As a veteran performer, Kazuo is fully aware of what he is doing; he possesses the

Food

for the

Soul

———

33. Ohno at the
Hijikata Commemo-
rative Performance,
Yamagata, 1987.
© Munusuke
Yamamoto.

know-how and critical acumen necessary to reinvent himself physically the moment he treads the boards. Of course, he has to pay attention to his back and torso, for they determine how the body
projects itself and in how the audience perceive him, ultimately. In
particular, the torso plays a crucial role in how he shapes his body
image.

At other times, one can observe how (see fig. 34) Kazuo bends
backward. Here, his body seems to be thrust upward by a vertically
rising energy rushing through him. This powerful force is what
causes his back to arch and displaces his center of gravity. At re-

2.

Performance

_____

53

34. Rehearsing *Ad-
miring La Argentina*
in Madrid, 1987.
© Sachiko Takeda.

hearsals many years ago, Kazuo used to constantly admonish us with directives such as "Steady up" or "Pull yourself together and stand firmly on your feet!" The point he was trying to make was that we require a solid core, both physically and psychologically, so as to ground and center our lives. This, in turn, plays a determining role in how we become responsible both to ourselves and others. Interestingly, the Chinese character for "core" 芯 (shin), written by placing the radical for the character "grass" ⺿ (kusakamuri) above the character for "heart and mind" 心 (kokoro), suggests that the essential nature of a stem or a stalk is to grow upward. Human beings also require their feet to reach upward. This core or kernel to which Kazuo alludes unquestionably exists both in our bodies and in our relationship with our ordinary, everyday lives.

In the past, it was often remarked that those families living in houses centered around a *daikoku-bashira*—the heavy post that serves as main support for the frame of a traditional Japanese wooden house—tended to prosper and thrive. Years ago, these posts were even considered sacred objects and accorded great respect. Nowadays, the term refers, albeit more prosaically, to the central and most important structural post in a building or sometimes to the person who ensures a household's economic survival. Although individual family members mightn't necessarily have taken much notice of this post, they were nonetheless very aware of the indispensable role it played in the household's survival. The post was treated like a living entity. Figuratively speaking, this traditional core of a Japanese house acted as the family guardian down through the generations.[8]

To create such an unwavering core in our performances requires that we constantly engage ourselves in a process of trial and error. Students of Indian classical dance, for example, devote an entire lifetime striving to imbue their recitals with a spiritual quality. When it comes down to it, the credibility of any performer pivots on whether he or she exudes a sense of reality or not. Anyone wanting in this respect can never, in my reckoning, truly dance. If, let's say, a performer deliberately raises his head to express happiness and joy, or looks downward to indicate sorrow, she or he is merely going through the motions involved in communicating those particular emotions. The audience is confronted with a caricature, for such gestures are superficial and completely lacking in depth. The essential thing to get across is the innermost nature of the character portrayed, not the surface trappings.

2.

Performance

55

35–36. "Something thrusts Ohno upward." Teatro Nacional, Brasilia, 1986. © Carlos Menandro.

Walls

Yet another distinguishing characteristic of Kazuo's use of the scenic space is the way he unexpectedly transforms himself into an inanimate object. He does this by clinging on to solid surfaces such as a wall, a door, and so on (see fig. 37). In this photo, Kazuo's body seems to be walled in by something. By simply standing still in front of a wall, he finds himself utterly dehumanized; it's as though he's been transformed into a lifeless form.

37. "Ohno becomes one with the wall." Madrid, 1987. © Sachiko Takeda.

At times, one is left with the disturbing impression that Kazuo has been cast into stone. Tatsuhiko Shibusawa[9] once remarked after seeing one of his performances: "The human aspect of his dance is terrifying enough, but to witness him being transformed into some sort of lifeless object is a truly fearful experience." On such occasions, Kazuo's body comes within close reach of becoming pure matter; his gaze acquires the look seen in a dead person's eyes. Watching such a radical change of appearance is indeed frightening.

I suppose that Kazuo, in attaching himself to a wall, can completely erase all his individual and human characteristics, and thereby banish all traces of his personal psychology. Watching someone turn into a wall, or something not even remotely related to one's everyday image of that person, can provoke quite a disconcerting effect. And, just as in our daily lives we hide our faces behind a social mask so as to conceal our true identities, our social body, by the same token, wears an armor that renders our real body invisible. In the noh theatre, for example, the player eradicates any hint of his individual and human identity by putting on a mask of the character to be portrayed before he sets foot on the bridge leading from the greenroom to the stage. In that respect, a noh mask acts as a wall between the public and the player; it effectively conceals his body from view.[10]

On clinging to a wall, Kazuo doesn't grow into a human or plant-like figure but turns instead into an inorganic formless mass. That his physical appearance undergoes such a radical change underpins the fact that the human body inherently possesses the potential to alter the image it projects. Even though this modified body image is an clearly an illusion, it can still provoke a deep sense of disquiet among the public. As an analogy, think of the mechanical manner in which the Nazi storm troopers marched in goose step. The way Kazuo abruptly transforms himself from an ordinary, everyday human being one moment into a totally alien object the next re-

2.

Performance

minds me, in its own peculiar way, of how those troops became
utterly dehumanized.

In classical ballet or even mainstream dance one rarely, if ever,
sees a dancer perform the *atozusari,* a movement in which a
dancer bashfully retires to the wings or out of sight. Still, we are all
familiar with how it feels to be shy or embarrassed, or of wanting
to slip quietly away like a child whenever a stranger intrudes on its
private space. In this movie still (see fig. 38) taken on an outdoor
shoot with the film director, Werner Schroeter[11] during the 1980
Nancy International Theatre Festival, Kazuo's hand has ostensibly
transformed itself into a bird's claw clutching at the wall. Given
that this was his maiden voyage to Europe, he was understandably
somewhat anxious at being displaced from his habitual surroundings. No longer resembling a human hand, his fingers have tensed
into a bird's claw. Further, in observing this shot closely, we can see
how Kazuo stares vacantly into thin air. Unconsciously, his body
language reveals those cat- or bird-like creatures inhabiting him,
or perhaps even those animals dormant in each of us. On such oc-

Food

for the

Soul

60

casions, his movements are astonishing: they display an animal's instinctive reaction to being suddenly confronted with an unfamiliar environment. Kazuo cannot conceal his utter bewilderment at finding himself in such a far-flung place. He doesn't seem to really take it in; his whole body language betrays the feeling of being completely lost.

I recall another remarkable instance of such spatial and temporal displacement when we performed *The Dead Sea* at Lyons Théâtre de Célestins (1986). I should mention that even before setting foot onstage, Kazuo already has a preconceived image of the universe he is about to inhabit. On that particular occasion, Kazuo's hand started feeling his way along the stone wall of the stairway leading from the dressing room to the performing space. It was as though his hands were listening to something very carefully. In one sense, I suppose this gesture helped put him at ease in unfamiliar surroundings. Yet at the same time, it struck me that his hands were more than an expressive tool; they were also guiding him toward something. On being questioned about the suite *Ghost Dances* that he performs in *The Dead Sea,* Kazuo answered: "They are like the wandering footsteps of the dead in search of or love." The spirits of the dead, in his view, are in a constant state of yearning. Watching him listen carefully to that wall made me realize how his hands had transformed themselves into the ears of those spirits living in him.

39–40. "Ohno creates dramatic tension through a subtle use of 'empty' space." Improvisation, Montreal, 1981. © Jack Udashikin.

2.

Performance

Fluidity

Any attempt to predict how Kazuo will move, or what he will do onstage, is fruitless. On the whole, his individual movements are so inextricably intertwined that it's virtually impossible to break them down into separate segments. While each step and gesture plays an integral part of a larger whole, they somehow manage to remain self-contained. Seamlessly linked, they create a flowing continuity.

Kazuo does make the occasional what one might call "mistake" during the course of a public performance. Normally, a dancer would swiftly attempt to camouflage such misses by making whatever adjustments were necessary. Kazuo, however, intuitively takes advantage of such opportunities to explore the great unknown. This come-what-may attitude, even in public performance, enables him to thrust deeper into himself. Given that such happenings are by their very nature unpredictable, he has no control over how they unravel.

A close study of how Kazuo utilizes the various possibilities offered by performing spaces reveals clearly that his performances do not pivot exclusively on physical movement. If anything, non-movement and a bold use of the scenic space actively contribute to how he engages the public's imagination. By restricting, lets say, his movements to one side of the stage, Kazuo thereby creates a vacuum laden with potential on the opposite side. The India ink sketches known as *suibokuga*[12] provide a perfect model for the constructive use of emptiness. In these sketches, the brush artist's effective use of blank space performs a crucial role in breathing

Food for the Soul

62

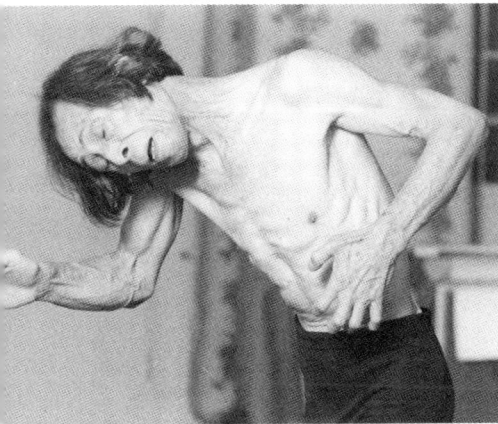

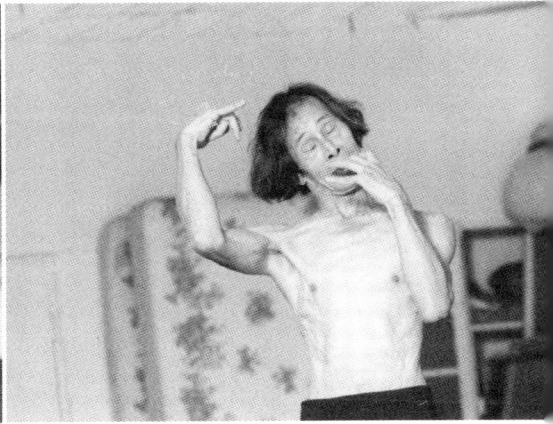

life into the image. Similarly, Kazuo's intuitive grasp of how and where to place himself onstage bears considerably on the public's overall perception. Those seemingly empty spaces in the India ink sketches, albeit primarily employed as a compositional device, are what ultimately render the black lines vibrant. Such resourceful use of what is often considered "nothing" is truly inventive. The impression Kazuo creates is one of effectively blending certain elements of the *suibokuga* tradition and the Western choreographic school—in particular, German expressionist dance. Endowed with a rare ability to freely draw on both idioms without leaning unduly toward either, Kazuo thoroughly commands all the means at his disposal. The influence of German expressionistic dance, in my view, is most visible in those movements that are slightly too demonstrative.

Yet another remarkable example of this come-what-may approach was to be seen at a performance at the Eglise Saint Jacques du Haut Pas in Paris[13] on his first visit to Europe in 1980. An awkward moment, in which Kazuo became unsure of what to do next, arose during the course of the recital. He seized upon the occasion by approaching a nearby statue of the Blessed Virgin and Child and started to tickle the sole of the infant Jesus' foot with the flower he happened to be holding in his hand. "In the circumstances," he remarked, "it was the only thing I could do."

As for me, I'm completely unable to step into the unknown with his sense of abandon. I would absolutely hate to find myself in such a predicament onstage. Yet somehow, I must admit that in daring to take that leap into unfamiliar territory, I might perhaps

2.

Performance

———

63

45. A blind organist
accompanied Ohno
at the Salle Poirel,
Nancy, 1980.
© Teijiro Kamiyama.

reveal what the public genuinely long to discover—the body's hidden truths. Letting the body move of its own accord, however, doesn't necessarily imply physical movement; this can happen even within immobility.

Makeup

From butoh's early days white makeup has been an integral feature of its aesthetic. In some respects, a butoh performer's objective in applying makeup to the face and body is similar to the noh player's intent in using a mask. While noh in all its refined elegance might strike one as being unrelated to the more primal butoh, the two dance forms do nonetheless have some principles in common. In wearing a mask, the noh actor-dancer supposedly becomes one with the character of the person or spirit he is to portray and, as such, brings that character or spirit to life. Applying *shiro-nuri* (white makeup), however, doesn't confine a butoh performer to a specific role. If anything, it offers the scope to transform himself with greater freedom.

When it comes to choosing which color makeup to use, white is the obvious choice, for it erases all superficial expression. Whitening oneself from head to toe could be viewed as an act of neutralizing and converting the body into a blank canvas. In applying makeup, we aren't, as often presumed, painting something onto the body. Rather, we're erasing something, namely, our private history. This process of self-obliteration, in effect, makes it possible us to become someone or something else. In concrete terms, it helps us to transform our sense of body. In conventional drama and theatre, makeup primarily functions as a means to fabricate an immediately identifiable expression for the audience. In butoh, however, our aim is completely the opposite. In applying *shiro-nuri*, we long to remove all trace of natural expression. And white makeup is what facilitates this deconstruction.

Kazuo often distorts the shape of the eyes through the use of thick black eyeliner (see fig. 46). By accentuating his facial features, he renders them more clearly discernible, even when viewed from a distance. His gaze, for example, can be distinctly perceived. Though it might strike one as contradictory, Kazuo's simultaneous need to highlight his facial features, on the one hand, and to neutralize his body, on the other, do not run counter to each other. We, as performers, must be attentive to how the "fictional" body we create onstage is perceived by the public. Given the essential role makeup plays in the image-making process, Kazuo uses

whatever means at his disposal to fabricate this illusion. And yet, it must be said that his true objective is to render himself invisible.

Photographic Subjects

In preparing a new piece, we inevitably reach a point where we feel the need to call in a photographer to attend a run-through at our rehearsal studio. Customarily, we invite one along once the basic structure is in place. For some inexplicable reason, the work in progress does not begin to jell until we go through what has become an almost ritual-like process of having a rehearsal captured or recorded on film. We only commence adding body and substance to the skeletal structure after first taking that indispensable step.

In effect, by exposing ourselves to an objective appraisal, we also assume the role of a photographer's subject matter. Over time we've come to realize that we could never grasp the underlying reality of our work were we not to go through the experience of being observed from without. Indeed, while Kazuo and I clearly comprehend the differences between looking at and seeing one another, or between being a spectator and being the spectacle, we would still be at a loss to decide how the various physical and psychological elements of a piece should fall into place without first of all coming under the objective scrutiny of a camera lens. Remarkably, once we go through that ritual, it all comes into perspective. In the normal run of events, we invite a photographer interested in shooting a rehearsal to our workshop studio in Kamihoshikawa, or very occasionally, as was the case with Eikoh Hosoe,[14] we visit his studio. After we see the results, an overall image finally begins to emerge. We can then start moving forward with the project, and commence building upon the skeletal structure. Obtaining an objective appraisal is an important step in the evolution of the work in progress.

A dancer's natural disposition to perform in public is obviously related with his or her need to "be seen." The novelist Yukio Mishima, for instance, once played a role in a performance at Tokyo's Nissei Theatre, in which, if my memory serves me well, he wore a hat. Sometime later, he confessed that he could never give up the stage, or, as he put it himself, "The moment I stood out under those ramp lights, I felt that this is what I was born for." Such is the seductive power that the stage holds over us. Regardless of how painful exposing ourselves to public scrutiny might be, we, as dancers, nonetheless continue putting ourselves through the

2.

Performance

67

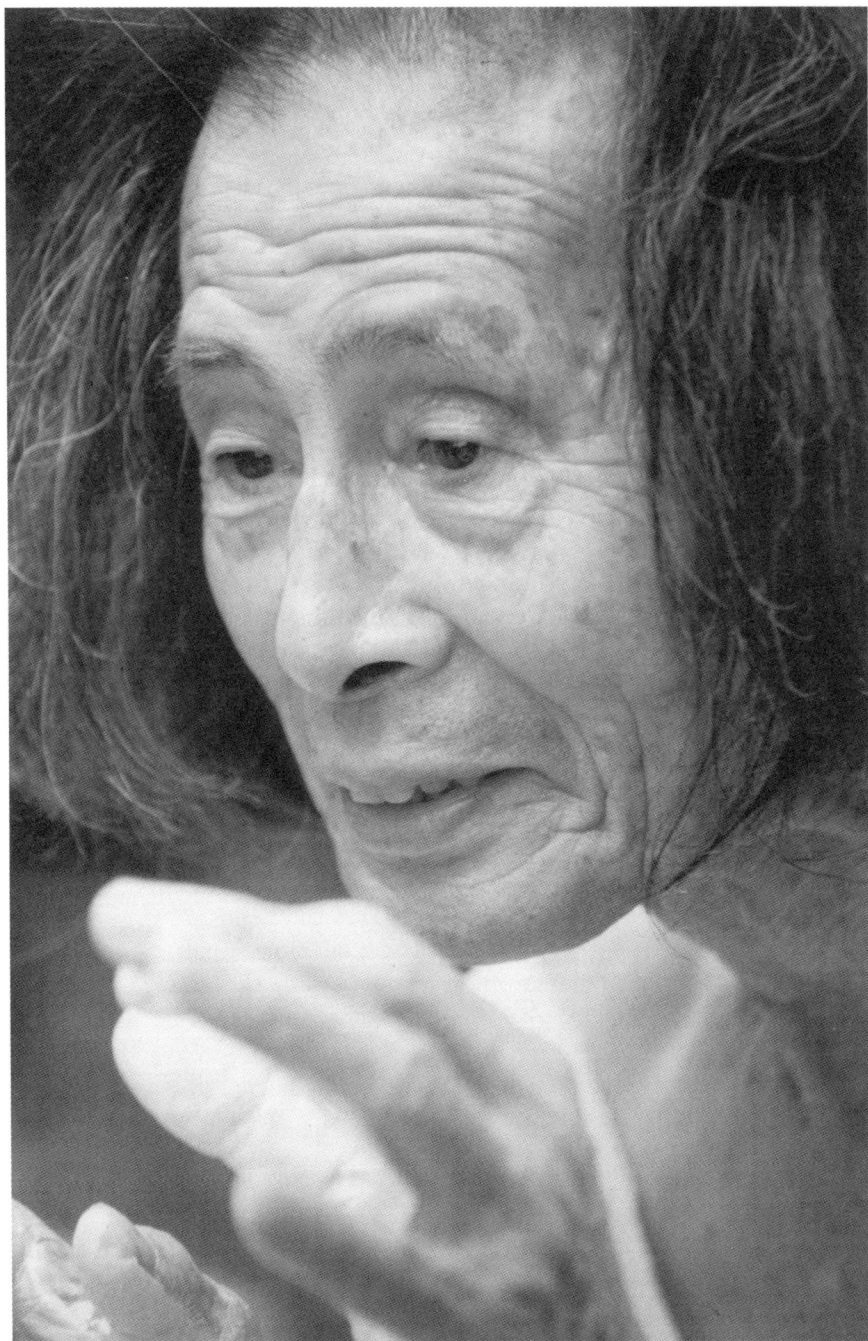

47. Pre-makeup
portrait, workshop
studio, 1988.
© Alain Denis.

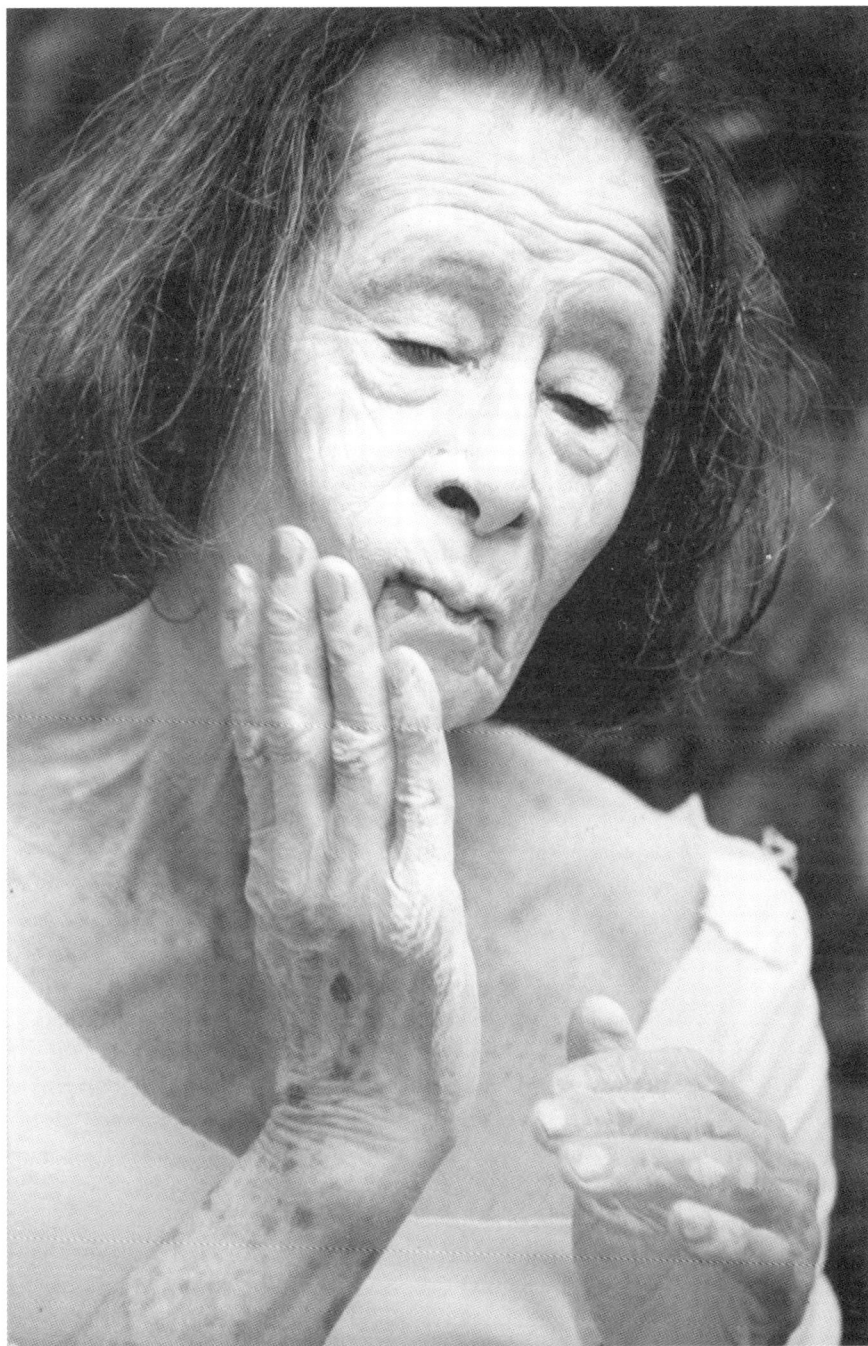

48. "Ohno erases his everyday self by means of white makeup." Workshop studio, 1988. © Alain Denis.

ordeal. Even if we consider performing as a form of masochistic behavior, we still derive some pleasure from the experience. Obviously, we wouldn't continue doing so without some form of psychological gratification.

Kazuo has always enjoyed having his photograph taken. If at all possible, he would even have photographers come onstage so that they could keep clicking away. He has no problem with them coming right up beside him if they require a better angle. This fondness for being photographed also explains why there are many shots of him preparing in the dressing room. The flash or click of a camera doesn't bother him in the slightest. I would go so far as to say that he gets even a certain thrill on being stalked in this manner. For Kazuo, the boundary between dancing onstage and sitting beforehand in a dressing room is as good as nonexistent.

He displays exactly that same nonchalance in his ordinary, everyday life. On many an occasion, just as we are about to bid good-bye to a guest at our home, Kazuo gets it into his head to invite them into the workshop studio. On stepping into the rehearsal space, he picks out a CD and proceeds to dance without the slightest hesitation. He's always ready to dance at the drop of a hat, irrespective of the setting, whether it be an opening party at a gallery, among his students at the workshop, at an outdoor location, for an encore call, wherever. Once he gets into the flow of things, he just keeps on dancing. Kazuo makes no distinction whatsoever between dancing on- and offstage; he puts his heart and soul into it, no matter what the circumstance. As far as he's concerned, the stage and life are one and the same.

At times Kazuo has been described by the public as being "playful." Does that, I wonder, mean that he has the sense of wonder of a child? The responses to the questionnaire at the recent performance in Osaka would seem to indicate that the younger members of the audience see him in this light. The respondents were, for the most part, in their late teens or early twenties. One sixteen-year-old went so far as to describe him as "mischievous Mister Ohno." He appears to be full of fun, even seen from their youthful perspective.

It apparently doesn't bother Kazuo to be photographed during the rest periods between performances. I, on the other hand, decline such offers because, for me, dance involves a process whereby I undergo a transformation. Needless to say, Kazuo is completely indifferent to such concerns and is willing to be photographed at almost any time. This, I suppose, accounts for why he has been photographed so often over the years.

"In preparing a new piece, the day comes when we need a photographer to come to a run-through at the studio." Ohno at a civic reception in Nancy City Hall, 1980. © Ohno Dance Studio Archives.

Food

for the

Soul

To change the subject, I recall an incident that occurred back in the sixties when Kazuo was still participating in Tatsumi Hijikata's happenings. Just as the performance was about to begin, Hijikata told one of his students, Kishi Ono, to run down to the dressing room and see what was keeping Kazuo. It turned out that my father was listening to the stock market report on the radio. Apparently, he was concerned about some shares he held at that time.

I must admit that I've had occasion to become pretty vexed with him for the way he chatters incessantly in the dressing room. I often wonder what on earth he could be prattling on about. Here we are in the midst of getting ready for a performance, and he just keeps on talking away. On listening more carefully, it often turns out to be nothing more than idle chatter and small talk. Kazuo's spontaneity remains unconstrained in any situation; it makes no difference to him whatsoever whether he's applying makeup to his face, dancing onstage, or going about his business in his everyday life—he remains imperturbably himself at all times.

Femininity

For the second day of a run, we occasionally ask Kazuo to consider trying on a different costume so that we can see how it compares with his choice on opening night. What matters most, however, is not variation for the sake of variation in itself, but rather the response the costume evokes in him. Kazuo's dance doesn't come to life unless he's deeply charmed by what he wears. In making a selection he must, above all else, take his subjective response into account. A gown, lets say, that doesn't become a second skin, won't do anything for him, no matter how much his dressing assistant tries to render it more attractive. His instinctive response to the costume is what really counts, not the garment itself.

In reply to the often asked question why he performs dressed as a woman, Kazuo has repeatedly stated: "My intention in dressing as a woman onstage has never been to become a female impersonator, or to transform myself into a woman. Rather, I want to trace my life back to its most distant origins. More so than anything else, I long to return to where I've come from." Kazuo's separation from his mother, in my view, has been not only a constant source of pain but also the driving force behind this spiritual journey back to his roots. More specifically, Kazuo's dance embodies both the joy and the anguish of a newborn baby separated from its prenatal environment. His performances constantly revolve around two fundamental facts of life: death—the severance of biological links with his mother—and birth, the beginning of an autonomous existence.

Death and life, in that order, are the predominant themes in the opening scenes of *Admiring La Argentina*,[15] in which Kazuo poignantly portrays Genet's prostitute's last moments. While death is often seen as being the ultimate rupturing force in the continuity of mortal existence, at the same time it unearths a more profound continuity of existence. Climbing up onto the stage from the auditorium, Kazuo symbolically departs this life, only to return later, reborn as a young girl. When he quietly rises to his feet on the exact spot where in the previous scene he had collapsed and died as a prostitute, one has the impression that a different person has been born before one's very eyes.

Food for the Soul

This photograph captures something truly awesome (see fig. 54). Watching Kazuo onstage, we tend to miss such fleeting facial expressions, as more often than not we're captivated by his movements. In fact, photographs have that peculiar capacity to catch what eludes the naked eye. In this particular sequence from *Ad-*

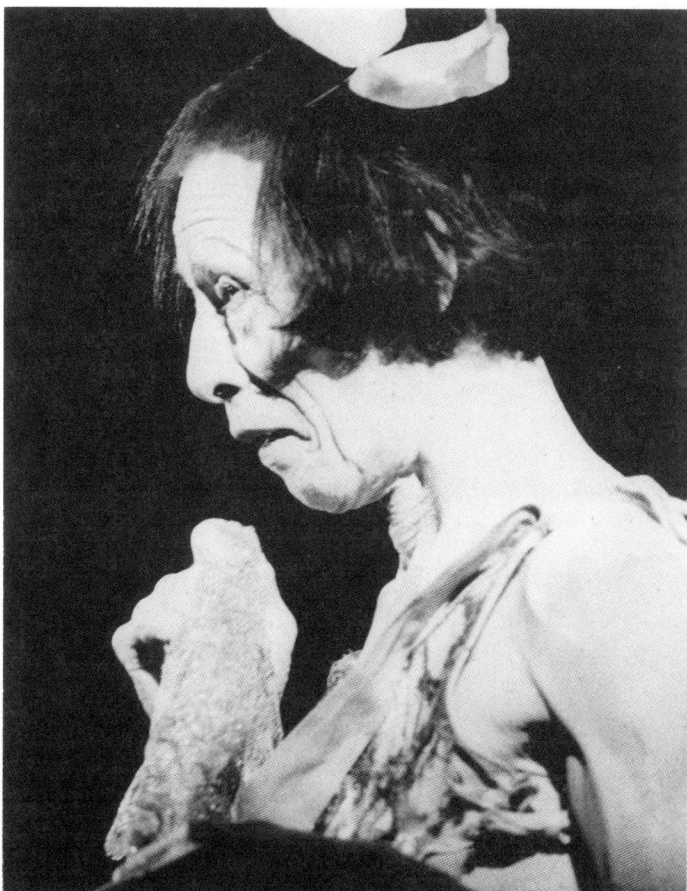

54. "The telltale signs of old age are already present even though he has been reborn as a young girl." *Admiring La Argentina*, 1977. © Hiroaki Tsukamoto.

miring La Argentina, Kazuo emerges into our deranged world, a world in which life engenders death and death gives birth to life. While he is ostensibly portraying a young girl, one can see how his face is marked by old age.

Over the years, Kazuo has portrayed a variety of female types. His dance aesthetic doesn't restrict him to merely emulating or impersonating the conventional mannerisms of beautiful women. This approach starkly differs from the hackneyed attempts of some other female impersonators. I would even venture to say that Kazuo has enlarged the scope of his dance aesthetic so as to give expression to a flesh ravaged by time, illness, and infirmity. His portraits are not only confined to aging beauty; he has appeared at times in the guise of a wicked woman or an old hag.

Food

for the

Soul

———

78

With regard to the choice of costume for his female "roles," we find that a dress, more so than any other form of woman's clothing, offers the most potent symbol of love and beauty. Inevitably, it symbolizes a mother's unconditional love for her offspring. No doubt that's why Kazuo repeatedly speaks of the symbiotic relationship between mother and child. In his own words, "My dance is born from love." Seen from a filial perspective, his habit of wearing female garments onstage is nothing other than an instinctive response to a yearning to rejoin his mother. In a sense, he can't help but wear similar clothing, for, in doing so he feels that he's drawing closer to her. Kazuo's intention isn't to cross-dress, nor, for that matter, would I say that he's even conscious that he's dressed as a woman. If anything, he wants to reveal both the feminine and masculine aspects of the universe.

Kazuo opinions on the gender issue have evoked some interest. His basic tenet is that all of us contain both female and male energy, irrespective of gender. As far as I can see, he doesn't emphasize his masculinity by speaking harshly, or deliberately acting in a so-called manly way in his day-to-day life. I, at any rate, haven't caught glimpse of such behavior. He doesn't by any means indulge himself; nor for that matter does he hide his shortcomings. Mind you, he doesn't make a point of revealing his weaknesses either. Being openly himself, he is somebody completely devoid of social defenses.

Until quite recently my father never carried a coin purse. He would simply put whatever cash he needed in his pocket. As a child, I recall being envious of my classmates. I kept imagining to myself how their fathers would beckon to them and say, "Hey, boy, come over here," so as to give their children some pocket money. That wasn't Kazuo's style. Even at home he was wholly oblivious of what it meant to be the mainstay of the household. He never sat imposingly at the head of the family table or behaved in a father-like manner.

Speaking of life in the womb, Kazuo often claims: "Before birth, there is no such thing as being a man or a woman. Bodies long forgotten, the bodies of those long gone astray in memory are still living inside of me." By wearing female clothing, Kazuo says that he wants to shed the masculine role he assumes in his troubled everyday existence. When he puts on a gown, he can discard the social conventions inhibiting him and thereby fulfill his deeply held longing to return to where he originally came from. His body, through dance, is able to come into contact with its true nature.

2.

Performance

55. "I was neither man
nor woman before
birth." *Room*, Tokyo
1966. © Ohno Dance
Studio Archives.

However, Kazuo can't encounter all of the spirits alive inside of him by dressing as a man. That, in my view, underlies his choice of female clothing for some dances.

Masculinity

In selecting a costume for his male "roles," Kazuo Ohno frequently chooses formal black attire along with a man's starched, white, dress shirt. His choice of such clothes in *The Dead Sea* clearly illustrates this tendency to don mourning wear for dances thematically dealing with the fundamental questions of human existence, namely, life and death. Apparently, he prefers the formal attire worn traditionally at marriages, births, and funerals over the plainer two-piece suit. Ceremonial wear, in his view, is what is really needed for dances on such a solemn theme. Given that clothing also functions as a nonverbal idiom, Kazuo's ritualistic use of a tailcoat, for example, provides an audience with an instantly recognizable symbol of how life and death are finely interwoven (see fig. 56).

Naturally, a dancer's scope in movement varies considerably depending on the choice of costume. Needless to say, the impressions evoked by a suit and a gown are poles apart. For one thing, the body responds differently, and the performer's appearance undergoes an outright transformation as well. In Kazuo's case, however, we've got to keep in mind that the reason behind his choice of formal attire is that it makes it possible for him to create a perceptibly "phallic" image. An ordinary suit would be totally out of place on such occasions, for it makes him appear too delicate. Regardless of gender, we all exude both male and female energies. Even though Kazuo effortlessly renders incarnate contrasting masculine and feminine traits such as stiffness or softness, it is his choice of costume that ultimately determines his overall expressiveness. In his masculine dances the costume has to elicit an erotic image.

Depending on whether the character portrayed is male or female, Kazuo's movement style noticeably alters. With regard to his choice of musical accompaniment, he tends to prefer the Viennese waltz or Franz Liszt's piano works for male "roles," because he feels that such romantically charged works are fitting for dances brimming with dynamism. The Viennese waltz, in particular, remains a personal favorite for him. As a musical form, the waltz, for Kazuo, has an air of finality about it that somehow summons up a "death image" of sorts, one that fits very well with his dance

2.

Performance

aesthetic. Incidentally, I recall how an evening's entertainment at Hijikata's cabaret club[16] would invariably conclude with a waltz-like number. The audience was left in no doubt that the show would soon come to a close.

After completing *Admiring La Argentina*, which incidentally featured a small orchestra playing a suite of tango accompaniments, I suggested to Kazuo that he use the waltz as the backing soundtrack for his next production. As things turned out, the principal musical accompaniment for our next creation, *The Dead Sea*,[17] was none other than the Viennese waltz. Once rehearsals got under way for that piece, Kazuo became totally engrossed with this musical form and ended up training with it for a full five years. I will never forget having to practice to that waltz-time pum-pa-pa, pum-pa-pa rhythm over and over again.

When Kazuo dances as a man, one sometimes feels that he is being trailed by a shadow (see fig. 57). One might describe it as "the shadow of death" looming in the background. It is being drawn upward, or so it seems, at least. Though its trunk floats through midair, the head alone is being pulled into the surrounding darkness. The public is confronted with a specter of sorts, a mind- and bodiless presence personified by this mysterious shadow rising delicately from out of nowhere. Witnessing such a full-blooded human being and its "dancing" shadow right in front of their very eyes, people in the audience are forced to ask themselves which of them is real. Perhaps, Kazuo's deliberate choice of formal mourning attire is his way of voicing the sadness of those spirits inside of him whose lives were cut short. In donning the outward tokens of sorrow, he at once embodies their unquenchable yearning for life, and renders incarnate their grief.

Kazuo has often portrayed those women who played determining roles in his life. La Argentina and his mother readily come to mind as pertinent examples. Strangely, in performing as a man, he doesn't personify his father or any other corresponding male figure. In my view, he doesn't, as such, leave the door open for them. If anything, I would say that he embodies the spirits of those who haven't made it to this world. Human beings, as seen from Kazuo's evolutionary perspective, are born as a result of death, the death of others.

The expression Kazuo assumes in the scene depicted in figure 56 epitomizes suffering. Formal attire imposes a serious demeanor on the part of the person wearing it, especially given the circumstances in which it is customarily worn. Whether on- or

2.

Performance

83

57. "The shadow of
death appears as
Ohno shunts his
head aside." Ohno
dancing with a frying
pan. © Ohno Dance
Studio Archives.

offstage, the undertones attached to wearing a symbol of mourning are the same. In fact, such an open expression of mourning and grief necessitates that Kazuo psychologically brace himself ahead of a performance.

As Kazuo, dressed in a black tuxedo, danced to a recording of Liszt's *Liebestraum* in the closing scene of *My Mother*,[18] he was trying to show his gratitude, not solely to the audience, but also to his mother—something he had been unable to do during her lifetime. By his own admission, Kazuo considers those male characters he portrays onstage to be "someone else." They are, as he puts it, "the lingering souls of the sperm who didn't survive the fight for survival."

That male figure we see so lovingly devoted to his mother is not, however, the everyday flesh-and-blood Kazuo Ohno. Personally speaking, I am terrified to witness the outright transformation that comes over Kazuo. I just cannot relate this utterly alien being, who suddenly appears in front of me onstage, with the everyday Kazuo I know. I feel as though I'm looking at someone coming from a long way off in time. It's hard to conceive how such a person could even exist. It is truly frightening to see such a change occur.

Formal black attire is also Kazuo's first choice for performances of what he refers to as the "Spirit" or "Ghost Dances." In these particular pieces, his attention isn't specifically directed at the immediate world. He describes the suite *Ghost Dances* in *The Dead Sea* as "embodying the wandering footsteps of spirits in search of love." In his own words, "Those dead spirits denied themselves the chance of birth so that a single human life could evolve in the womb." Essentially, Kazuo performs out of gratitude to the countless sperm who sacrificed themselves for him.

Quite recently, before a performance, Kazuo happened to speak about that two-year period he spent in captivity in New Guinea jungle at the end of World War II.[19] Of the eight thousand or so soldiers initially interned along with him, some six thousand lost their lives. They often perished as a result of starvation, or the hardships endured after losing their way in the depths of the jungle. Kazuo was among the few survivors who narrowly escaped such a fate. This experience made him face the fact that he was indebted to his colleagues who died during the war and its aftermath, and how, in that respect, he owed his life to them. Surrounded by suffering and death, he was forced to strike against the limits of his own being.

2.

Performance

58. Ohno performing at *Poetry, Butoh, and Jazz* with bassist Keiki Midorikawa, Sound House, Tokyo, 1980. © Ohno Dance Studio Archives.

Avatar

By embodying palpable characteristics of other life forms, Kazuo exemplifies his conviction that one can transform oneself into an animal, a demon, or even the incarnation of a ghost.[20] At one point many years ago, he repeatedly rehearsed insect movement and gesture; paying particular attention to tiny and almost imperceptible ways of moving. His close affinity with other forms of life, and the role this phenomenon plays in his performances goes a long way back. On his return from the war, for instance, the first public recital he gave featured a piece called *The Jellyfish Dance* (1949). Indirectly, this dance echoed the harrowing homecoming sea voyage that he, along with several thousand other former prisoners of war experienced on being repatriated from detention camp in New Guinea.

At the workshops, Kazuo consistently stresses the importance of expanding our physical awareness beyond the limits of our deeply ingrained human sensibility. He encourages participants with off-the-cuff comments such as "Try to turn into an insect" or "How about becoming a fly?" Kazuo, in fact, considers the ability to adapt one's physical responses to one's immediate surroundings as crucial in one's development as a dancer.

59. Ohno wears black formal attire when performing "Ghost Dances." The poet Kazuko Shiraishi is on the right. © Ohno Dance Studio Archives.

2.

Performance

A concrete example of such an outright transformation could be seen when he performed as an insect in *Mushibiraki,* at the commemorative performance for Hijikata in Yamagata prefecture (1987; see fig. 60). At this open-air event, Kazuo's gestures unified the workings of mind and body to such an extent that he virtually became an insect. His immediate response to the surroundings was purely instinctive. One could see how his body was already in motion ever before it started reacting to mental dictates. The initial sensory response was swiftly followed by a physical one. His movements were completely spontaneous and not just calculated to make him resemble an insect. Kazuo's constantly stresses the importance of awakening such an awareness. He encourages us to thoroughly study an insect's response to its environment; he believes it fundamental that we grasp how an insect's sensory awareness functions. In his view, we should first acquire the insect's tactile sense before attempting to physically move like one.

Flowers

In Kazuo's aesthetic discourse, a flower is constantly cited as the ideal mode of existence, one, in fact, that every dancer should aspire to. Speaking in relation to his own dance, Kazuo insists that his physical presence must at all times be flowerlike. One sees him in this image clasping a white paper flower in his right hand—he took to holding a flower in this hand from around the time he first staged *My Mother* in 1981 (see fig. 61). By becoming an integral part of the body's nervous system, a flower functions much in the same way as an insect's antennae do: constantly palpitating the air. Not only does it receive and respond to incoming stimuli, it also acts as a natural extension to the hand, and, in doing so, becomes a point of contact with the outside world. It functions independently, as though it were an external eye detached from the trunk of the body. In that respect, it exists both as an autonomous entity and as a sensory organ.

Tatsumi Hijikata would occasionally perform using a flower, but, in contrast to Kazuo, he tended to hold it in his left hand. Hijikata's attitude differed in the sense that while he created an intimate relationship with a flower, it didn't assume the function of an independent sensory organ. If anything, it became an intrinsic part of the body.

Kazuo repeatedly stresses that one should rise from a chair, for instance, in the way a flower blossoms. A flower, he explains, inevitably opens itself out on rising forth from the earth. By the

2.

Performance

89

same token, a dancer needs to arrive at a physiological level of awareness where his or her physical responses are no longer shackled by deliberation. In everyday life, we customarily tend to lean slightly forward before rising to our full height, whereas a flower simply reaches upward without the slightest hesitation. Dance, in his view, should never be reduced to mechanically replicating routine daily movements and postures; it should instead allow us experience within ourselves how a flower blossoms. In speaking of the necessity of "becoming a flower," as Kazuo in fact often does, he lays particular emphasis on how we should strip ourselves of everything—habits, technique, vanity.

When it comes to choosing a flower, the Buddha's sacred lotus seems to be Kazuo's favorite.[21] His particular attachment to this species of water lily is largely due to the fact that they don't all flower at once; they do so one at a time, and moreover, they do so calmly, without indulging in any flashy display. Once, during a visit to a temple in Kamakura on the anniversary of Tatsuhiko Shibusawa's death, Kazuo turned to me as we stood there admiring the lilies on the pond and said that one day he, too, would like to be able to dance the way the lotus did.

Kazuo used to enjoy pottering about in the garden at home, cultivating cosmos and other such flowers. I was happy to see him busy himself in this way, as it struck me as being a fruitful exercise for dance making. Working in the garden brought him into direct contact with plant life, and thus with life itself. He wasn't really cultivating flowers as such but learning at firsthand how they interacted with their environment. This assimilation of, and rapport with other forms of life constitutes a fundamental element in his dance, and its evolution over time. Needless to say, Kazuo's performances would never encompass the scope they do had he simply gone to the workshop studio to compose a choreography. Reading or studying books would never have provided him with that kind of vital knowledge.

A photographer who specializes in shooting a particular flower once remarked that no matter how closely one approaches it, its appeal never weakens—even if shot at very close range. Dancers and people, however, unavoidably lose some of their magnetism if put under such close scrutiny. In looking through this collection of photos, I'm struck by how Kazuo's expressive range and depth holds its own with a flower. In this respect, he can truly be called flowerlike.

Now, at over ninety years of age,[22] Kazuo isn't nearly as physi-

61. Ohno clasping a paper flower in his right hand in *The Dead Sea.* © Naoya Ikegami.

2.

Performance

cally agile as he once was. Though he used to have as much energy as required to create a vast universe onstage, nowadays he is somewhat restricted by an inevitable decline in his physical powers. Speaking in terms of a flower's life cycle, one could describe Kazuo's as gradually approaching that season where it withers and falls. While some might consider him as well past his prime, his inner vitality has not forsaken him. Even in this physically diminished state, he remains fully alive. The intensity of these waning moments, as the divide between life and death starts drawing in, has generated a lyricism and fragrance hitherto unknown in his work. At an age when most dancers have long abandoned their careers, the essential strength of his dance emerges even more forcefully despite the fact his body is progressively weakening.

Obviously, as performers age, the uglier they become, outwardly, at any rate. Yet the onset of old age shouldn't blind us to another, truly invaluable, form of beauty in their withering away. In classical ballet, for example, dancers who are no longer considered superficially attractive—those who are tired and ravaged from the all the wear and tear that the years have inevitably taken on their faces and bodies—are ignored and forced to abandon their stage

Food

for the

Soul

_____

63. "Ohno, in play-
ing with flowers,
'becomes a
flower.'" Nancy,
1980. © Teijiro
Kamiyama.

careers. They should never, in my estimation, be cast aside in this way, for they have still something truly precious to offer. Decrepitude offers the public a fleeting glimpse of another form of beauty, a beauty that a young performer could never render incarnate.

Twosome

Irrespective of how accomplished or talented one may be, one inevitably remains incomplete without some form of interaction with others. Tatsumi Hijikata, for instance, always stressed the importance of form in dance; he believed that once the structure and choreography had been established, the content would subsequently emerge of itself. In his own words, "Life catches up with form." Kazuo, on the other hand, even to this very day, holds the diametrically opposite view: form comes of itself, only insofar as there is a spiritual content to begin with. While both approaches sound like viable working practices, one and the same person could never employ such conflicting methods.

A similar dramatic tension underlies my working relationship with my father. It is Kazuo who places the utmost significance on the spiritual aspect of dance. For him, movement is utterly dependent on a spiritual presence. I, on the other hand, invariably emphasize the more physical aspects; I concentrate in as much as possible on the form dance assumes.

A good illustration of our differing approaches could be seen in when we performed *A White Lotus in Bloom* at Tokyo's FM Hall accompanied by the pianist Miyake Haruna. There was a grand piano onstage, whose beautiful curved lines struck me forcefully. I wanted to try to incorporate its arresting shape into the visual backdrop. Yet Kazuo, in typical fashion, wouldn't have anything of the sort. He said he wanted to dance more freely and not be in any way constrained by what he considered an unnecessary prop. Though our opinions openly clashed on this issue, I nonetheless was determined to avail of its beautiful shape in the scenic space. I thought to myself at the time: "If Kazuo isn't going to dance with that piano in the background, well then, damn it, I will!"

Also, our conceptions of space clearly differ: Kazuo is inclined to take advantage of the entire scenic space; he freely utilizes the auditorium, the aisles, the floor, the seats, or wherever he deems fit to create his universe. I, on the other hand, dance in a restricted area within the confines of the stage. But I consider this is a positive feature of our working relationship, in that having contrasting viewpoints and ways of relating to space only enriches our work.

Food

for the

Soul

——

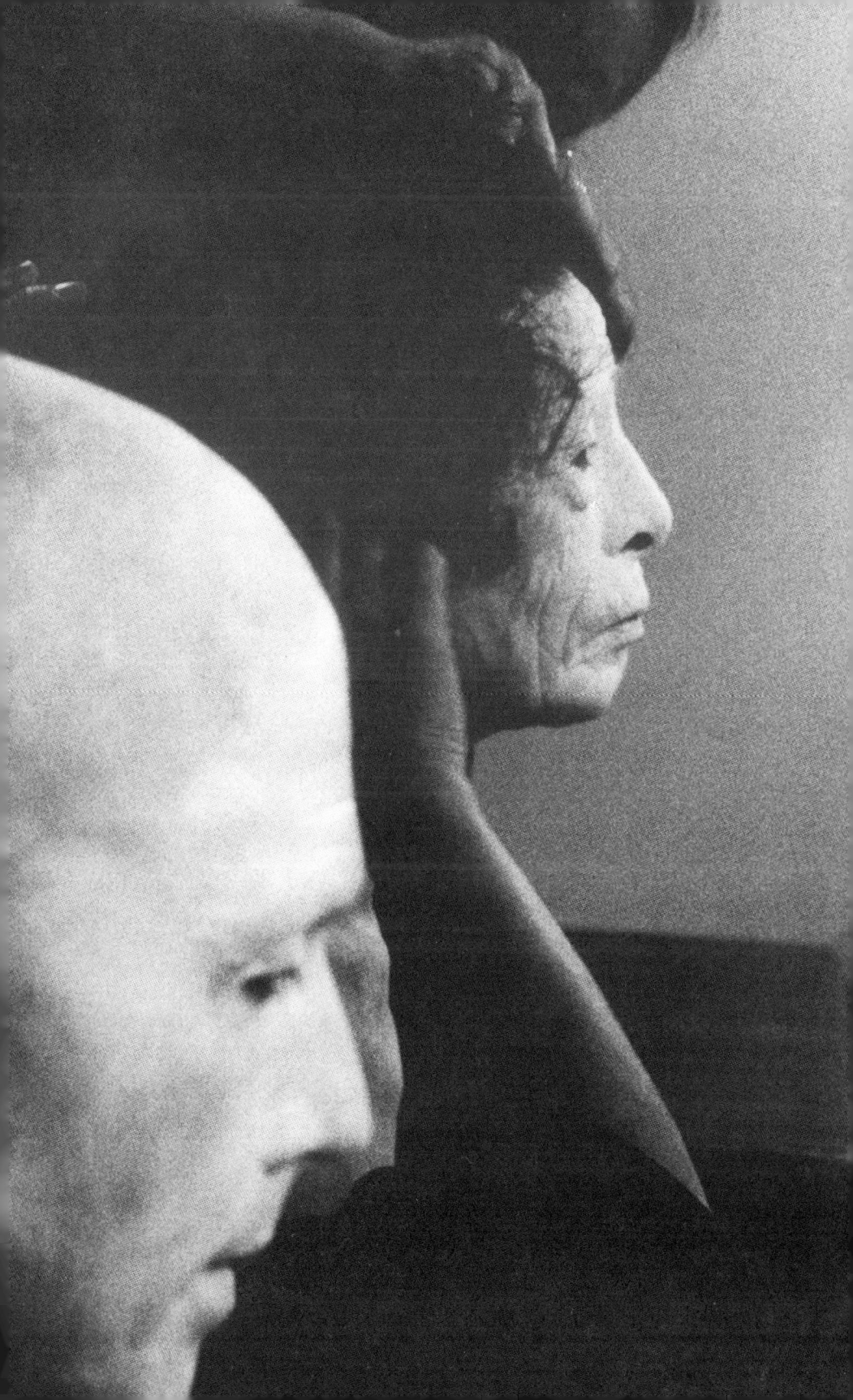

Kazuo frequently quotes from Swedenborg's tale of a man and wife who, despite their inherently different, and often clashing personalities, went on to become reconciled and united as a single angel in heaven on their departure from this world.[23] Our relationship onstage could be described in somewhat similar terms. While having separate identities and completely opposite approaches both to rehearsal and performance, we nonetheless successfully merge into a larger whole. And yet we somehow manage to retain

Food

for the

Soul

——

our individual voices. Ultimately though, when it comes to setting foot onstage, we both realize that our separate identities must merge as one. We don't try to upstage each other or engage in rivalry. Notwithstanding that we are two individuals, with very independent streaks, the public is left with the impression that we jointly strive to create a single entity in our work.

66. "We remain incomplete without interaction with others." Kazuo and Yoshito Ohno in *Room*, 1966. © Ohno Dance Studio Archives.

Chapter 3

Beginnings and Family Life

Modern Dance Recitals

My earliest recollection of watching my father dance dates back to the time I was in third grade of elementary school. That was around 1947, a period in which Japan was still haunted by the war and its aftermath.

My father was demobilized shortly after his release from internment camp in 1946.[1] Upon his return to Japan, he soon reoccupied the teaching post he had held at the Mission school before the war. As a staff member, use of the gymnasium was free of charge, so he availed himself of the opportunity to resume dance practice, accompanied by a pianist. Money, needless to say, was in scarce supply during those early postwar years. For some reason I, too, ended up attending training sessions. I can distinctly remember having to dance to a motif he gave us: "Dance the sun's bigness!" we were told. From around the time I became a junior high school student, rehearsals moved to the Soshin Girls Baptist High School. I was very embarrassed at having to rehearse together with schoolgirls. Besides, seen in the social context of that time, dance was not regarded as a suitable activity for men.

I became conscious of the fact that Kazuo was a professional dancer on the occasion of his public recital at Tokyo's Kanda Kyoritsu Kodo hall in 1949.[2] I was amazed that so many people—some two thousand spectators—would come to a dance recital given by *my* father. His early recitals were entertaining in a lighthearted vein. He would do things like appear onstage riding a bicycle or dance to a tango accompaniment played by a pianist (see fig. 69). At that time, Kazuo had no choice but to rely on live musicians for accompaniment because he didn't have the means to buy a record player. One should remember that there was nothing like cassettes or a cassette player in those days.

(facing page)
67. Ohno in *The Honeybee's Song*, Tokyo, 1951.
© Ohno Dance Studio Archives.

68. Ohno wearing a mask in *The Devil's Cry*, at his first public dance recital, Kanda Kyoritsu Kodo Hall, Tokyo, 1949. © Ohno Dance Studio Archives.

Funding these recitals was another matter, however. It was our family who had to keep borrowing large sums of money to pay for the expenses incurred in producing these public performances. In the postwar years the government introduced a luxury tax, whereby if an entrance ticket to a performance were to cost, let's say, 300 yen, the performer would then have to pay a corresponding 300 yen tax on every ticket sold. This, in effect, meant that Kazuo was legally obliged to part with the entire takings from the door and hand them over to the tax man.

70. Ohno dances the spirit of an apple in *Fruit from Heaven*, a piece inspired by Jun Takami's poem "Heaven," at the fourth recital, Dai-ichi Seimei Hall, Tokyo, 1953. © Ohno Dance Studio Archives.

In practice, this entailed Kazuo having to visit the tax office prior to a recital so as to have the tickets officially numbered and registered. Occasionally, luck would be on his side, as some kind-hearted tax clerk would tell him: "Please go ahead and number the tickets yourself." Effectively, this allowed him to conceal the actual number of tickets in our possession. We could never have afforded putting on those recitals had we strictly obeyed the regulations in place. I can still recall how, on returning from the tax office, my father would regale us about his dealings with the officials. Some of them, fortunately, went easy on him and overlooked the amount of tickets we issued; others, however, would insist that he count and stamp every last one.

Given such trying conditions, there was absolutely no way Kazuo could eke out a living as a dancer. A recital's production costs came to almost a full year's salary. He would end up spend-

ing on a single recital what he earned in a full year as a teacher. Performing in front of a paying public became a luxury that could be afforded only by those with independent means. In fact, I would say that during those early years, my father never picked up his full wages on payday, for he had always borrowed it in advance. Once payday passed, he would immediately start drawing on the following month's salary. In normal circumstances the strain of such constant borrowing and financial hardship would break anyone's nerve, yet Kazuo remained determined to continue producing the recitals. Come to think of it, I doubt that he ever handed over a full monthly pay packet to my mother.

Those were indeed hard times for Kazuo himself and the family. To compensate for the lack of steady income, my mother went to work for the American army of occupation, at a nearby military base.[3] Faithfully, she brought home her monthly salary of about 14,000 yen.[4] At a later stage she supplemented her income by giving piano lessons. Her contributions toward the household's living expenses were invaluable: her earnings, in fact, made it possible to the pay the tuition fees at the private school that my elder brother and I attended. We were indeed fortunate, as the monthly fee came to about 800 yen each—quite a substantial sum of money at that time.

I now ask myself what spurred Kazuo on to such extremes? What drove his burning passion to perform; what motivated this tenacity to fly in the face of such adverse conditions. To my mind, the two shaping forces that perhaps have impacted on him most

3.

Beginnings

and Family

Life

___

72. Ohno in *Uni-
corn*, performed
at a Takaya Eguchi
recital, 1956.
© Ohno Dance
Studio Archives.

are: firstly, his battlefront experience in World War II. Then, naturally, there was the deep mark his mother left on him. Their relationship has undoubtedly been a primary driving force. A mother,
in Kazuo's view, sacrifices part of her own life so that the embryo
she carries in her womb can survive and develop. His mother
offered him the gift of life, and hence the possibility to grow into
the person he has become. This nurturing link between mother
and child underlies Kazuo's fundamental perspective on life and
dance.

Food

for the

Soul

____

(upper left)
73. Group perfor-
mance; Ohno is on
the extreme right.
© Ohno Dance Studio
Archives.

(middle)
74. Ohno in *Dove* at
the fifth recital at
the Dai-ichi Seimei
Hall, Tokyo, 1959.
© Ohno Dance Studio
Archives.

(upper right)
75 . Ohno in *Shoes,*
1959. © Ohno Dance
Studio Archives.

(bottom)
76. Ohno perform-
ing with Shinji
Kobaysahi, Tokyo,
1951. © Ohno Dance
Studio Archives.

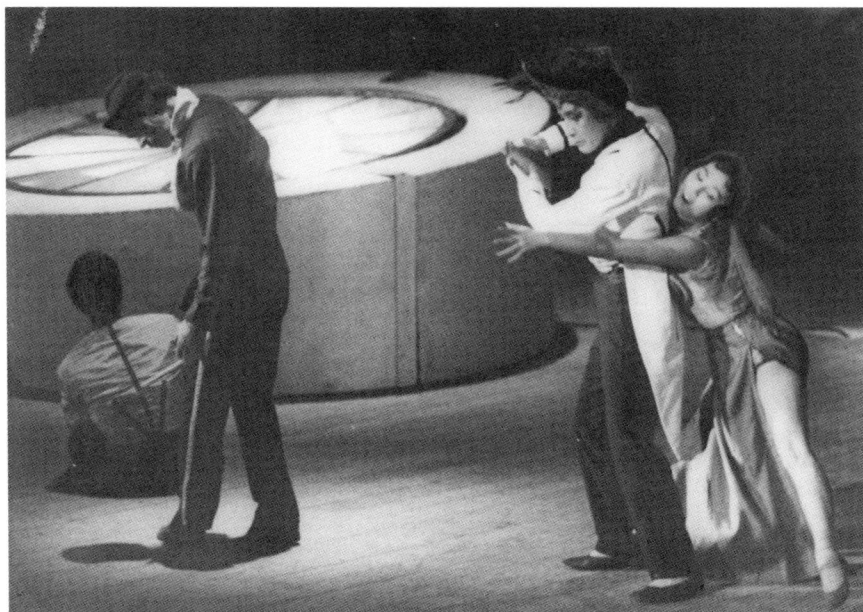

(top)
77. *Barking at the Moon*, 1959. Ohno is on the far left; Takaya Eguchi in the center. © Ohno Dance Studio Archives.

(left)
78. A group shot of an expressionist pose popular in the late 1950s; Ohno stands on the far left. © Ohno Dance Studio Archives.

(left)
79. Portrait, early
1950s. © Ohno Dance
Studio Archives.

(right)
80. Ohno in *Down-
town Rain*, Tokyo,
1951. © Ohno Dance
Studio Archives.

81–83. Ohno with
his group in a real-
istic adaptation
of Ernest Heming-
way's *An Old Man
and the Sea* per-
formed at the
Dai-ichi Seimei
Hall, Tokyo, 1959.
© Ohno Dance
Studio Archives.

World War II

Kazuo often likens himself to Judas Iscariot:[5] "As human beings,"
he maintains, "we couldn't continue to exist without the experience of sinning against God." It's impossible for those of us who
haven't experienced war at first hand to truly grasp the horror that
his generation suffered. It's my belief that Kazuo, along with his
contemporaries, remain in many ways traumatized by what they
went through during those tumultuous years. The subject is seldom discussed, for it would cause Kazuo almost unendurable suffering to be questioned in a judgmental manner about the war—
even by close members of the family.

Kazuo was conscripted in his early thirties, and the following
nine years of his life were spent on active service in the overseas
territories. Initially, he was stationed in western China, and later
sent to New Guinea. Being drafted into a reconnaissance unit, he
didn't, as such, have to engage in combat duty on the battlefields.
His remit didn't involve his bearing arms or getting directly involved in the conflict. Kazuo witnessed the war from behind the
front lines. Over the years, he has given us fragmentary accounts
of his wartime experiences.[6] There were times, he recalls, that he
was so terrified that the hair on his head would positively stand on
end. The enemy would suddenly jump from out of nowhere and
start besieging their positions. He could never forget the cries of
the wild dogs emerging from under the cover of darkness as they
devoured the abandoned corpses that lay strewn about the perime-
ter of their encampment.

Apparently, the infantry would routinely open fire like utter lu-
natics in the war-torn zones. Further, some of troops plundered
money and goods belonging to the local population and then
brought the spoils to Kazuo, who happened to be their senior
officer. He, in turn, would then go and return the loot to their
rightful owners. That was just a taste of what he had to put up
with.

Backstage, before a recent performance, Kazuo gave us an account of the repatriation of the prisoners of war on their release
from the internment camps in New Guinea. He, along with several
thousand other returnees, was crammed onto a ship like sardines in
a tin. The vessel's cramped conditions led to the death of several persons during the homebound passage. Rather than being brought
back to the mainland, the dead were given a sea burial. The ship's
horn was sounded three times as the corpses, wrapped in cloth,
were dropped into sea. The ship would then circle about the spot

Food

for the

Soul

___

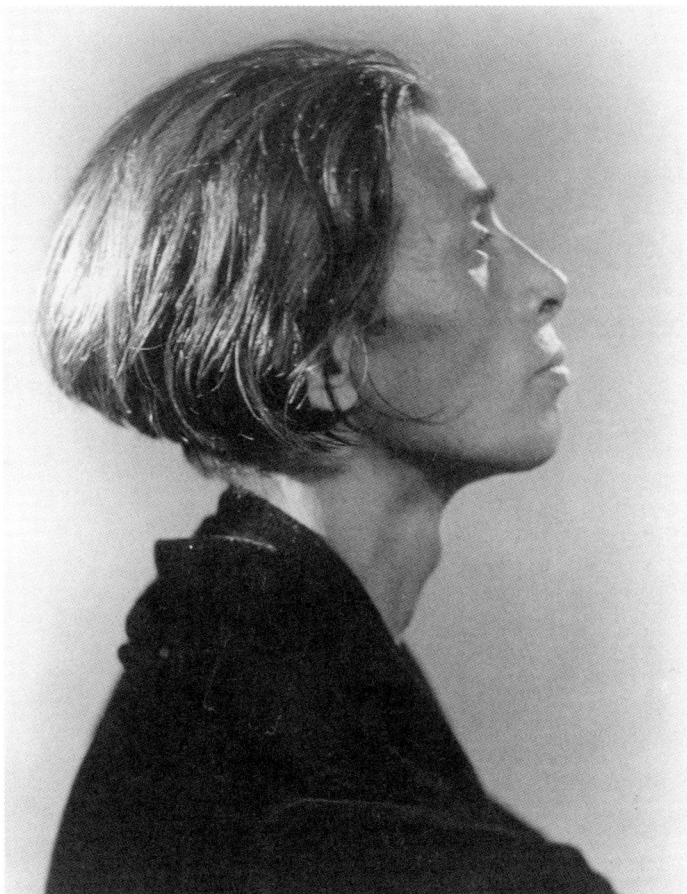

where the bodies had been lain to rest before continuing its journey homeward. The sound of that farewell salute has forever remained with him.

Incidentally, the first choreography Kazuo composed on his return to civilian life was a piece called *The Jellyfish Dance*. Presumably, the sea burials he witnessed had some bearing on the creation of this performance.

Given that most Japanese Christians were inveterate pacifists, and that Kazuo himself had converted to Christianity even before being drafted into the armed forces, we still haven't got around to asking him what he actually did on being sent off to the war zone. Then again, considering what he suffered, he probably couldn't really give us an answer. Or, he might simply respond by saying,

Food

for the

Soul

___

"That's the reason I dance." On the face of it, his strongly held convictions with regard to how life and death are inextricably linked arise from his war front experiences. And yet one can clearly discern that behind these concerns that he still agonizes over what he lived through. Kazuo himself has testified to this in similar terms on numerous occasions.

As I mentioned Kazuo converted to Christianity before the war; in fact, he became a follower of Baptist faith. It was Tasuke Sakata, principal of the Kantō Gakuin,[7]—the school where Kazuo held his first teaching post,—who was ultimately responsible for his conversion to Christianity. Notwithstanding the fact that he was a member of a distinguished military family, Sakata was a devout Christian and, moreover, a disciple of the Christian philosopher

3.

Beginnings

and Family

Life

___

113

Kanzo Uchimura.[8] Kazuo held Sakata in very high esteem and would visit him several times weekly to discuss religion.

Spiritual guidance, in my view, clearly ought to be passed on from one person to the next. Unbeknownst to ourselves perhaps, we all innately possess a spiritual dimension to our lives and a capacity for religious faith if guided accordingly. In Kazuo's case, the person who awakened such a spiritual awareness just happened to be a Baptist.

Mothers

Just recently (1997), I suffered the loss of a mother, and Kazuo that of a wife.[9] Time and again, I've come across friends and acquaintances coping with the death of a parent; I've attended wakes and funerals, offered condolences and sympathy, but I must admit that I never fully realized the true meaning of death until my own mother passed away. I never understood the depths of sadness and grief suffered by the bereaved until having experienced such piercing sorrow, personally. My mother's departure brought it home to me what the loss of a parent really means.

Since my mother's passing, I've started constantly thinking back over the anger and sorrow she endured during her lifetime. In view of all she put up with, I must confess that, next to hers, my troubles are of little importance. I now realize only all too well that my personal frustrations, joys, and sorrows simply pale in comparison.

Kazuo, too, greatly misses not having my mother around, for she was a constant companion at his side. He could always ask her for her impressions of a performance, about the costumes, music, and so on. If she said nothing, we took her silence as a sign of tacit approval. I'm pretty certain, however, that she would not have hesitated to voice her discontent had she felt embarrassed by his work. Now that she's no longer among us, I, too, have no one to whom I can ask for guidance. In terms of character, my mother was never one to grumble, regardless of the circumstances. She instinctively understood her husband, both as a performer and as a human being.

Midori Ohno,[10] Kazuo's mother and my paternal grandmother, was another extremely influential figure in his life. Once, Kazuo dreamt of a hairy caterpillar that kept crawling over his hand all night long. On recognizing this creature to be his mother, he screamed out her name in his sleep. This nightmare, he claims, was what made him finally realize that his selfishness as a child

Food

for the

Soul

_____

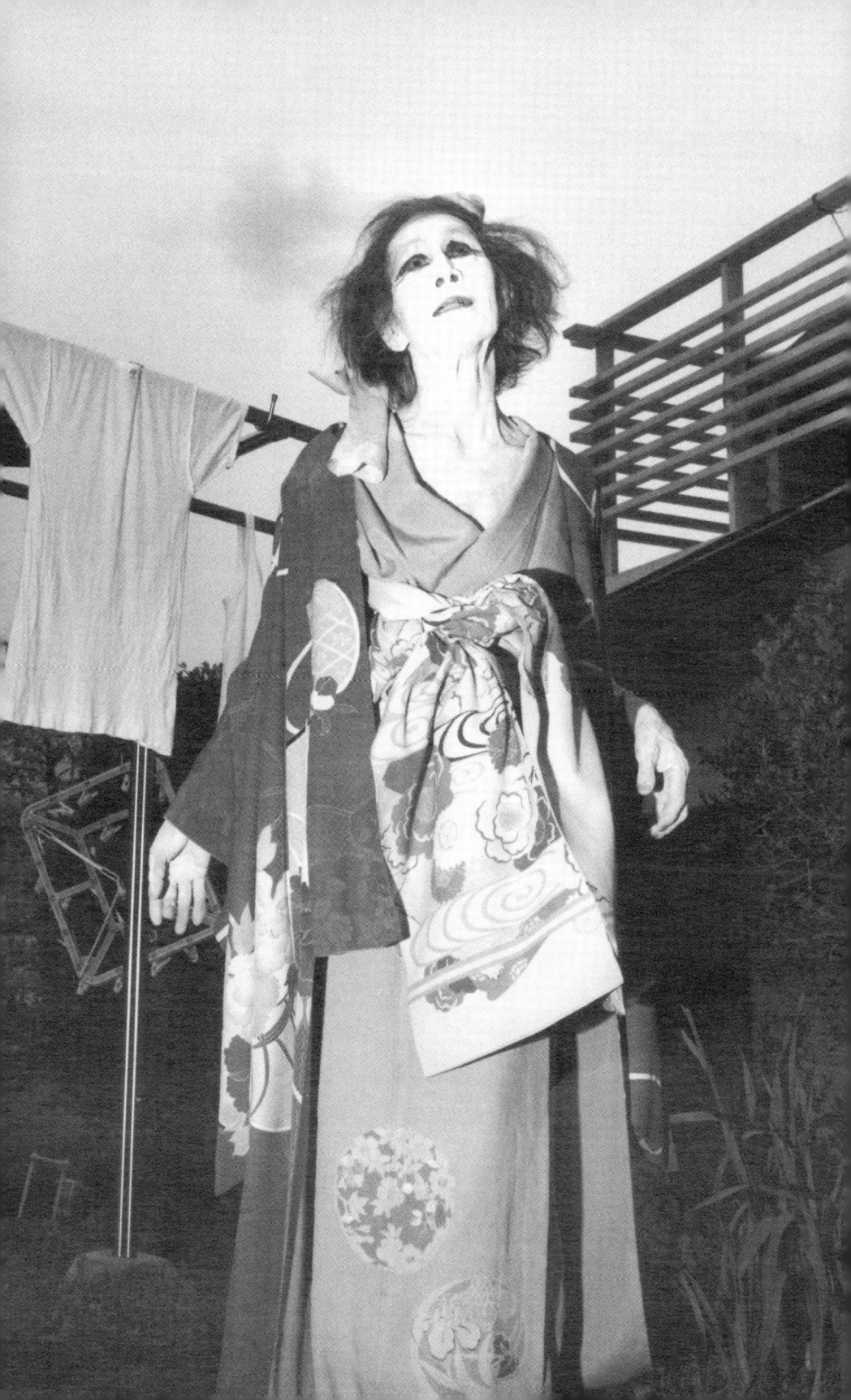

had driven her into becoming an insect. Kazuo, by his own admission, was always dead set on getting his own way.

At fifty-eight years of age and having just lost my own mother, I must admit that I somehow understand his feeling of remorse. Given that we are the fruit of our mothers' flesh, we owe our lives to the sacrifices they made on our behalf. Our innate tendency as human beings to inflict harm upon others is, to my mind, what original sin is all about. Kazuo is deeply aware of the debt of gratitude he owes to his mother. Indeed, he frequently speaks of how she shortened her life by giving of her flesh and blood so as to nourish him in the womb.

Dance, as I see it, is my father's way of telling his mother that he has come to realize the full extent of her sorrow; this became clear to him when he was haunted by that image of her being driven into becoming an insect.

Perhaps this explains why Kazuo often ponders over Sōga Shouhaku's *The Witch under the Willow Tree,* a portrait of an emaciated witch with a truly devilish face standing beside a willow.[11] He is deeply attracted to something in that image. In looking at a painting or a scroll, my father's initial response is invariably a visceral one; it's only subsequently that he begins thinking about what it represents and how it's been conceived. Shouhaku, in my father's view, most likely started out with the intention to depict his subject as a beautiful woman. And yet he delved so deeply into himself that he ended up portraying her as a devil. For some inexplicable reason, he was driven to transform her into something completely unrecognizable. Shouhaku, as Kazuo sees him, added the willow tree to the composition in a sudden fit of compassion after it dawned on him that he had utterly disfigured his subject.

On occasion, Kazuo tries to portray something akin to a mother's lamentation. Once, he even danced as a courtesan. That particular piece was inspired by the story of a courtesan's intimate relationship with a samurai who was attending the Shogun's court in Edo (Tokyo). During the Tokunawa shogunate, the *daimyos,* or feudal lords, were under strict obligation to attend the imperial courts in Edo and in Kyoto, alternately. Upon completing his assignment, the samurai had to return to the court in Kyoto. The courtesan couldn't bear the fact that he had gone and left her and consequently went out of her mind. She ended up becoming completely deranged, staggering about in despair, muttering crazily to herself.

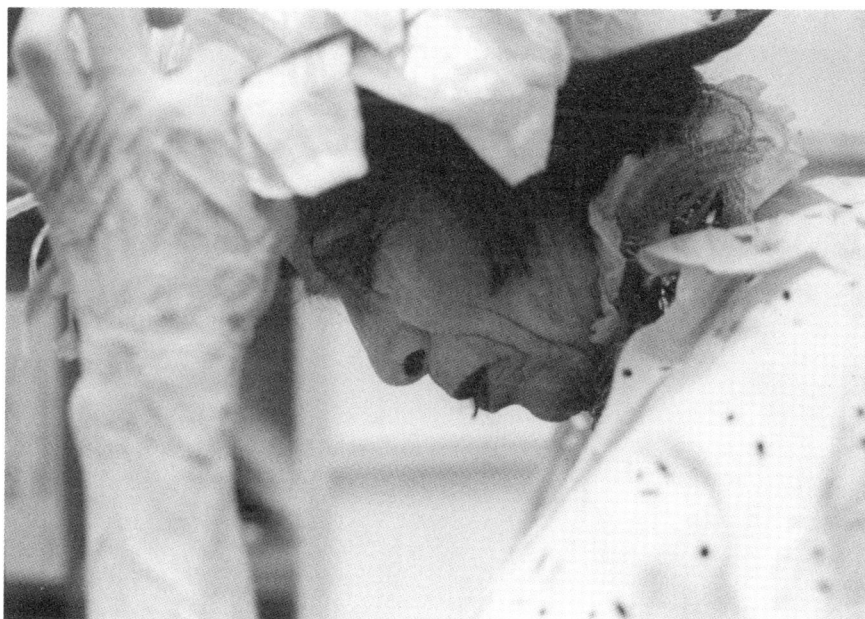

Kazuo has always been deeply attracted to such tragic heroines. In fact, tragic tales depicting madness and sorrow have often provided him with an impetus to perform. A story, however, based on an ordinary, run-of-the-mill woman would never kindle his imagination to create a dance. His performances are enriched by an in-depth grasp of the causes of madness. By plunging into their deranged worlds, Kazuo longs to embody the sufferings endured by these tragic figures.

Kazuo frequently refers to the human reproductive process as the epitome of madness itself. Of the millions of sperms attempting to fuse with the unfertilized egg cell, only one succeeds in penetrating the ovum's membrane to form an embryo. Birth, as seen from Kazuo's perspective, is the result of a process of elimination in which the millions of sperm that don't succeed in fertilizing the egg are cast into oblivion. We, as victors and survivors in the fight for survival, carry that memory embedded in us. He even describes the act of birth itself as giving form to madness.

Kazuo doesn't, however, consider the lives of these "rejects" to have been in vain. In his estimation, they are none other than the source of one of our human emotions. His outlook on life is based

88. "Ohno admits how utterly selfish he was toward his mother." In the dressing room of Seibu 200 Theatre, Ikebukuro, Tokyo, 1981, before a lecture-demonstration in which he presented an excerpt from *Divinariane*, the opening sequence in *Admiring La Argentina.* © Ohno Dance Studio Archives.

3.

Beginnings

and Family

Life

89. Ohno lying on the floor in a fetal position during a rehearsal of *My Mother*, 1981. © Teijiro Kamiyama.

on the belief that this prenatal experience makes us truly aware of the meaning of sorrow and loss. On that subject, I can now understand what led Yutaka Haniya,[12] on seeing Kazuo lying in a fetal position on the stage floor in *My Mother*, to laconically comment that a Kazuo Ohno butoh performance was like "an embryonic meditation" (see fig. 89).

One could perhaps say that, for Kazuo, the stage itself becomes his mother's womb. It offers him the freedom to dance, just as he played without restriction in the womb. In *My Mother*, the *ozen*—a miniature lacquered table used for serving food—becomes the very embodiment of his mother (see figs. 90, 91, 92). Watching this scene, it's hard to say whether he is playing with or annoying her. For Kazuo, that table is clearly not a stage prop; it's nothing other than the personification of her presence. He frolics about just as he did when playing with her on the tatami mats during childhood. As he becomes totally engrossed in play, his gaze turns childlike and innocent. His expression isn't in any way studied or contrived. Kazuo is genuinely playing with his mother, just as a child would.

Food

for the

Soul

118

90. "Perhaps
the stage itself
is a womb." In
rehearsal for *My
Mother*, Kami-
hoshikawa, 1981.
© Teijiro
Kamiyama.

(next 2 pages)
91–92. "Personify-
ing his mother,
Ohno becomes
engrossed in play
with the table."
Rehearsal for
My Mother, Kami-
hoshikawa, 1981.
© Teijiro
Kamiyama.

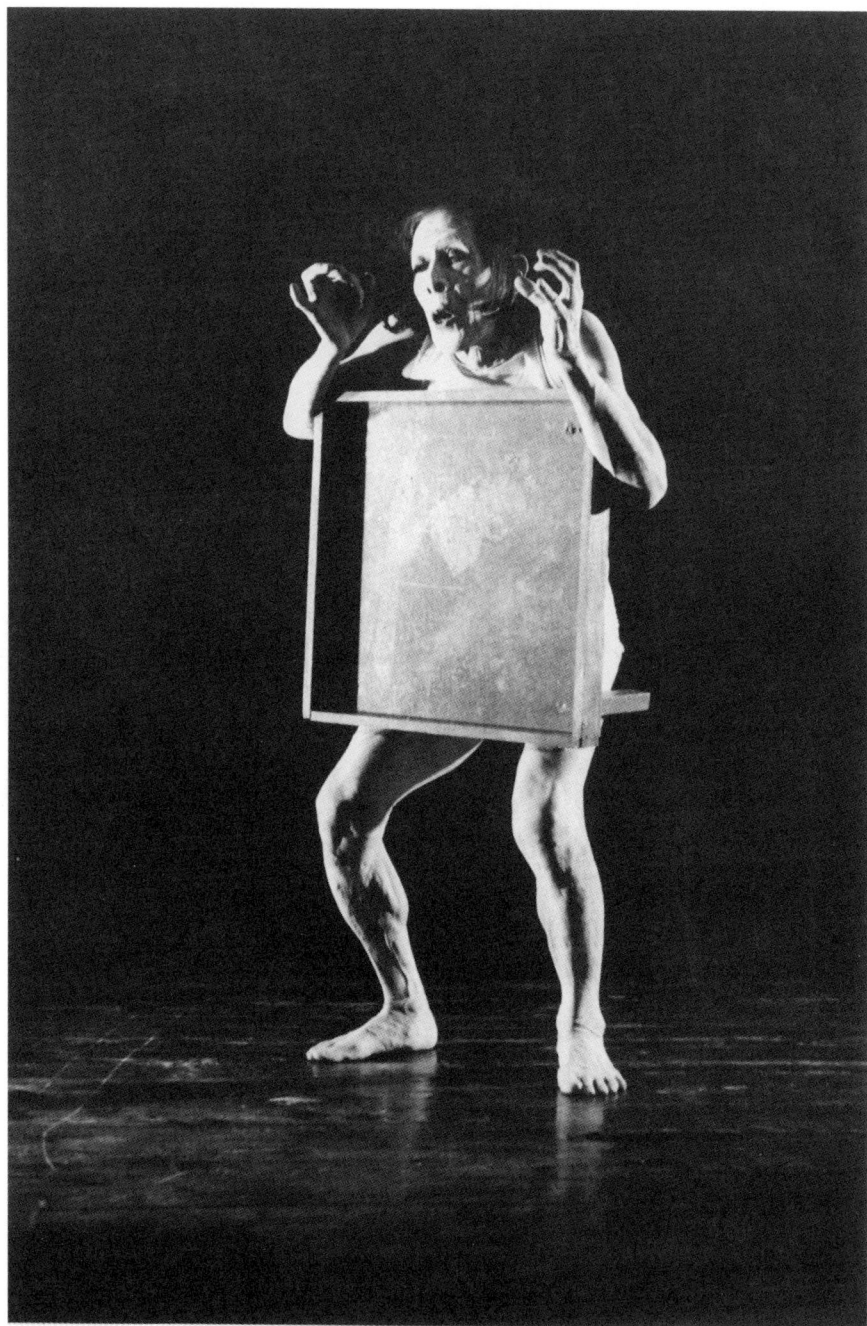

Fathers

It mightn't exactly be a nice way of putting it, but, for me, Kazuo
Ohno as a father, was someone for whom life revolved solely
around dance. I recall how in my school years, he would get quite
angry with me for not attending practice. If I skipped a dance lesson he wouldn't speak a word to me afterward at mealtimes, and a
gloomy atmosphere would descend over our home. To this very
day he talks of hardly anything other than dance. As a young
schoolboy, I was never greeted with "Hey, how did you get on at
school today?" or something of the sort. He was in his element
whenever the subject of conversation turned to dance, given that it
was the only topic that held any real interest for him. Dance was,
and remains to this very day, the be-all and end-all of his life.

Sitting around table at mealtimes, for instance, he instantly becomes all smiles at the mention of dance. If, however, we family
members happen to discuss another subject he remains sullen, as
he has absolutely no interest in anything else. Regrettably, it was
only in my mother's later years that I finally became attentive to
her predicament. I deeply regretted that she had to put up with
such self-centerdness all along.

A while ago, one of my father's former pupils, a woman several
years my junior, told me of having heard how on the days it would
happen to rain that Kazuo would propose to his students in physical education class that they transform themselves into frogs. I immediately blurted out an apology to her for his behavior. But now,
on reflection, it strikes me that my father was so truly filled with
passion for dance, so much so in fact, that he couldn't get it out of
his system even when he was meant to instruct his pupils.

Perhaps, it is exactly this unshakeable attachment to dance that
saves him from any form of embarrassment when it comes to performing in public. I've never known Kazuo to hold himself back
either on or off the stage. Indeed, this very lack of self-restraint has
frequently led us to argue. Even just the other day, for instance, a
workshop student who accompanied him to a nearby nursery
school where he was to dress up as Santa Claus suddenly came
running back to the house to tell us that Kazuo was wearing some
outlandish get-up. Seemingly, he was putting on strange makeup
in his preparation for the Christmas show for the children. On
reaching the school, I found my father wearing a brunette wig that
we used to sell in our store[13] quite some time ago. Apparently, he
had gone and chosen the wig from among the leftover stock stored
away in the workshop studio.

Food

for the

Soul

___

It would never dawn on him that a nursery school is a public place. The children's parents and teachers aren't accustomed to meeting with performers or artists; nor, for that matter, are they in the slightest bit aware of the fact that Kazuo is a dancer of international renown. Naturally enough, they would think his behavior somewhat odd were he to turn out in some outlandish get-up and wearing makeup.

On that subject, Kazuo used to dress up as Santa Claus for the annual Christmas celebrations in his early days as a staff member at the Soshin High School[14] (see fig. 94). Although my father likes to say he is fond of children, I have to qualify that statement by saying the children he has in mind are not everyday children but instead those who inhabit his imagination or those whose spirits he renders incarnate on stage. While he would do anything under the sun for these imaginary children, he never plays with or takes a true liking to children in real life. I must admit that I'm still puzzled by these apparent anomalies in his character. The Kazuo Ohno the public see stepping out on stage epitomizes a form of love almost beyond human reach. In day-to-day life, however, he does not exemplify such affection for others.

Recently, we were forwarded the questionnaires distributed at Kazuo's performance of *The Road in Heaven, the Road on Earth* at

Food

for the

Soul

_____

95. Ohno on the
nursery school
stage, 1950s.
© Ohno Dance
Studio Archives.

Osaka's Torii Hall (1996). The replies, completed mainly by the younger members of the audience, were full of phrases like "Kazuo's love" and "gentleness." Each and every one described how his performance had deeply moved them. In all likelihood, they assume that the Kazuo they see onstage is equally as compassionate in everyday life, but they might be in for a surprise were they really to get to know him.

Even so, having said all that, I've lately come to believe that a performer needs to mask his or her true nature. When it comes down to creating a thoroughly convincing performance, there are no halfway measures. A performer must be totally captivating if the audience are to be become fully engaged. In that respect, Kazuo's radical contradictions in character play a vital role in the way he creates that necessary illusion.

Someone, who incidentally knows Kazuo very well, often remarks at how distant he can be. On hearing that comment, I have to agree to a certain extent. At the same time, however, in examining closely what lies beneath the surface, I can see that, paradoxically, Kazuo's seeming unfriendliness and indifference conceal a love and gentleness. His warmth and love are not those of mortals, though; his warmth and tenderness are not those of flesh and blood. The form of love he epitomizes is one that pierces the pub-

3.

Beginnings

and Family

Life

———

lic's heart. That explains why his performances provoke such an emotional response from the public; some members of the audience rise from their seats at the end of a performance feeling grateful for being alive; others feel cured of their sufferings; others again are deeply filled with thanks.

Tōzō Ohno,[15] Kazuo's father and my paternal grandfather, was a fisherman with the salmon fleet on the Sea of Okhotsk. On returning to Hakodate after many long months at sea,[16] he would apparently pass his time at the local geisha house. Though only a young boy at the time, Kazuo would, as the eldest son, have to go and fetch him in the morning. On reaching the geisha house, he would seemingly find his father and some other patrons chanting in low rumbling voices along with the gidayū players.[17]

Because of her husband's continual absence, Kazuo's mother would spend her lonely evenings in conversation with the children before falling off to sleep. At that time, it was common for menfolk to leave the home place for lengthy periods to earn the where-

Food

for the

Soul

_____

126

withal to feed their families. They would spend months on end either at sea or in some distant urban center on Honshū, the country's chief island to the south of Hokkaido. On their homecoming, they were looked upon as something of a wonder. My own experience of growing up was somewhat similar: I wasn't even three months old before my father was conscripted and sent off to the war front. I wasn't to meet him again until I was nine, as he had been away from home during all those intervening years.

Because Kazuo invariably created performances inspired by the influential women in his life, we suggested to him one day in jest that his next performance should be based on his father. At that point in his career he had already paid homage to Antonia Mercé in *Admiring La Argentina* and staged *My Mother,* a tribute to his own mother. I can detect definite traces of my grandfather's life in the subsequent creation *The Dead Sea.* The title itself refers to a sea; moreover, the choice of costume also was significant, for Kazuo dressed in formal black attire for this piece. The choice of a black costume hinted at a man's strength.

Leaving those obscure aspects of his character aside, Kazuo gets on with daily life as though totally indifferent to such matters. Despite his age, he continues to regularly eat fatty foods such as eel and tempura fried fish and vegetables. Remarkably, he never tires of eating the same thing over and over again. With regard to meat, he likes it fatty, and for that reason dislikes the pork ribs bought at the market because he maintains that they contain too little fat. Nor, for that matter, is he keen on pork loin chops; he prefers the boned rib of pork for making *tonkatsu,* a deep-fried breaded pork cutlet.

Even if a guest happens to drop by at mealtimes, Kazuo generally invites them to come and watch him perform a short dance in the studio as soon as he rises from table. Ordinarily, one wouldn't get up and dance just after having eaten, but Kazuo is made of something different.

As far as household chores are concerned, he has never done the laundry or helped with the housecleaning. His bedroom would soon turn into a dust-covered universe unless somebody occasionally straightened it out. Apparently, he dislikes having his room thoroughly cleaned, for tidiness makes him feel uncomfortable. My father does, however, cook for the family now and then. He told us that ever before he started dancing he had seriously wanted to become a professional chef.

3.

Beginnings and Family Life

97. Four generations of Ohnos at table in the family home, Kami-hoshikawa, 1993. From left to right: Yoshito Ohno's wife, Etsuko Ohno; Kazuo's great-grandson, Yuki Ohno; Yoshito Ohno's daughter, Mikako Ohno; Yoshito Ohno; Kazuo Ohno's wife, Chie Ohno; Kazuo Ohno. © Xavier Lambours/Métis Images.

98. "Paradoxically,
Ohno's character com-
bines warmth and
aloofness, love and
indifference." Ohno
speaking in public,
1970s. © Ohno Dance
Studio Archives.

Curtain Calls

Opening nights are always sheer hell for Kazuo and me, not to mention the rest of the crew. At times, we have had to ask ourselves on coming offstage, where did it all go wrong? Had we come this far merely to make a proper show of ourselves? On the second day, things are slightly more composed, and generally the overall impression is not as disastrous as that of the previous day. We, along with the different members of the stage crew, discuss the forthcoming performance, taking each other's observations and comments about opening night into account.

On the closing day of a run, we don't get involved in any further discussion. At that point, nothing remains to be done but to leave it up to one another's discretion. Once beyond that critical juncture, our performances begin to breathe naturally. Kazuo and I actually look forward to the opportunity to perform without constraints, as do the lighting and sound engineers.

A performance only comes to life when dance is spontaneous—our physical responses need to be spur-of-the-moment and not simply mechanical reactions to preset arrangements. Imposing a structure, in itself, does not give birth to dance: we have to create the dance within ourselves. In going with the flow, we enable a performance to follow its own course and yet take advantage of all the potential offered by the specific time, location, music, costumes, and so forth.

Speaking as a performer, I feel that a dance born of the moment is never static, it doesn't end at a particular point, for, in being true to its spontaneous nature, it always needs to explore a little further. A ready-made dance, on the other hand, leaves me feeling limited by its built-in constraints. By letting the dance itself take hold of him, Kazuo overcomes the restrictions imposed by a performance's structure. To some extent, this perhaps explains why certain members of the public deliberately choose the day on which they come to see a performance: some prefer opening night, some the final performance, others the second day.

On being presented with flowers at curtain call, Kazuo releases all the pent-up tension built up over the course of the performance and instantly transforms into a naïve, and as some spectators have remarked, mischievous figure. Often, he goes so far as to lie down amongst the flowers and petals strewn about the stage floor after having deftly lain aside the bouquets given to him by members of the audience (see fig. 100). Unlike Kazuo, the vast majority of performers are unable to act on a sudden impulse. He doesn't, mind

3.

Beginnings and Family Life

_____

100. Ohno lying down among flowers at curtain call for *Admiring La Argentina*, Nancy, 1980. He was accompanied by Hiroshi Yamasoe (piano), on the left, and Mitsuo Ikeda (bandoneon), on the right. © Teijiro Kamiyama.

(facing page) 101. Ohno and Tatsumi Hijikata in the lobby of Tokyo's Marion Asahi Hall, during the Butoh Festival, 1985. © Munesuke Yamamoto.

you, consciously set out to close a performance on this impromptu note—it just happens that way.

Tatsumi Hijikata

Kazuo first met Tatsumi Hijikata[18] in 1954, when they both appeared in Mitsuko Andō's performance *Crow*. Hijikata already knew of Kazuo, having attended his first or second recital at the Kanda Kodo Kyoritsu hall some years earlier. Apparently, it was Hijikata who made the initial approach with an invitation to Kazuo to join him for a cup of tea.

As rehearsals got under way early in 1959 for a group performance based on Hemingway's *The Old Man and the Sea,* the scenario writer Nobuo Ikemiya used to drop by at the studio everyday with revisions to the stage notes. It was from around this time that Hijikata also started paying regular visits in the afternoon to rehearsals so as to offer advice on stage directions. Later the same year, Hijikata went on to both direct and stage *Kinjiki* (Forbidden Colours) whose title was borrowed from the Yukio Mishima novel. The following year he specifically choreographed *Divinariane* for Kazuo, a solo dance inspired by Divine, the hero/ine of Jean Genet's novel *Our Lady of the Flowers*. This performance was

to mark the beginning of an intense working partnership that lasted the best part of a decade. It was also around this time that Yukio Mishima and the literary critic Tatsuhiko Shibusawa began attending Hijikata's Dance Experience recitals. They would often meet together to discuss his ongoing projects.

Kazuo's encounter with Hijikata was to spark off a radical change in his approach to dance. Beforehand, Kazuo had been primarily interested in modern and expressionistic dance. As their collaborative efforts evolved, however, he began seriously reflecting over the meaning of death. Up until that point, his dance had portrayed life as seen and felt by one of the living. Considering the human condition from the viewpoint of the departed provoked this crucial turnabout in Kazuo's attitude to both life and dance.

Initially, Hijikata and Kazuo were reserved toward each other; they retained a certain distance and would avoid getting deeply involved in discussion. I remember how Hijikata would deferentially ask Kazuo if he wouldn't mind putting on, for example, a dress whenever he performed *Divinariane,* or he might politely suggest that he wear the chemise he had worn on a previous occasion, and so on. Kazuo responded favorably and willingly followed whatever advice was offered. They rarely disagreed or clashed in their opinions. As their working relationship evolved, Kazuo increasingly accepted what was said to him. Hijikata, too, it must be said, had complete confidence in Kazuo. Their professional relationship was one built on complete mutual trust. So, whenever Hijikata made a request, Kazuo willingly obliged.

Both Hijikata and I were envious of the size of Kazuo's enormous hands. Kazuo used to liken the human hand "to a rose whose stem is formed by the arm." Speaking of roses, in 1965, they performed a duet entitled *Rose-Colored Dance: A la Maison de Civeçawa,* in which Hijikata replicated Kazuo's movements (see fig. 103). In broad terms, the choreography consisted mainly of suggestive movements such as lying on top of each other in an embrace, or dancing in each other's arms. They did occasionally separate and step forward into the foreground individually. Seemingly, Hijikata had always wanted to dance with a similar costume to Kazuo's in a scene where they appeared together.

Once, however, a heated discussion over the meaning of God led them to spend an entire night thrashing the matter out. Hijikata persisted in asking: "*Sensei,*[19] seeing that you are the Christian, please explain to me what God is?" Kazuo, instead of replying to the question, didn't utter a single word; he simply remained

silent for quite some time. Although the discussion dragged on until morning, Kazuo never answered him in the end. He didn't try to extricate himself by saying that God exists in each of us, or offer any other such explanation. As Hijikata didn't know who or what God was, or perhaps, didn't even believe in one, he was curious to know the reasons for Kazuo's religious convictions. He would never have blindly believed in God just because Kazuo did so. In that respect, Hijikata made no concessions whatsoever; he was entirely his own man in his beliefs and approach to life.

While preparing for a performance, the day would invariably come around when they seemed to reach a dead end. They would then, strangely enough, spend the whole evening relentlessly discussing how to find a way out of the impasse. In view of the fact that they weren't talking on the same wavelength, the discussion just continued turning in circles. As they became utterly exhausted, it would dawn on them that they had been talking at odds all along. Only on reaching that point, beyond which all further talk was futile, were they able to clear the air. A joint abandoning of the ego permitted them to start afresh and effortlessly recreate the sequence from scratch. In fact, those scenes that initially gave them most trouble turned out in the long run to be the best that

102. Ohno in the forefront on the left, Tatsumi Hijikata is to his right, Yoshito Ohno is on the extreme right, in the finale of *Divinariane* at Tokyo's Dai-ichi Seimei Hall, 1960. © Ohno Dance Studio Archives.

3.

Beginnings and Family Life

——

135

103. Ohno and Tatsumi
Hijikata wearing identi-
cal gowns in *Rose-
Colored Dance: A la
Maison de Civeçawa*,
Tokyo, 1965. © Ohno
Dance Studio Archives.

they had thus far composed. The strange thing was that these head-on confrontations between Hijikata, the freethinker, and Kazuo, the believer in God, would drag on until they jointly abandoned their deep-seated principles. Before they knew it, it would be four or five in the morning, with dawn about to creep up on them.

However, many years later, when I visited Hijikata in hospital a few hours before his death, he confessed: "Yoshito, all I'm afraid of is God." I was deeply struck by the ambivalence of his stance. Here was somebody who had been so adamant in grilling Kazuo about his religious beliefs, and yet his parting words to me were that the only thing he was afraid of was God. Later that same day, he was heard to say: "In my last moments, God's light . . . ."

Another curious thing about Hijikata was that he would disappear the day after a performance ended. He simply vanished into thin air and would not be seen for some time. Meanwhile, the printers and other tradesmen involved in the project would come around to collect their dues. Obviously, a rumpus broke out as he wasn't to be found. In the 1960s, the Japanese economy was in a phase of rapid expansion, so the tradesmen were never lacking for work. Hijikata's crew simply resigned themselves to collect whatever was owed to them at a later stage.

Hijikata would, of course, sooner or later show up, and ask them to cooperate on an upcoming project. It must be pointed out, however, that the printers, graphic designers, and other tradesmen gained by working with him: they enhanced their reputations considerably, for it added luster to their status in the artistic milieu to have collaborated on the making of his performances. This explains why they willingly placed their talents at his disposal. In a subtle way, this continuing interdependency between the artisan's know-how and Hijikata's talent as a director enabled the Japanese performing arts to flourish in the 1960s.[20]

The sixties was the decade in which Kazuo's dance typified those ideas that attracted him to Hijikata's intensely experimental approach to dance. When they eventually went their respective ways, this influence became far less marked. Hijikata and Kazuo stopped working together when they felt that there was no point in going any further. It simply finished of its own accord; they had no need to wait for each other to make this decision. After their collaboration had run its course, they parted. Moreover, I had the impression that Hijikata had, on the whole, squeezed as much out of Kazuo as he could.

From around 1967, Hijikata became more interested in choreographing for others than in performing himself. He started inviting boxers, ballerinas, and other untypical physical types to his
rehearsal studio, the Asbestos-kan, so that his students could ap-
preciate the potential offered by different bodily shapes. Mitsutaka
Ishii[21] and I served as a screen upon which he projected the physical images he conceived. In parallel to the studio rehearsals and
training sessions, he immersed himself deeply in music and literature. He had always been attracted to French literature, in particular to the works of Jean Genet and le comte de Lautréamont.
All these diverse elements stimulated Hijikata's creative drive to
shape a world based on his unique conception of the human body.
His later years were spent entirely focused on choreographing
others.

Food

for the

Soul

Still, I do remember being puzzled during a particular performance by an emblematic shape suddenly appearing from out of
nowhere onstage. Taking a closer look, I realized it was none other
than Hijikata doing a handstand.

Toward the close of the 1960s major changes started taking

105. Ohno spent
part of his youth
in Akita prefecture
in northern
Honshū. *The
Dead Sea*, 1985.
© Kenichiro Aita.

place. At this juncture an internal revolt broke out. Hijikata's body revolted; the pent-up seeds of discord within him could no longer be restrained and finally exploded. His subsequent performance *Hijikata Tatsumi and the Japanese: Rebellion of the Body*[22] was symptomatic of the inner turmoil through which he was living. As time went on, he became increasingly more interested in "things personal." *Rebellion of the Body* focused on his individual physical identity as a native of the remote Tōhoku province in northern Japan. But, despite a theme dealing explicitly with regional identity, and the placing of a fake animal on the stage as a prop, his gestural vocabulary continued in a similar vein to the one he had employed before undertaking that crucial journey back to his native Tōhoku in the company of his friend, the photographer Eikoh Hosoe.[23] Just as in his previous performances, he wore a gown and movement remained heavily influenced by Western dance.

Some time after that watershed performance he once again withdrew to the rehearsal studio and started secretly choreographing for Yōko Ashikawa[24] and her group. From this point onward his work demonstrates a growing awareness of how one's body is constructed and defined by the region where one is born—in his case, the forbidding and remote Tōhoku. Choreographically, he went in search, within the body itself, of gestures and memories buried under the veneer of everyday life.

(facing page)
106. Hijikata with Ohno rehearsing *Tango* before the première of *Admiring La Argentina*, 1977. © Tōjun Okamura.

107. Backstage with Hijikata before the première of *Admiring La Argentina*, Tokyo, 1977. © Hiroaki Tsukamoto.

3.

Beginnings and Family Life

Chapter 4

Admiring
La Argentina

Some Background

To recapitulate on Kazuo's formative years, he first took dance lessons at the Baku Ishii dance school in Tokyo in 1933.[1] The following year he went on to study Ausdruckstanz [German expressionistic dance] under the guidance of Misako Miya, continuing until time such he was drafted into the Japanese armed forces in 1938. During those prewar years, he thoroughly explored the various idioms of modern dance both in style and in substance. On returning to Japan from detention camp in 1946, he resumed taking lessons under Miya for a further three years. The upshot of all this experimental research was a loosely grouped series of what Kazuo termed "contemporary dance recitals" presented over a ten-year period. Launched in 1949, with both group and solo performances at the Kanda Kyoritsu Kodo hall in Tokyo, the series culminated a decade later with a group performance, in which I also participated, in a realistic adaptation of Hemingway's *The Old Man and the Sea* presented at Tokyo's Dai-ichi Seimei Hall.

As previously mentioned, Kazuo initial contact with Tatsumi Hijikata was in the mid-1950s when they both participated in *Crow,* a piece choreographed by Mitsuko Andō. In 1959 Hijikata and Kazuo began collaborating on what were later referred to as *Ankoku butoh* performances, or "Dance Experiences" as they were then known, which they continued producing and staging until about 1967. Incidentally, the term *Ankoku butoh* ("Dance of Utter Darkness") was borrowed from Yuko Haniya's description of a Hijikata dance in which he likened the dance to an obscure image moving about in the womb. After that juncture, they eventually went their separate ways. For Kazuo, a hiatus in creative activity ensued. He wasn't to produce himself on stage again until 1977. It wasn't that he retired from performing as such; he simply couldn't face standing in front of an audience.

108. Ohno about to enter a pigsty. Still from Chiaki Nagano's film *Mr O's Book of the Dead,* 1973. © Ohno Dance Studio Archives.

Away from the public eye, Kazuo began working with the experimental filmmaker Chiaki Nagano on the making of the *Trilogy of
Mr O*. Nagano had previously attended the workshops for more
than a year and thus was familiar with Kazuo's working methods. In
1969 the first part of the triptych, *A Portrait of Mr O*, was completed, to be followed two years later year by its sequel, *Mandala of
Mr O*.[2] The final part of the trilogy, *Mr O's Book of the Dead*, was produced in 1973. Working on these films allowed Kazuo to plunge
into his own emotional turmoil and to rediscover his interiorized
landscapes. In my opinion, this self-searching phase was, ultimately, to prove cathartic in instigating a renaissance. Had he not
undertaken this inner voyage, I doubt he would ever have danced in
public again.

During the making of these films, Kazuo was particularly fascinated by the notion of squalor and filth. On set at a local pig farm,
for instance, he would, without the slightest hesitation, step into a
pigsty and start sucking on a sow's teat. In Nagano's films the images
are for real: there was no pretence whatsoever involved. Kazuo is
seen behaving exactly as a pig would.

Food

for the

Soul

___

144

Occasionally, Nagano and he would board a plane and fly up as far as Hokkaido in search of a lake or some such suitable setting to use as a location for their films. They traveled the length and breadth of Japan to places, mountains, temples, shrines that even we—his family members—didn't know about. At weekends, the pair of them would just suddenly disappear with a group of workshop students. By making these journeys into the wilderness Kazuo was, on one level, reexploring his life's landscapes, the landscapes of his childhood in Hokkaido and school years in Tōhoku. But this dung-smeared figure was not only physically ploughing through cinematic-like backdrops of muddy chaos and swampland; he was also, in effect, simultaneously exploring his own lower depths.

On emerging from this identity crisis, Kazuo was to create his quintessential work: *Admiring La Argentina*. Initially, we were all taken aback, for nobody had ever heard him speak of this La Argentina[3] until that momentous day in 1977 when he went to view Natsuyuki Nakanishi's one-man show in a Tokyo gallery. The story goes that just as Kazuo was about to leave the gallery he was dumfounded by an abstract painting hanging on the wall close to the exit. Inexplicably, he cried out: "La Argentina, it's you!" Afterward, he said that he had shouted her name to himself.

On returning home later that evening, he excitedly told us all about this mysterious encounter. When we questioned him as to what on earth had provoked such a passionate reaction on seeing Nakanishi's painting, Kazuo explained that, as a young man of about twenty-three, he had seen a performance by a Spanish dancer known as La Argentina at the Imperial Theatre in Tokyo.[4] She cast such spell on him that the emotions he felt at that time had lain dormant in him throughout the intervening forty-seven years. These feelings, he told us, had been rekindled and drawn into consciousness by something in Nakanishi's painting at the gallery.

Insofar as I recall, Kazuo had never spoken about La Argentina or her dance until the "happening" that day. Though he had frequently cited and referred to such well-known modern dancers and teachers as Harold Kreuzberg and Kurt Joss, he had never uttered a single word about this Spanish dancer who marked him so deeply. La Argentina was the stage name for Antonia Mercé, born in 1890 in Buenos Aires to parents of Spanish descent. As a mark of his deep devotion and respect, Kazuo decided to dedicate his comeback performance, *Admiring La Argentina*, to her memory.

We were to learn later that her performance had so over-whelmed him that he could never forget that evening way back in 1929. Out of curiosity, I asked him what kind of music La Argentina had used for her onstage accompaniment. Given that she was Argentinean by birth, I wondered whether she danced to tango music. Unwittingly voicing my aspirations, Kazuo then hinted that he might possibly perform in public yet once again, seeing that he himself had often used tango music as an accompaniment for the modern dance recitals he staged in the forties and fifties. Interest-ingly, the tango, as a form of musical accompaniment, had long been a favorite with Misako Miya and Takaya Eguchi. In fact, they were partially responsible for the popularity of the tango among young Japanese dancers in the postwar years. In the wake of our discussion, Kazuo began seriously thinking of reviving his stage career.

Then, another miracle of sorts occurred. Kazuo received by post some reading material about La Argentina from the New York–based dancers Eiko and Koma. This package, too, had inexplicably fallen out of the blue. Apparently, until the moment he started looking through those old program notes, he had been convinced that he could never dance again. But, on seeing a portrait of La Argentina in the program notes, he had a change of heart. Kazuo related that Argentina's voice seemed to implore him: "Ohno-san, let's dance. I, too, am going to dance, so let's dance together." He says that hearing her speak these words is what impelled him to come out of retirement.

And yet Kazuo hadn't the slightest idea about how to go about fulfilling this wish. Apart from a strong emotional impulse, he had nothing concrete with which to work on the idea. We didn't even know where to find suitable music for the project. We first of all decided that I should find some musicians capable of playing the necessary tango accompaniment. With this in mind, I approached Shinpei Hayakawa, leader of a small orchestra called Argentinean Tango. At one point in the past, Hayakawa's group had been very popular, but with the changing trends in music tango no longer seemed to be the in thing. Moreover, he informed me that the tango, as a musical form, was technically very demanding. Finding a violinist capable of interpreting it as it should be played would in itself be quite an accomplishment. In his estimation, we would need a musician the caliber of the leading violinist in the NHK (Japanese Broadcasting Corporation) Philharmonic Orchestra. On Hayakawa's recommendation, I went to meet his friend Mitsuo

110. Ohno climb-ing a post in a pigsty. Still from Chiaki Nagano's film *Mr O's Book of the Dead*, 1973. © Ohno Dance Studio Archives.

4.

Admiring

La Argentina

111. Ohno caked in
gypsum. Portrait,
1960s. © Ohno Dance
Studio Archives.

Ikeda, leader of the Los Amigos tango orchestra. Ikeda very kindly agreed to attend a run-through at our rehearsal studio, at which Kazuo danced several sequences to a tango accompaniment on tape. Ikeda was undoubtedly somewhat shocked by the fact that Kazuo would use taped music and immediately requested that he and his orchestra be given the opportunity to play for him at the performance. "It would be an honor for my tango orchestra," he said, "to play alongside Kazuo Ohno."

It was then agreed, as far as the musicians were concerned, to discuss the necessary arrangements during a run-through onstage. Kazuo, at any rate, was going to improvise during the performance, so there was no need for them to attend practice sessions at the workshop studio. We did nevertheless decide that the musicians should wear black tuxedos for the actual performance. As things turned out, it was Mitsuo Ikeda's seven-member orchestra, featuring two bandoneon players, who accompanied Kazuo at the première in Tokyo's Dai-ichi Seimei Hall on 1 November 1977.

Opening night was truly unforgettable:[5] the members of the au-

4.

Admiring

La Argentina

dience were not only genuinely aroused by Kazuo's performance, they were also stunned by the juxtaposition of his very personal dance with the Latin strains of a tango orchestra. The poet Kazuko Shiraishi along with other poets and artists in the audience, were completely bowled over. The framework of *Admiring La Argentina* was devised in such a way that the opening half focused on the sum and substance of Kazuo's individual trajectory through life. By means of a series of intimate tableaux, he draws an authentic self-portrait before our eyes. He then proceeds to introduce the public to another influential figure in his life, namely, La Argentina, in the second half. The brief lull between acts was abruptly interrupted by the tango orchestra bursting into a boisterous prelude even before the echoes of a Bach fugue, lingering in the air since the close of the first half, had had time to fully fade away.

Admiring La Argentina, Part 1: Self-Portrait

Admiring La Argentina opens on a tense note: from the moment hall lights are dimmed, the audience is plunged into a state of disarray. In the first scene, Kazuo grapples with the most crucial problem we have to face in life, namely, our inevitable mortality. After depicting his vision of individual existence as nothing other than a facsimile of collective experience, Kazuo gradually unveils, over the course of the subsequent scenes, a more intimate portrayal of his own life.

Admiring La Argentina was indeed Kazuo's initial step toward a stage comeback; one could perhaps even call it his first ever butoh performance. Hijikata, who directed the première, was likewise of this opinion. Unlike those one-off happenings and the "Dance Experiences" that they coproduced during the sixties—performances whose very concept excluded them from ever being revived—this tribute to La Argentina was deliberately structured in such a way as to allow it be repeatedly presented to the public. In doing so, Hijikata and Kazuo molded the prototype of a butoh performance that could be staged over and again.

The opening sequence, *Divine's Death,* is a revival of an extract from Hijikata's 1960 creation *Divinariane,*[6] which had been specifically choreographed for Kazuo. Inspired by Divine, the antihero of the Jean Genet novel *Our Lady of the Flowers* (see figs. 114, 115, 116, 117), this particular dance, more than any other that I have seen Kazuo perform in a career spanning over five decades, embodies the essence of a lifetime's work. Kazuo readily agreed to Hijikata's request to revive this inimitable portrait of Genet's aging male pros-

Food

for the

Soul

_____

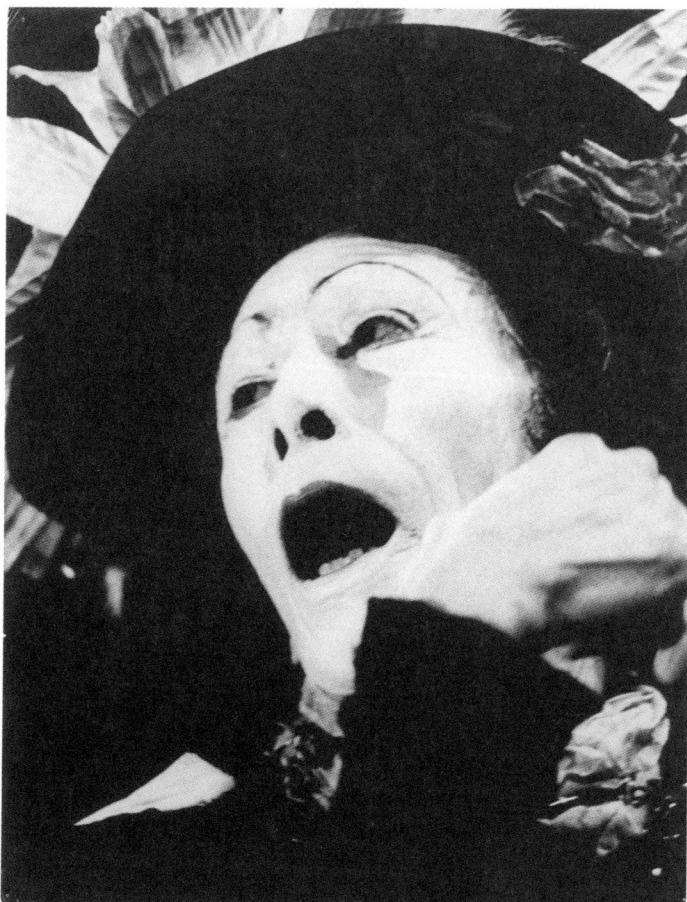

titute. In fact, Hijikata went so far as to suggest that the evening open with this particular piece. Before the house lights are switched off, Kazuo, in costume, takes a seat in the auditorium just like any other member of the public. After the blackout, a spotlight catches Kazuo rising from his seat and tracks him all the way down the aisle in what could be described as a symbolic passage toward his demise. Purposefully heading toward the proscenium, he none-theless hesitates, tottering to and fro on the steps before slowly climbing onto the stage for an encounter with destiny.

In Genet's novel *Our Lady of the Flowers*, Divine contracts pul-monary tuberculosis and eventually meets his end vomiting blood, with his head stuck down a toilet bowl. Set to Bach's Toccata and

Food

for the

Soul

_____

Fugue in D minor, Kazuo evokes the prostitute's waning moments in life as he makes his way anxiously from the auditorium to the stage. While thoroughly tainted by vulgarity, this low-living prostitute is nonetheless blessed with a spiritual dimension to his life. In rising from his seat in the crowd, Kazuo personifies both the criminal and saintly aspects of Genet's antihero, both the male prostitute hustling on the sidewalk and the saint in everyone. He brings to the surface a hint of the divine hidden within each and every one of us. Up until the moment the spotlight reveals him sitting in the audience, Kazuo is simply another face in the crowd. In some respects, he is the everyman, or the everywoman. When he stands up, it's just as though a member of the public rises to his or her feet.

4.

Admiring

La Argentina

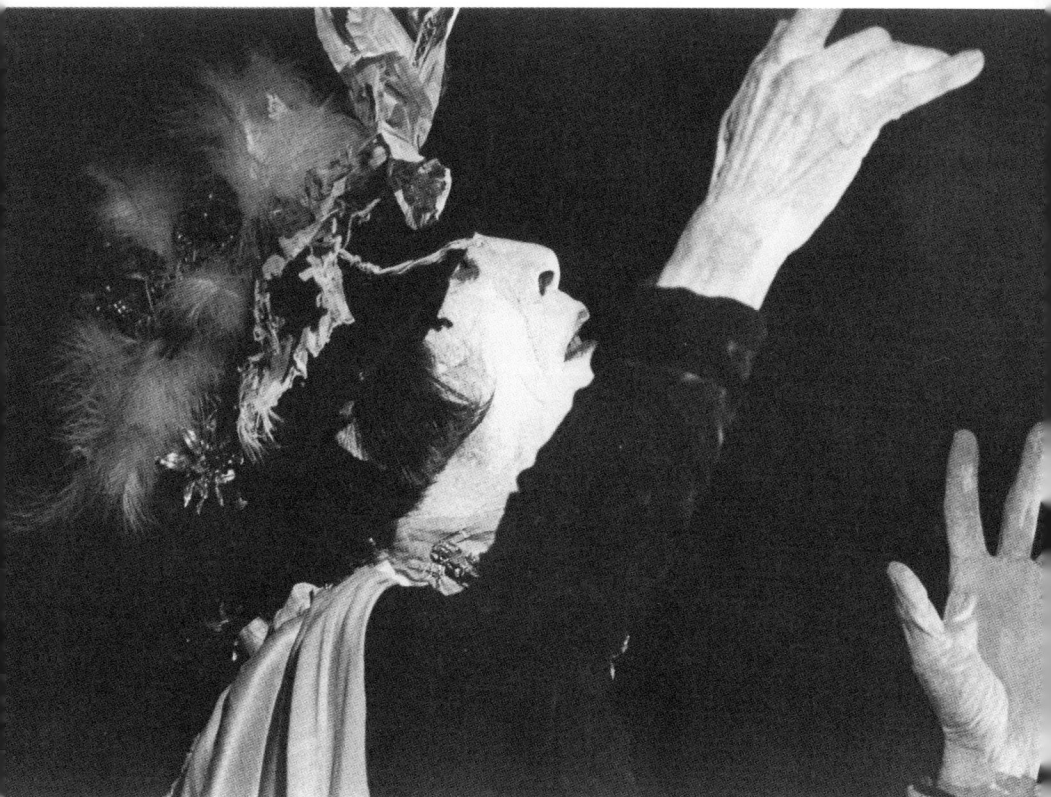

As the organ sounds the Toccata's high opening note, Kazuo rises from his seat like a flower about to burst into blossom. On setting his foot in the aisle, the atmosphere in the auditorium abruptly transforms; it becomes saturated in the prostitute's raging anger and fury at God's injustice. He eventually makes his way up onto the stage as though climbing the stairs of a church belfry. In a figurative sense, the steps joining the auditorium to the stage aren't merely physical steps leading from one area of the scenic space to another but a bridge between our profane human existence and a spiritual plane above.

As that "flower" bursts into bloom, one has the impression that *death* itself, as personified by Kazuo's presence, truly rises in our midst. Possessed by an invisible presence, he is set in motion as though in a trancelike state. Though physically climbing up onto the stage, he is gradually winding down toward his life's final moments. As he lies down on the stage floor, a concentrated beam of

Food

for the

Soul

____

154

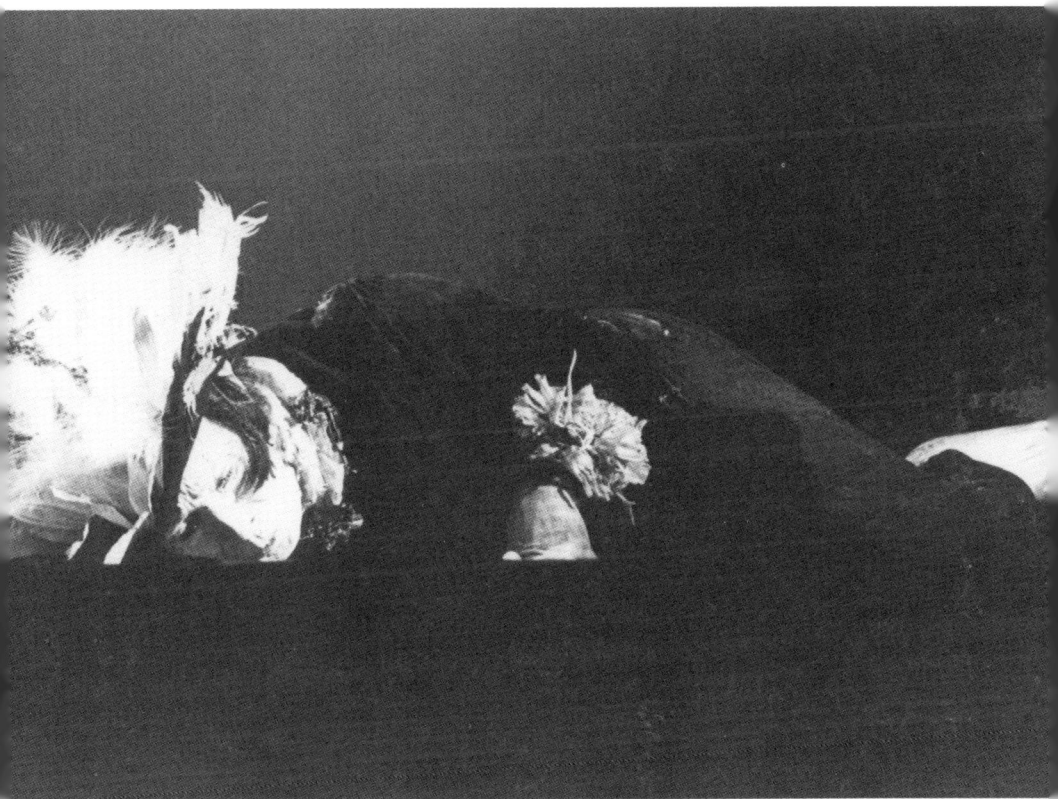

light pinpoints his face from above. Under its constant and almost merciless scrutiny, Divine slowly passes away in full view of the audience's gaze, exposing a face scarred by deep suffering.

During the blackout that follows Kazuo slips into a chemise in the wings before coming back out on to the stage, his hair adorned with a flower made from a ribbon of soft paper (see fig. 118). Maria Callas's rendition of Puccini's "Senza Mamma" provides the musical backdrop for this tableau, titled *Rebirth As a Young Girl*. Kazuo, in the guise of a young girl, rises to his feet in precisely the same spot where the elderly prostitute died in the previous scene. The sequence comes to a close as this frail and childlike figure delicately vanishes into the upstage shadows.

The following scene, *Daily Bread*, introduces a dramatic change in tone. As Kazuo walks out onto a silent stage, he's no longer an aging male prostitute, nor a young girl; but just his everyday self (see fig. 119). Clothed in nothing but a pair of black trunks, he is ex-

117. "Rising from his seat, Ohno personifies both the sacred and the profane in each of us." Première of *Admiring La Argentina*, Tokyo, November 1977. © Hiroaki Tsukamoto.

4.

Admiring La Argentina

155

tremely powerful in this scene. He makes us feel that we are watching the *body* itself dance. Each movement and gesture, though fragmented and eventually coming to a standstill, nonetheless remains contingent on what comes before and after. Each and every instant is thoroughly unique, and yet they all flow into one another to create a seamless flow of images.

Given that Kazuo was seventy-one years of age, this comeback performance provoked outright astonishment. He genuinely succeeded in making the audience feel how the human body, in itself, is a living entity. His movements in *Daily Bread* are ones of pure physical expression: the body's every organ, every limb and joint,

**Food
for the
Soul**

_____

156

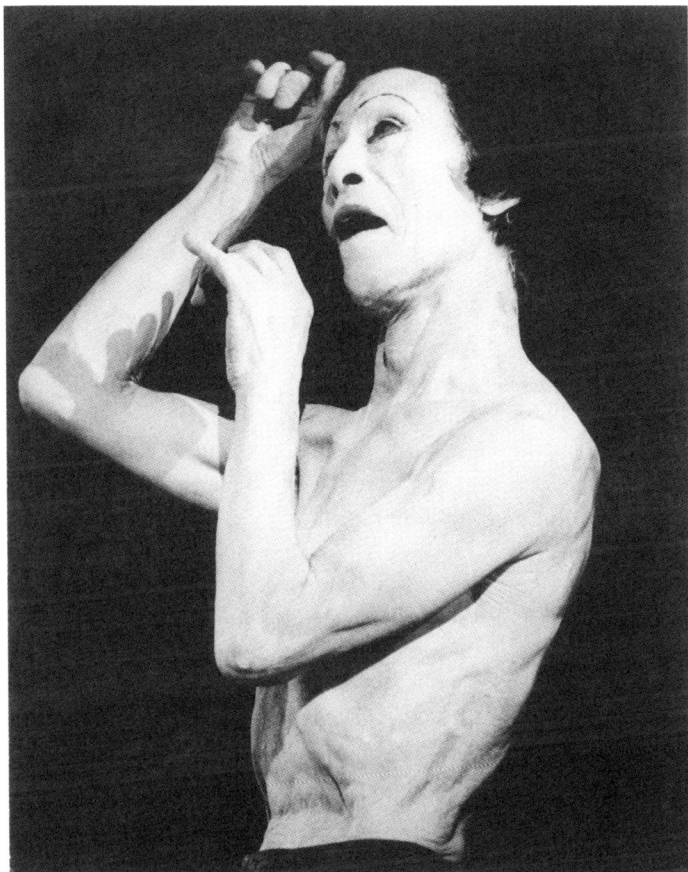

119. Ohno in *Daily Bread*, from *Admiring La Argentina*, 1977. © Hiroaki Tsukamoto.

from the intestines right through the veins and arteries are palpable. Here, Kazuo structures his dance by emphasizing the physical and material nature of the human body as an object.

Kazuo, as I mentioned earlier, is a Christian. Generally speaking, reciting the Lord's Prayer plays an integral part of the faithful's routine religious obligations. Kazuo, it must be said, worships in another manner. Dance has become his way of reciting "Our Father, who art in Heaven." He strives at all times to invest his performances with the true spirit of prayer, because, for him, dance springs from his faith in God and his belief in the healing capacity of art. He rarely, if ever, worships in the conventional sense. He wouldn't, let's say, kneel down and pray. Strange though it may seem, I doubt that those who believe in the power of prayer do so

4.

Admiring

La Argentina

———

in that way. As for me, I'm completely the opposite. Though basically an irreligious sort of person, my basic response on feeling the need to repent over something is, inadvertently, to call upon God through prayer. A true believer, however, wouldn't express remorse in that way.

I would go so far as to say that Kazuo's everyday movements and gestures actualize a physical statement about his life experience. His gestural language, more so than any words ever could, faithfully conveys the remorse he feels. His movements divulge the hell he went through while roaming through the carnage on the battlefields, not to mention the hell that we, as human beings, know in the depths of our hearts. An entire life's experience has been compressed into his commonplace actions, and habitual movements. Whether walking on stage, squatting on the ground, falling suddenly to the floor, or even chewing his food, Kazuo's routine movements and gestures bear vivid testimony to his individual experience of life.

Kazuo still held the post of caretaker at the Soshin Girl's High School in 1977, the year the première of *Admiring La Argentina* was staged. Though no longer a member of the teaching staff, he nonetheless continued working, looking after the school's general maintenance, cleaning the boilers and so forth. Visible traces of movements involved in carrying out his routine janitorial duties are evident in *Daily Bread:* manual movements used in cleaning gutters, repairing water pipes, and other maintenance activities. These routine physical activities have consistently played a determining role in the way his movement style has evolved.

A good dancer, in my view, always enables us to perceive his or her everyday reality. Their physical presence, even with a simple gesture such as raising an arm reveals a distinct truth about their lives. Their movements awaken us to things that cannot be read on the surface, to something inherently invisible. They create no artificial distinction between their personal lives and performance. I don't believe that dance can be mastered solely by means of regular workouts in a rehearsal studio. Kazuo is a case in point: it's only when dance and everyday life merge as one, that an authentic portrait of the dancer emerges. As for the title *Daily Bread*, it, more so than any other title in *Admiring La Argentina*, is probably the most symbolic. Considering the tangible relationship between his everyday existence and the truths inherent in his movements, it reflects the ultimate purpose of Kazuo's dance: to nurture and comfort our souls.

Food

for the

Soul

_____

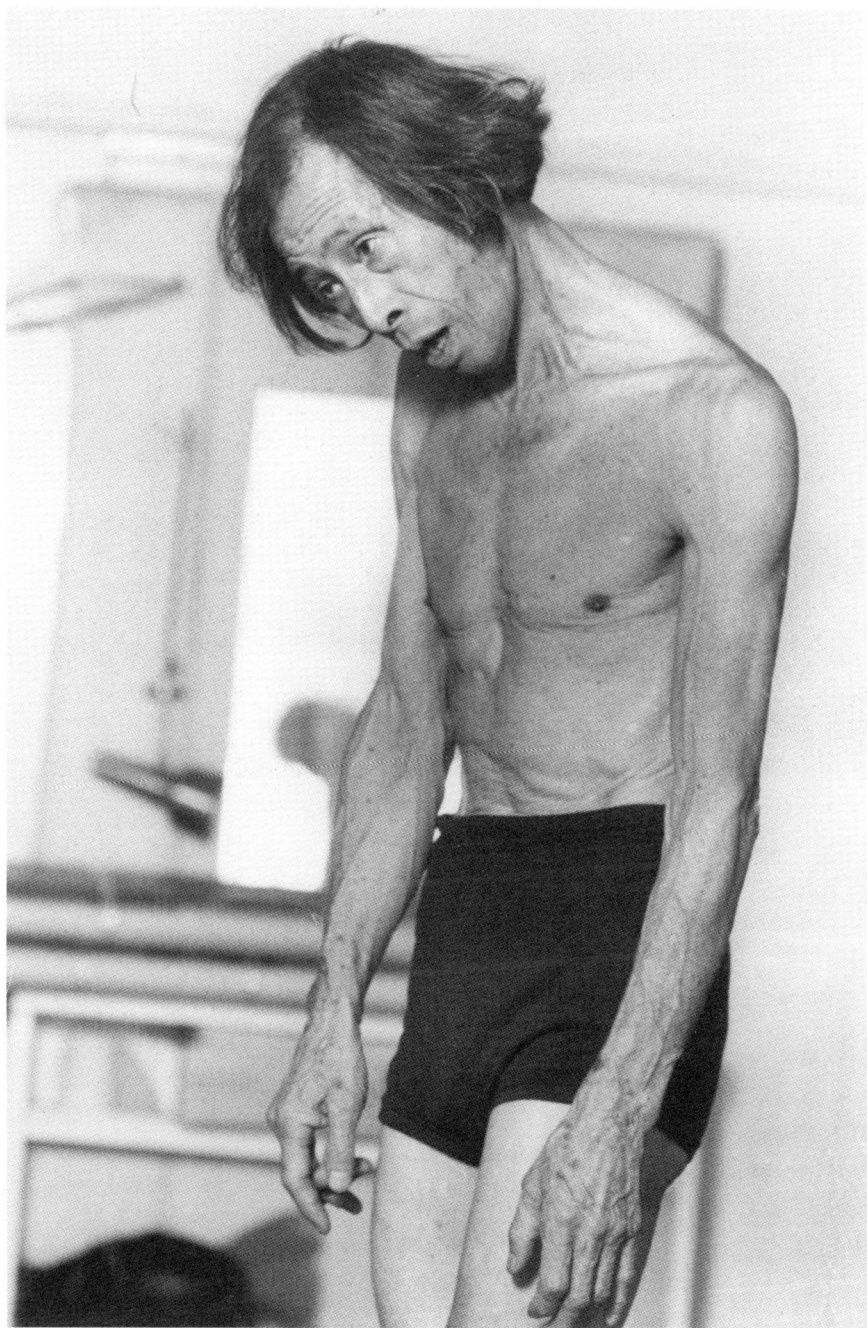

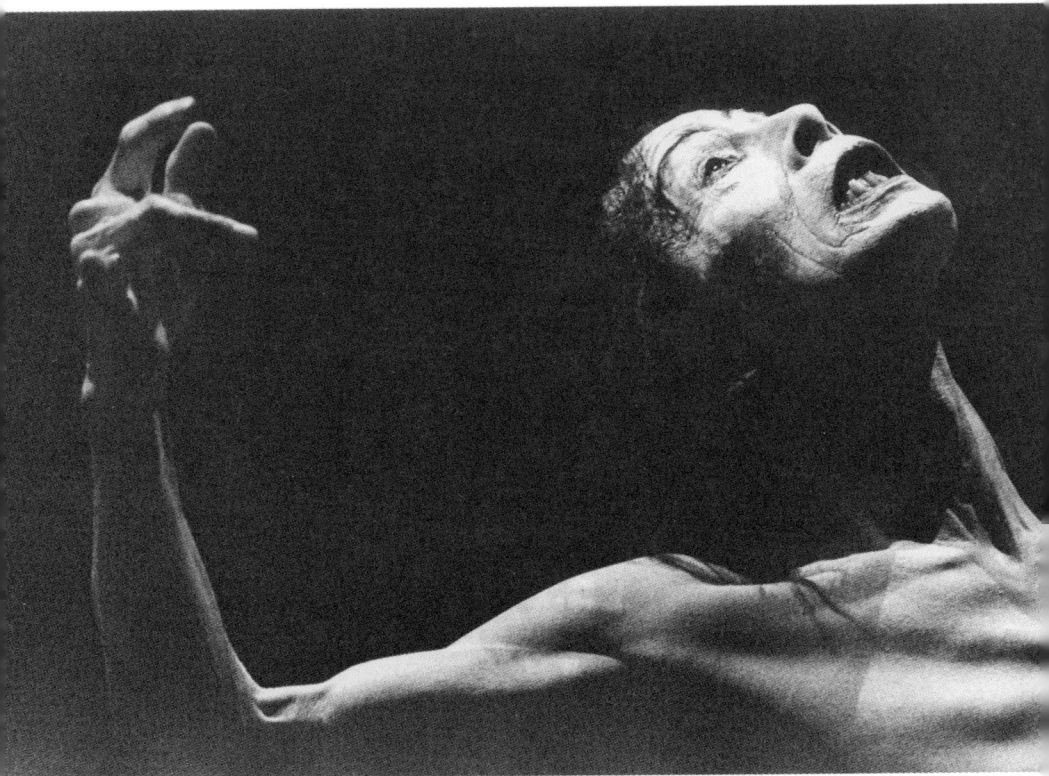

As Kazuo slowly disappears into the wings at the close of this tableau, he culminates a series of dances thematically dealing with death and rebirth. Through the grace of dance, he longs to reach out and nourish our everyday spiritual needs. The final scene of the opening act, *The Marriage of Heaven and Earth*,[7] unfolds with Kazuo, his back leaning against a grand piano, rolled out onto center stage as though he were a phantom. Propped up against the bend of the piano, Kazuo stands motionless like a figure in a life-size painting, his arms outstretched as though crucified, whilst a live pianist plays a Bach prelude, followed by a fugue from the *Well-Tempered Clavier*.

The ensuing blackout marks the conclusion of a cycle of symbolic dances portraying the life of a single human being. Unquestionably, this larger-than-life portrait would be incomplete without all the constituent parts, whether it be Kazuo breathing motionlessly at the close of *The Marriage of Heaven and Earth*, or exploring

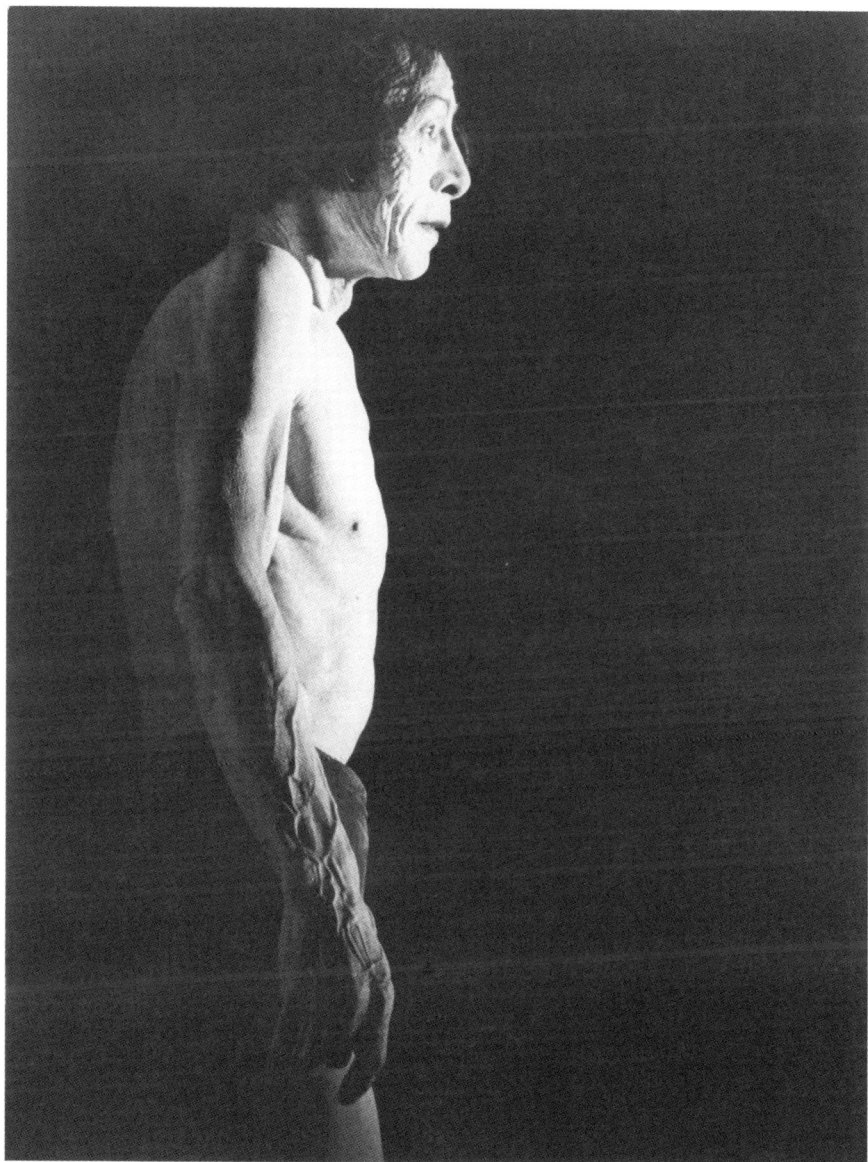

121–122. Ohno in *The Marriage of Heaven and Earth*, a symbolic dance portraying the life of a single human being. Première of *Admiring La Argentina*, Tokyo, November 1977. © Hiroaki Tsukamoto.

his inner depths as in *Daily Bread,* or grappling with the existential questions posed by death and rebirth as in *Divine's Death.* In fact, now that I come to think of it, I would say that never before has Kazuo been so nakedly honest as in that opening scene. Here, his performance is completely devoid of anything spurious.

Admiring La Argentina, Part 2: La Argentina

The closing half opens with the tango orchestra bursting into a lively overture, setting the pitch for Kazuo's arrival onstage in a flowing costume to dance *Flower.* Set to a very suggestive accompaniment, this intimate reverie unfolds meditatively with Kazuo creating the effect of staring into his inner world. In the following dance, *Bird,* his relationship to the world around him becomes a little more apparent. As his awareness shifts between his inner life toward the outer world, one can sense intimations of anger and revolt rise to the surface.

An abstract piece in a modern dance vein follows, in which the emphasis is more on visible form. Kazuo, who studied Ausdruckstanz in the immediate prewar years, performs this dance in period costume—a dark green dress evoking the 1930s—using movements authentically replicating the Teutonic severity characteristic of this expressionistic dance form.[8] Curiously, while the romantically strained tinges of Argentinean tango and the abstract tones of German expressionistic dance might strike one as realms apart, they are an ideal combination in the context of a Kazuo Ohno performance.

As part of his preparations, Kazuo routinely rehearses in his workshop studio using recordings of various tango pieces. This habit has resulted in his finding himself facing a dilemma: his dance invariably peaks on his first hearing of any given piece of music. The initial attempt is nearly always flawless. The problem is that he can't seem to recapture that sparkle whenever dancing to that same piece of music on an ulterior occasion. The magic simply vanishes. Rehearsals become increasingly difficult as we try to find a way to rekindle that spark. His dance is so truly outstanding the first time around that it inevitably outshines all subsequent attempts. We are forever painstakingly trying to figure out how Kazuo can recreate the same intensity on the illusory world of the stage. He was eventually forced to plot a variety of schemes so as to find that sparkle again.

As a solution, we decided to use different musical settings for our run-throughs at the rehearsal studio and performances on-

Food

for the

Soul

———

stage. For rehearsals, Kazuo confines himself to recorded versions of the more refined continental tango, which at one time was very popular in Europe, whereas in performance, he has live musicians play a simpler form of tango accompaniment with its characteristically cha-cha cha cha cha dotted rhythm. This approach, in effect, has led to genuine differences emerging in both his physical and emotional responses in rehearsal and in onstage appearances.

The tango orchestra's version of Alfred Hauze's tango air "Olé Guapa!" provides the musical backdrop for *Flower*. By way of tonal contrast, this is followed by the two bandoneon players' rendition of "Memory" as an accompaniment for *Bird*. On Kazuo's retreat into the wings at the end of these two numbers, the orchestra

Food

for the

Soul

_____

launches into an instrumental interlude. As he reemerges, this time dressed in a large flowing gown, the mood changes as they introduce the mournful tones of the Juan de Dios's "Quejas de Bandoneon."

After a final costume change, Kazuo returns to dance to a recording of Maria Callas singing the Puccini aria "O, mio babbino caro." Musically, the performance closes with the Callas version of the aria "In quelle trine morbide," taken from Puccini's *Manon*

125. "La Argentina's dance embodies the Creation of Heaven and Earth." Ohno performs *Finale* at the première of *Admiring La Argentina*, 1977. © Hiroaki Tsukamoto.

Lescaut. In this scene, Kazuo, dressed in a white ruffled gown, represents the epitome of womanhood (see fig. 125). While skillfully exploiting his whole stage know-how and craft to create this quintessentially feminine image, I nonetheless don't believe that Kazuo is conscious of being dressed as a woman.

In analyzing the overall framework of this tribute piece, I'm struck by the fact that the opening half of *Admiring La Argentina* is primarily a self-confession. Kazuo unveils an authentic portrait of himself to the public. After first offering an insight into his inner world and into the person he is, he goes on to evoke the spirit of La Argentina in the closing half.

In many ways La Argentina is like a lover for Kazuo. That potentially beautiful creature we see coming to life on stage is none other than La Argentina. Kazuo identifies himself totally with her. Unquestionably, she is the source of the beauty and emotion so characteristic of his dance. In fact, it was she who influenced him most with regard to his "intuitive" approach to performance. Watching this piece, I'm never sure whether Kazuo is quietly possessing her spirit, or if La Argentina herself has entered his body. One has the impression that he dances both for and with her. I've had to ask myself on many an occasion if it's not a case of mind over nature.

Admiring La Argentina has on occasion been labeled a stage adaptation of the Spanish dancer's life, with Kazuo cast in the leading role. And yet one can clearly see La Argentina taking bodily form in his dance. As they begin to merge and become as one, a metamorphosis takes place. Kazuo becomes La Argentina.

That partly explains why the public's initial response to this performance is an emotional one. Kazuo would prefer that an audience respond on a visceral rather than cerebral level to his performances. The essence of dance, or butoh performance, as he sees it, lies exactly in that emotional linkage the dancer creates with the public.

Kazuo's heartfelt wish in making this comeback performance was to pay homage to La Argentina.[9] Her tombstone inscription in Neuilly, in the outskirts of Paris, reads: "She was born for art, and she died for art." His profound admiration for her was the prime motivating force to come out of retirement and create this tribute. Moreover, he wants to impart to us what La Argentina revealed to him about the deeper significance of dance. Both physically and spiritually, Kazuo seeks after truth in art and in dance. In his own words, "I would somehow like to share what I discovered through

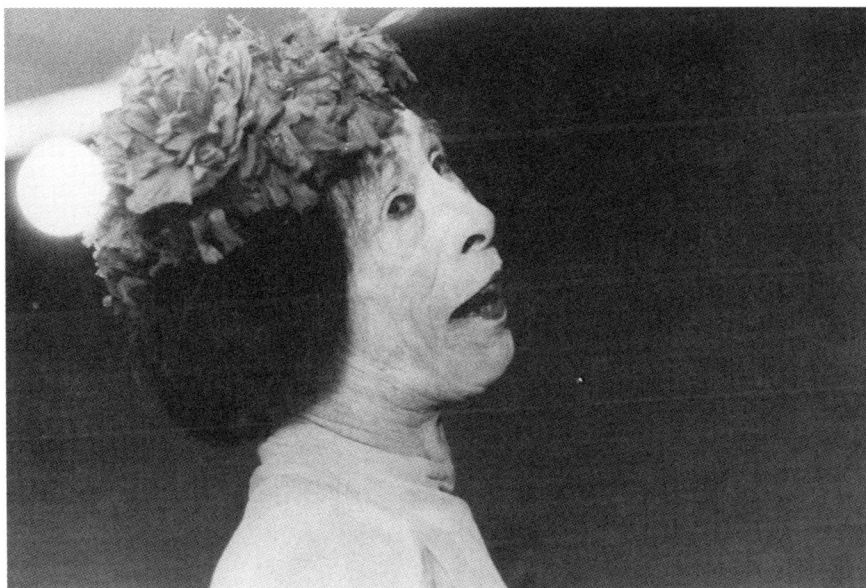

my encounter with her." Kazuo considers La Argentina's dance an illustration of creation as described in the Old Testament's Book of Genesis.[10] In her work, he witnessed the genesis of this world right before his very eyes. That is what he so desperately longs to convey—that dance is a life-generating experience.

I've often been struck by the manner in which a good work of art, be it a performance, a choreography or whatever, is well crafted. And yet, in observing Kazuo, I must say that he never deliberately sets out to create a good performance or intentionally compose it in an artful way. Given that a dance, for him at any rate, has no need for predetermined sequences or movements, his modus operandi doesn't require him to establish a choreographic structure or vocabulary.

If anything, our fundamental approach has been to focus primarily on the substance of a performance. Once we grasp what lies at the core of a work, the individual components, such as the music, the costume, the lighting, and so on emerge of their own accord without having to be forced. As an illustration of this point, consider how a certain scene in a performance might strike us as being flowerlike. The scene, however, embodies just one particular aspect of Kazuo's stage persona. Though unique in itself, it only becomes part of a true-to-life image when combined with the other

126. "Onstage, Ohno becomes La Argentina." Rehearsal of *Finale*, from *Admiring La Argentina*, Ohno Studio, 1977. © Tōjun Okamura.

4.

Admiring

La Argentina

127. Ohno clasps
a bouquet of flow-
ers presented to
him by the audi-
ence. Première of
*Admiring la Ar-
gentina*, Tokyo,
1977. © Hiroaki
Tsukamoto.

aspects that go into creating the whole. Imagine how strange it would be were flowers, for instance, to exist in a birdless world. If related by an inner necessity, the individual elements constituting a performance fall naturally into place.

Another determining factor is the lingering influence of Ausdruckstanz. As I mentioned earlier, Kazuo studied this dance form under Misako Miya on her return from Germany in the mid-1930s. Kazuo's technique could, I suppose to a certain extent, be considered as something of an acquisition. Artificial, perhaps, in the sense that it has been grafted onto him, it nonetheless has played an indispensable role in his evolution as a dancer.

Watching how the second half of this performance unfolds, it becomes clear that all these random elements, his spiritual encounter with La Argentina, the decades working as a schoolteacher and caretaker, his battlefront experiences during World War II, Ausdruckstanz, and so on, are the fundamental building blocks upon which Kazuo's dance and stage persona has been built. As with any performer, Kazuo needs to constantly focus on his personal experience of life and not merely dwell on superficial mental constructs.

As I watched a short film of La Argentina dancing, I was struck by her disarming simplicity. Her dance was so pure and devoid of any artifice or pretence. I felt as though I was looking at an innocent young girl floating in the air like a butterfly. Kazuo's dance, likewise, is imbued with that innocent and direct quality. La Argentina, however, is not the only female dancer who inspires him; he is also enthusiastic about Martha Graham and Mary Wigman, to name but two. Yet their dances are contrived and extremely intellectual in content. La Argentina's creations, by comparison, hadn't the slightest trace of artificiality; they came across as being completely free of pretence.

128. Ohno with his
wife, Chie, look out
over Lisbon harbor
on a free day during
his 1994 European
tour. © Hiroko
Oishi/Ohno Dance
Studio Archives.

Endnotes

1. Haiku: The word literally means "play verse." It is the shortest among the traditionally accepted forms of Japanese poetry. Consisting of three unryhyming lines of five, seven, and five syllables each, this poetic form presents a pair of contrasting images. One suggests time and place; the other introduces a vibrant, albeit fleeting experience; and the two images in unison give rise to mood and emotion. Haiku cultivates its images in such a way that they take on a meaning beyond the very precise observations of which they consist; they sometimes suggest much more than the poet consciously intends, almost to the point that it is not really possible to catch their ultimate meaning.

2. Tatsumi Hijikata (real name Kunio Motofuji): Born 9 March 1928 in Akita prefecture in northern Japan, he died of liver cancer in Tokyo in 1986 at the age of fifty-seven. A prominent figure in the Japanese experimental dance scene in the 1960s, Hijikata, along with Ohno, is widely regarded as the founding father of butoh. See "Food for the Soul," pp. 132–41.

3. *Universal Restaurant* was performed at Kushiro, Hokkaido, in May 1983.

4. *Jigokuemakizoshi:* A series of late twelfth-century hand scrolls depicting the horrors of hell. Alternating paintings and textual descriptions of the torments and punishments encountered by sinners in the Buddhist hells, these narrative paintings occasionally verge on the comical.

5. Both Yoshito and Kazuo Ohno frequently use the term (*mushin*), to describe their working approach to performance. A combination of the kanji for nothingness (*mu*) and mind (*shin*), translated literally it signifies lacking heart or depth of feeling, or even mindlessness. However, in this particular context, "intuitive" or "intentionless" come closer to the meaning they have in mind. In aesthetic discourse or in Buddhist texts, *mushin* assumes yet other meanings. As an aesthetic term, it refers to an absence of

refinement or elegance in expression or concept. It also sometimes means a positive attempt to be amusing or vulgar. In Buddhism, it denotes a person who is free from mundane attach-
ments or desires. A guileless or innocent child could also be
described as *mushin*.

6. *My Mother,* filmed at Yokohama's Teatro Fonte in November
1995, was broadcast by NHK, the Japanese Public Broadcasting
service, in April 1998.

7. Tamotsu Watanabe: Author, theater critic, and specialist in Japanese traditional performing arts. In his book *What Is Dance?*
Watanabe asserts that dance is the body's voice. Around the time
the commentary for this book was recorded, Yoshito Ohno happened to attend a lecture given by Watanabe on the role of voice
in performance

8. Ohno speaks at length on this subject in "Workshop Words" (see
p. 203).

9. Ohno frequently speaks on this theme at the workshops. See
"Workshop Words," p. 205.

10. Koi Nagata (1893–1997): Haiku poet.

11. Sekitei Hara (1886–1951): Haiku poet.

12. Ohno makes frequent reference to the fox in his workshop talks.
Japanese folklore also features many stories about foxes; they are
said to have the ability to bewitch and possess people. See "Workshop Words," p. 260.

13. Ohno uses the Japanese term for ghost, *yūrei,* which generally
refers to the spirit or soul of a dead person. A *yūrei* is the departed soul of a dead person, which appears as a shadowy resemblance of the deceased. It is thought to have a specific purpose
for coming back to the world of the living and reveals itself only
to a particular few, most often surviving relatives or intimate acquaintances. *Yūrei* are commonly depicted as having elongated
dangling arms, disheveled hair, and no legs.

14. Lacfadio Hearne (1850–1904): Writer of Greek-Irish descent. An
author of fiction, essays, and accounts of his travels in Japan, he
was one of the forerunners in making Japanese culture known
in the West. Arriving in Japan in 1890 as a correspondent for
Harper's Monthly, he became a naturalized Japanese citizen in
1895, taking the name Koizumi Yakumo. In all, he wrote twelve
books on the customs and folklore of Japan. He devoted much
time and energy to the study of Japanese life and was particularly
interested in Buddhism. Hearne's ghost stories had a marked
influence on the young Ohno. Apparently, Hearne was one of
Ohno's mother's favorite writers.

15. Kyouka Izumi (1873–1939), distinguished writer of grotesque
and fantastic tales. He was particularly fascinated by the super-

natural, borrowing and embellishing themes from the noh plays and Japanese folklore.

Chapter 2 Performance, pp. 41–97

1. *Divinariane:* Tatsumi Hijikata was deeply inspired by the work of the French novelist and dramatist Jean Genet (1910–86). In July 1960, as part of the "Dance Experience" recital, Hijikata specifically choreographed a piece for Ohno based on the character Divine, the aging male prostitute in Genet's novel *Our Lady of the Flowers.* This piece was revived in 1977, when Ohno performed it as part of *Admiring La Argentina* under Hijikata's direction.

2. An interesting parallel to Yoshito Ohno's commentary is to be found in Tatsuhiko Shibusawa's essay *On Hijikata,* featured in Tatsumi Hijikata's *Yameru Maihime* (The Ailing Dancer [Tokyo: Hakusuisha, 1983]). Describing a Hijikata performance, Shibusawa wrote: "At once stooping his back and curling his hands and feet inward, this naked figure fell to the floor without struggle, simultaneously suggesting life and death. He embodied not only the sleep of an unborn child but also those insects creeping out from between the pages of a Kafka short story" (p. 224; trans. Barrett).

3. *Tendo Chido* (The Road in Heaven, the Road on Earth) was initially performed at the Art Summit in Indonesia in 1995. After restructuring the piece, Kazuo and Yoshito Ohno presented it in Ferrera in 1997. It subsequently took its place as one of their repertoire pieces.

4. Misako Miya and her husband, Takaya Eguchi, both studied at the Mary Wigman Institute in Dresden between 1931 and 1933. On their return to Japan, they opened a dance studio where they taught the techniques they had learned in Germany. They had a marked influence on the evolution of modern dance in the pre- and postwar years. In an interview with Richard Schechner (*Drama Review* T110 [summer 1986]: 167) Ohno relates that on his return from the war in 1946 he became an assistant at the Eguchi studio. He was a student for only the first six months or so of his five years at the studio; he was promoted to teacher rank because he was such a good dancer. See "Food for the Soul," p. 143; and p. 184, note 8.

5. The lyrics of this popular old Japanese song lists the name of every station linking Tokyo's Shimbashi station to Kyoto on the Tokaido line. During the prewar years, an excursion on the Tokaido line was considered a pleasurable outing. Hijikata probably suggested this particular song because it offered Yoshito the

wherewithal to enter a totally different world, and, moreover, it made no reference to the act of standing up.

6. Hijikata was often vociferous in his opinions about how a dancer should not allow himself to be constrained by rigid techniques: "Learning to dance is not a matter of knowing how to position an arm or a leg. I don't teach dance in that way. I believe neither in methods nor in controlling movement. I've never believed in systems; I've been mistrustful of them since the day I was born" (trans. Barrett; an excerpt of Hijikata's writings published in *Shades of Darkness*, by Jean Viala and Nourit Masson-Sekine [Tokyo: Shufunomoto, 1988], 187).

7. Masakatsu Gunji: A noted authority on kabuki and traditional Japanese theater. His book on traditional Japanese dance in the Performing Arts of Japan Series, *Buyo: The Classical Dance*, is an authoritative reference on the subject (Tokyo: Walker/Weatherhill, 1970).

8. While Yoshito Ohno does not explicitly refer to ancestor worship, this passage underpins the prevalent belief that the welfare of the living is predicated on the well-being of the dead. Essentially, a Japanese household consists of both living and dead members of the family circle; the living ensure the ancestral line, while the dead, for their part, provide spiritual guidance. This echoes his father's belief that the departed inhabit his body and, as such, are a constant and loyal source of inspiration for his dances. The human body is at once corporeal and spiritual; together, they create an inseparable whole.

9. Tatsuhiko Shibusawa (1928–87): Noted theater critic and essayist, he wrote extensively on butoh and Tatsumi Hijikata. He also translated the writings of the marquis de Sade, as well as other contemporary French authors. He was particularly fascinated with the demonic aspect of human beings. Along with Yukio Mishima, he became a close adviser-cum-critic to both Hijikata and Ohno during the period they worked together.

10. The noh plays favor a figurative treatment over representational accuracy and naturalistic depiction; they are essentially nonrealistic in their expression. The world depicted on the noh stage consists of what cannot customarily be seen or heard in ordinary life, only what can be felt.

11. Werner Schroeter (1945–): German-born, feature-length documentary filmmaker, whose works are often influenced by operas.

12. *Suibokuga* (water ink paintings). A Chinese style of painting adopted by Japanese painters in the fourteenth century. Essentially, *suibokuga* is a monochrome painting characterized by the use of black ink.

13. Ohno performed an improvisational piece, *An Invitation to Jesus*, at this Paris church in June 1980. As a Christian, Ohno had

been hoping for many years to realize his dream of dancing in
a church. The program notes attest to his sense of devotion:

> Before I kneel down and pray,
> I long to share in Judas' sorrow.
> I was born of my mother's flesh,
> "I planted while Apollo poured water,
> yet, it is God who lets it grow."
> Jesus, this weathered stone hollow is your flesh.
> I lie prostrate before you, silently;
> It's so comfortable here,
> I ask myself, "Is this my mother's womb?"
> All the prayers that have permeated these walls
> Now echo in the dome like a mighty choir.
> That last remaining empty seat,
> Could it possibly be for me, a Judas?,
> I stand here believing that
> Jesus will answer my prayer.
>> (Program notes for *My Mother,* published by the Ohno
>> Dance Studio, 1981 [trans. Barrett])

14. Eikoh Hosoe: Japanese pioneer in an expressionistic form of
photography and one of the most distinguished chroniclers
of the butoh movement since its inception. As a child during
World War II, Hosoe sought refuge with relatives in Tōhoku
in the far north of Japan. His wartime experiences remained
with him, for he later collaborated with Hijikata on *Kamaitachi*
(Sickle-Toothed Weasel) over a three-year period in the mid-
sixties when they went in search of their individual pasts, as well
as something they shared in common, to that hinterland
of the Japanese countryside.

    Hosoe is currently working on a portrait series of Ohno,
which he started shooting in the early 1990s. Some of
them have been featured in *Kazuo Ohno* (Tokyo: Aoyanagisha,
1997).

15. Yoshito is referring to *Death and Rebirth,* the opening tableau,
which is performed in two parts. The first part, *Divine's Death*
(or *Divinariane,* as it was originally known), climaxes with the
symbolic death onstage of Genet's prostitute. After a costume
change, Ohno returns to dance the second part, *Rebirth As a
Young Girl.*

16. Hijikata operated an avant-garde cabaret show at a club called
Space Capsule in Akasaka, Tokyo, in which Yoshito Ohno performed from time to time.

17. *The Dead Sea* premièred in Tokyo in February 1985. It also
marked the resumption of Kazuo and Yoshito Ohno's creative
collaboration. Ohno's trip to the Dead Sea during his stay in Is-

rael in March 1983 made a very profound impression upon him. (See "Workshop Words," pp. 252–54).

18. *My Mother:* First performed in Tokyo in January 1981, at the Dai-ichi Seimei Hall. Below is an excerpt from the program notes:

> *The Flower Train*
>
> In 1914, my younger sister died after being run over by a streetcar. On that day, a festival to mark the launching of the streetcars was taking place in my hometown, Hakodate. The streetcar which knocked her down was decorated with flowers.
>
> Our maid, who accompanied my sister to the festival, suddenly burst into the house crying, "Madam, oh madam," and told us of the tragic news. At that very moment, my mother happened to be tidying up the kitchen, daydreaming about a procession of Buddhas. The maid's unexpected cry brought her back to reality. On seeing the maid's ashen face, she immediately realized that death had taken her daughter away.
>
> Again in 1916, my mother was to watch on helplessly as my newly born baby brother died in my arms. There was little she could do about it, for his chances of survival were poor. I was only in my first year of junior high school at the time.
>
> My mother departed this world in 1962. A truly devout person, her faith in Buddha carried her through life's ups and downs. She would kneel in front of the Buddhist altar, palms together, praying, swaying her hands from left to right. She would invariably spend a full hour in prayer before every meal.
>
> One day my son, Yoshito, asked her, "Grandma, why are you doing that?"
>
> She answered, "I am praying to Amitaba, to Jesus Christ, to all those that have passed away, for all those alive, for everybody." Death does not sunder our deep relationship with our parents and loved ones. My younger sister's death, my brother's death, my mother's prayers, her parting words; all these experience are still living inside of me. When I decided to give this performance, I knew that I could count on my mother to guide and help me. It has only been through the help of others that I have survived so far. I must admit that I have not always known happiness. I must admit that I've recklessly scattered the seeds of trouble, sometimes intentionally, sometimes not. My selfishness was to cause my mother untold pain. Saying, "I'm sorry" is but the first step. (Trans. Barrett; © Kazuo Ohno Dance Studio, 1985)

19. Ohno was held in detention in Menakawari, New Guinea, following the surrender of Japanese troops at the end of the war.

20. *Avatar:* Yoshito Ohno uses the term (*keshin*). It can mean either the incarnation of a deity, or the embodiment of an animal by a human being. *Keshin* also signifies the visible or even incarnate form taken by a supernatural being in order to manifest itself in the human world. A fusion of religious and folk practices are often evident both in butoh and traditional Japanese theater. In the noh plays, for example, elements belonging to both Shintoism and Buddhism are present. The spirits of those departed from this world manifest themselves through the medium of the actors.

21. The lotus flower is one of the most important symbols in the Buddhist tradition. Because it rises above the mud to bloom, the lotus symbolizes the human capacity to rise above the world's impurities and attain enlightenment. Moreover, another interesting correlation with Ohno's cosmological perspective is that its seeds are extremely long-lived; indeed, some believed to be more than two thousand years old have been successfully germinated. The flowers themselves, however, bloom only for a few days, opening at dawn and closing during the course of the afternoon.

22. Although Ohno was briefly hospitalized following a fall onstage in October 2000, he has since returned to participate in the twice-weekly workshops. Although he has increasing difficulty in walking and requires assistance to stand, he continues to dance, either by lying on the floor or sitting in a chair. Though his public engagements were canceled for some time, he has resumed performing, albeit in smaller and more intimate venues.

23. Emanuel Swedenborg (1688–1772): Swedish scientist, philosopher, and theologian. A man of considerable intellectual powers, he made significant contributions in chemistry, physics, and biology. He published *Economy in the Animal Kingdom* in 1741, a treatise on the relationship between the soul and matter. Swedenborg believed that the natural world derives its reality from the presence of God, whose divinity took human form in Jesus Christ. Ohno was very taken by Swedenborg's cosmological views. He speaks at some length on this subject in "Workshop Words" (see pp. 241–43).

Chapter 3 Beginnings and Family Life, pp. 98–141

1. Ohno was interned by the Allied forces in Menakawari, New Guinea, at the close of the World War II. On his return to Japan in 1946, he resumed his teaching career at the Baptist Mission School in Yokohama. He also took up the assistant teaching post he held before the war at the Eguchi Dance Studio for a further two and a half years.

2. Ohno's first dance recital in November 1949 featured both solo and group dances. He was forty-three years old at the time.

3. Ohno's wife, Chie, went to work in the U.S. army base at Oppama, close to Yokosuka in Kanagawa prefecture.

4. In the late 1940s, 14,000 yen was worth the equivalent of 40 dollars.

5. Ohno frequently refers to Judas Iscariot in his workshops and in his writings. See "Workshop Words," p. 212.

6. In 1938 Ohno was mustered into the infantry as a second lieutenant. He subsequently became a captain in charge of provisions. Initially stationed close to the military airport at Kai Feng in western China, he was later sent to New Guinea and remained there until his release from internment in 1946.

7. The Kantō Gakuin, where Ohno taught between 1930 and 1934, is located in Yokohama's Hinode-cho district.

8. Kanzo Uchimura (1861–1930): An influential Christian philosopher in prewar Japan. Converted to Christianity in 1877, he subsequently studied at a theological seminar in the United States. An outspoken pacifist, he believed that the church, as an institution, was unnecessary and at times even a hindrance to the Christian faith. He coined the term *mukyoukai* (Nonchurch Christianity) that is still used to distinguish his tradition. His ideas reflect his struggle to serve Jesus and Japan at the same time, and to develop a Japanese, though uncompromising, form of Christianity. Ohno was baptized in 1930; it has been claimed that it was a baptism of immersion in the sea water at Kamakura, but nobody can verify this assertion.

9. Chie Ohno (née Nakagawa) 1907–97: Born in Yokohama, married Ohno in 1933.

10. Midori Ohno (1884–1962): She migrated from Hokkaido to Honshū in the 1950s and lived with Ohno and his family in Yokohama's Tanmachi district and later moved with them to their present home in Kamihoshikawa, where she passed her remaining days.

11. Sōga Shouhaku (1730–81): In an interview with Mamoru Maruchi, Ohno recounts that he first came across Shouhaku's work in the monthly art revue *Mizue* shortly after the end of World War II. In his own words: "Shouhaku opened me up to the true nature of the universe." Ohno asserts in the same interview that he is a distant blood relation of Shouhaku's (Tokyo: Aoyanagisha, 1997; pp. 31–35).

12. Yutaka Haniya (1910–97): Novelist, butoh critic, and author of the monumental and unfinished *Shirei* (Dead Souls). A major

proponent of the idealist school in Japanese literature, his unusual existential theory of eternal revolution significantly influenced the intellectual climate of the 1960s.

13. Yoshito Ohno's retail business in Yokohama.

14. Ohno was a physical education teacher at the Soshin Baptist Girls High School in Yokohama. He retired from his teaching position in the early 1970s but remained on the staff as a janitor until 1980.

15. Tōzō Ohno (1880–1970): A fisherman by trade, at eighteen, he started to learn Russian, and later went to work at the visa section of the Russian consulate in Hakodate.

16. Hakodate: Ohno's birthplace, a seaport located in the southwestern Hokkaido. It was one of the first ports opened up to foreign trade under the Kanagawa treaty (1854). As an international port, it gave Ohno frequent opportunities to attend cinemas where foreign films were shown or to attend performances by traveling kabuki actors.

17. *Gidayū:* In this context, the word refers to the local singers and shamisen (Japanese plucked lute) players.

18. On first coming to Tokyo in 1952, Hijikata began studying dance under Mitsuko Andō. He subsequently went on to take lessons in modern dance at Takaya Eguchi's studio. His first public performance is reputed to be *Crow* in 1954, where he shared the stage with Kazuo Ohno and Mamako Yoneyama. In the late 1950s, he initiated the avant-garde dance form butoh. With powerfully erotic and violent dances such as *Kinjiki* (Forbidden Colours, 1959) and *Anma* (Masseur, 1963), based on stillness rather than movement, his style of butoh exerted significant influence on the artistic milieu during the 1960s. With *Nikutai no Hanran* (Rebellion of the Body, 1968), he started incorporating the gestures of Tōhoku folk culture into his performances and choreographic works. He later came to believe that the origins of Japanese folk dance are to be found in the cruel life the peasants endured. His dances often grappled with the roots of their suffering by tearing apart the superficial harmony of the traditional performing arts.

Hijikata is said to have first seen Ohno perform at Ohno's debut recital in 1949, in which he danced in a dress to a lyrical piece based on the Rainer Marie Rilke poem "Flower, flower, let's bloom—in the summer there will a great harvest." For additional material on Hijikata in English, see *Drama Review* T165 (spring 2000): 10–81, guest-edited by Nanako Kurihara.

19. *Sensei:* Respectful and honorific form of address for teacher, or master. The French term *maître* might perhaps come somewhat closer to the meaning.

20. The 1960s in Japan were a time of enormous intellectual ferment and persistent questioning of traditional values, both of which found expression in a new daring in thought and an outstanding diversity of artistic and literary manifestations. Hijikata is regarded by many as being one of those who spearheaded this movement.

21. Mitsutaka Ishii: A member of Hijikata's original company, based at the Asbestos-kan studio in Meguro, Tokyo. He subsequently went on to teach and give butoh workshops abroad and is currently is an advocate of dance as a form of therapy in psychiatric institutions. Ishii's dance was once described as "a primal dance, originating completely in the now, with neither beginning or end, where life rises forth in a simple dance leading to self-discovery" (E. S. Spor, quoted in Suehiro Tanemaru, *Kasabuta to Gyarameru* [Scabs and Caramel], in *Tatsumi Hijikata Butoh Encyclopedia* [Tokyo: Yushisha, 1993], from trans. by Stanley N. Anderson).

22. *Hijikata Tatsumi to Nihonjin: Nikutai no Hanran* (Tatsumi Hijikata and the Japanese: Rebellion of the Body) was performed at the Seinenkan, Tokyo, in October 1968.

23. This oblique reference alludes to the travels undertaken jointly by Hijikata and Hosoe in Tōhoku between 1965 and 1968, which ultimately led to the publication of Hosoe's photo collection *Kamaitachi* in 1969. A *kamaitachi* is a mythical weasel with very sharp teeth like sickles. This voyage was to be a turning point in both their lives. Outwardly a photographic record of a dancer tracing his footsteps back to his cradle, the book is at the same time a personal record by Hosoe of his own childhood memories and the complex feelings of love and hate he had for the countryside. As a refugee from the city, Hosoe was forced to take shelter with relatives in this region during the war. For him, the countryside seemed to be full of ghosts and other invisible creatures. With Hijikata as his guide, Hosoe realized he was able to record events that had already taken place in the past, something that, theoretically speaking, a camera cannot succeed in doing.

24. Yōko Ashikawa: She worked with Hijikata for the better part of two decades to develop a gestural vocabulary of minutely detailed movements. Hakutōbō, a group founded by Hijikata and subsequently trained by Ashikawa, was deeply influenced by this rigorous approach to understanding the body from within.

Chapter 4 *Admiring La Argentina,* pp. 143–169

1. Baku Ishii (1886–1962). Considered the forefather of Japanese contemporary dance. Like Ohno and Hijikata, he was a native of Tōhoku and was noted for his compelling stage persona. Though

trained in classical ballet, he sought to create his own particular style of modern dance. Between 1923 and 1928, he toured in the United States and Europe. Ohno studied under Ishii for a year in 1933 as part of his preparation to become a physical education teacher at the Soshin Baptist High School.

2. Nagano's program notes for *Mandala of Mr O* echo Ohno's voyage of self-discovery:

> This is a film of experience, or, it could be said, a film of a voyage into our inner consciousness.
> This film is the very expression of human love toward the universe.
> Our story unfolds in an old farm village. Actually, it is a world inside a mirror. There exists in the world around us healthy tensions full of uneasy and vicious pleasures, where anything can happen at any time.
> Poets, cherishing their sweet and cruel memories, continue traveling deeply into the mirror.
> This is a story about those wandering about in search of that dream and utopia taken away from us by our mechanized civilization. (Poster for film; translator unknown)

3. Antonia Mercé (1888–1936): Stage-named La Argentina, she was one of, if not the, most celebrated Spanish dancers of the early twentieth century. Born in Buenos Aires, she returned to Spain with her Spanish parents at the age of two. Her father was a leading ballet master at Madrid's Teatro Real, while her mother was a *première danseuse* with the same company. La Argentina's formative years were steeped in dance, and by the age of eleven she became a *première danseuse*. With her mother she traveled widely in Andalusia to study flamenco dance and gypsy life. She later emigrated to Paris. Throughout her career she collaborated with many of the leading figures of the Spanish vanguard, notably, the composer Manuel de Falla and the poet Federico García Lorca. She died of a heart attack in Bayonne in 1936.

4. Ohno's "meeting" with La Argentina is recounted in the program notes for *Admiring La Argentina*:

> More than fifty years ago, while a student at the gymnastic college in Tokyo, I saw La Argentina dance. I was invited to watch the Spanish dancer perform by a friend of mine, Yoshio Monden.
> Seeing her is something I could never forget. We were seated at the rear of the third floor of the Imperial Theatre. At the very first sight of her, I was spellbound, as though totally bewitched by her charm. It was a truly unforgettable experience. Some fifty years have now passed during which time I have lived through many ups and downs both in my profes-

sional and private life. Throughout those long years I've had flashbacks: I longed so much to see her again. Although I was never to again witness her intense presence before my eyes, her memory has lived in the depths of my soul.

Then, in 1976, I happened to visit a one-man show by the painter Natsuyuki Nakanishi. Just as I was about to leave the gallery I was stopped dead in my tracks by an oil painting of geometrical curves painted on a zinc sheet hanging close to the exit. I cried out to myself "Ah, Argentina . . . it's you!"

Nakanishi had never met with Argentina and, besides, knew nothing about her. And yet, he had somehow unwittingly captured her spirit. I could feel her presence; I could see her there dancing among those flowing curves.

This unexpected encounter with Argentina is what led me to resume dancing in public. I did so to express my profound admiration for her. Standing there, spellbound, I felt her come to life again. It came home to me that I will always seek after her, even after my ashes have been placed in an urn. (Trans. Barrett)

5. The Tokyo première took place on 1 and 2 November 1977 at the Dai-ichi Seimei Hall, Yurakucho. Ohno performed this piece on his initial trip to Europe in 1980 at the Fourteenth International Theatre Festival in Nancy.

6. *Divinariane* was originally choreographed by Hijikata for Ohno for the second and final public performance of *Kinjiki* (Forbidden Colours) in 1960.

7. Ohno was deeply influenced by William Blake's visionary art and makes repeated reference to him in his talks at the workshop (see "Workshop Words," pp. 241–43).

8. Ohno first took lessons in Ausdruckstanz under the guidance of Misako Miya and her husband, Takaya Eguchi, at their dance studio after seeing Mary Wigman's student Harold Kreuzberg perform in Tokyo in 1934. Ohno often remarks that while he was forcefully struck by Kreuzberg's sublime technique, it did not have the same impact on him that La Argentina's dance did. Her dance was so direct that he didn't even notice her technique. Another, albeit minor, influence on Ohno was Neuer Tanz. This movement, initiated by the German choreographer Kurt Jooss (1901–79), sought to create a modern dance idiom by reworking the excesses of classical ballet technique without completely abandoning its ingrained logic and discipline.

9. Following a performance at the Nancy Festival in 1980, a member of the audience mentioned in passing the whereabouts of La Argentina's grave in Neuilly, a Paris suburb. Ohno recalls:

On arriving in Paris I immediately went to her grave in Neuilly. I felt as though I were visiting my bride. A photograph, in a book I had been given, reminded me of her tragic and untimely death. In it, Argentina stood a wasteland clad in a fur coat. Life is a heavy burden for us all. That noble and most beautiful being, La Argentina, died at such a young age, even though she must have longed for eternity. As I stood by her grave, afflicted with pain, I realized the price she paid to live. It was so heartbreaking—I clung to her tombstone not wanting to leave her . . . ever. (*Admiring La Argentina* program notes, trans. Barrett, 1988)

10. In relation to La Argentina, Ohno commented: "I read about the Creation of the world in the Bible. I had always taken that passage for a legend, but in La Argentina's dance I saw it being realized right in front of my eyes. If this was what Creation was about, I felt, then I wanted to be part of it" (from the translator's workshop notes).

Part II Workshop Words

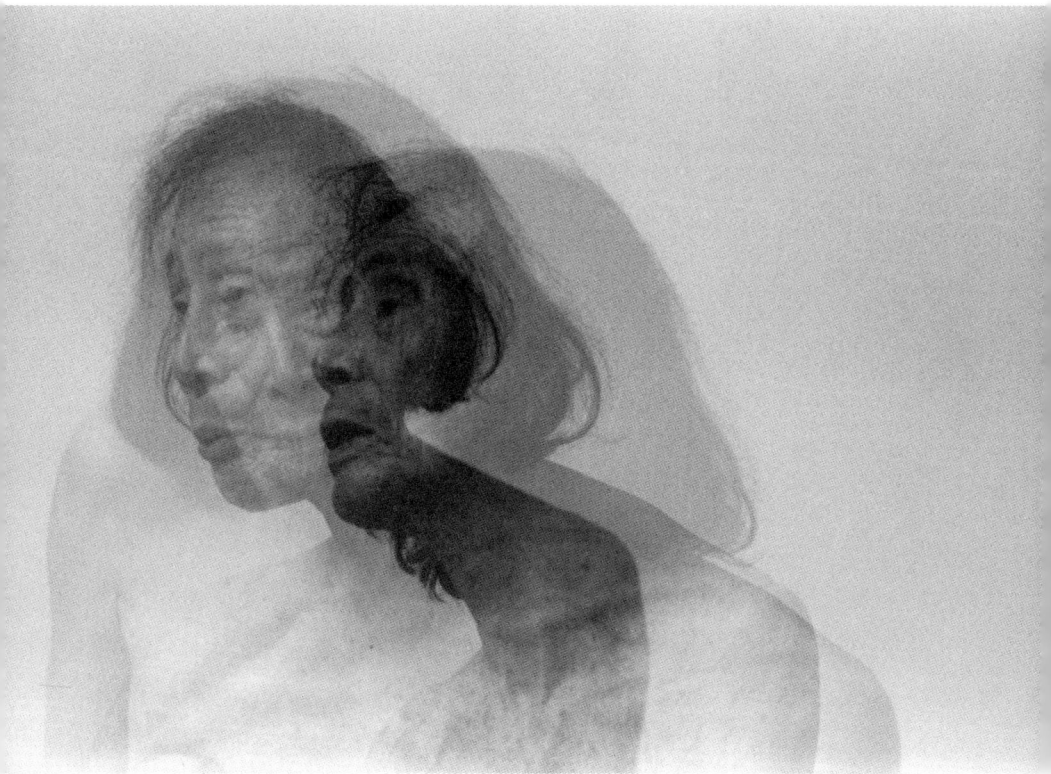

Introduction

Toshio Mizohata

The 154 aphorisms presented in this volume were originally transcribed from recordings made on cassette tape during Kazuo Ohno's workshops at his rehearsal studio in Kamihoshikawa, a suburb of Yokohama city. Recorded for the most part by individual participants of the workshops, the 120 or so hours of tape date from three periods: before and after the première of Ohno's watershed performance of *Admiring La Argentina* in November 1977; again in the late 1980s; and finally during 1995–96. The editors at Film Art Sha and I listened randomly to about a quarter of the tapes at our disposal, transcribing as much as could be deciphered. *Workshop Words* is the edited version of those transcripts arranged in five distinct segments that follow a schema we devised. No chronological order prevails; each segment freely presents Ohno's thoughts, ideas, and reflections on a specific theme. From the outset, we envisioned this collection as one in which the reader could immediately plunge into Ohno's universe on any given page. With the exception of chapter 3, the extracts were selected after a lengthy and in-depth study of the transcripts. Chapter 3 ("9 September 1989") is, by contrast, a verbatim record of Ohno's talk at the workshop on that day. Here, no abridgments were made, and editorial interference was kept to a strict minimum. That particular transcript is presented in its entirety to allow the reader to experience Ohno's natural flow of speech. The photographs sprinkled throughout bear little direct relation to the talks' contents. If anything, our choice leant toward the anecdotal or informal snapshot.

The workshop studio stands on a plot of ground at the rear of the Ohno family home. In 1961 the authorities at the Soshin Baptist Mission school where Ohno worked gave him the discarded wooden planks from the school buildings that were being demolished at the time. With these he constructed the roof, floor, and windows of the existing studio, which he has progressively renovated and refurbished ever since. This white wooden space, some seven meters in width by fourteen meters in depth, has served as his personal rehearsal space and is home to the twice-weekly workshops. This is no typical dance studio: costumes and props lie scattered about the floor and hang on the walls; there's neither a practice barre nor wall mirrors. On stepping into the studio, a visitor might feel that he or she has entered Ohno's private living quarters.

While we've never actually counted the numbers, it would be no exaggeration to state that a great many people have participated in Ohno's workshops during the thirty or so years they've been in existence. A considerable number of those who attend are not students in the strict sense of the term. They come from every walk of life, for the workshops are not exclusively designed for dancers or performers. They come from near and far; many have even traveled from overseas to study with Ohno. One sees the elderly, the middle-aged, and the young. Some attend a single session, others come faithfully to every workshop. Some simply watch and listen; others actively participate. No qualifications or stage experience are required of those wishing to attend. In fact, no questions are asked. There are no set courses or exercises, and new faces are to be seen at each session. On any given day it's impossible to predict who, or how many people, might attend. Regardless of these variables, Ohno's way of conducting the workshops never changes.

Perhaps the most confounding thing of all is that Ohno himself makes it perfectly clear to whoever attends that he has "nothing to teach." And yet, in planning a workshop, he has many questions to ask of himself. As a rule, he prepares his talk on the morning of, or possibly the day before, a workshop, by jotting down some ideas and rough sketches on a specific theme. When, however, it comes to actually addressing those present, everything that he has prepared just slips out of his mind. In his own words, "It simply vanishes." In his anxiety to get his message across he ends up talking on a completely different subject to the one he had prepared. Ohno nonetheless speaks with such overwhelming conviction that one feels that he is putting his life on the line. He gives the impression of desperately trying to create something new and not merely deliver a prepared speech.

Workshop

Words

_____

Ohno's long opening talk invariably lasts the better part of an hour; it frequently deals with the same topics repeated over and again, almost to the point of tedium. However, by repeating himself, Ohno doggedly perseveres in making the participants confront what he considers to be the most fundamental question for an aspiring performer: What is there to learn at his workshop? The starting line is the same for everybody—a workshop on workshops. At the close of the opening talk, he selects a piece of music to which he suggests themes or images for the participants to improvise on. This has been the established pattern for more than a decade: an inspired and inspiring Ohno encourages the participants while observing their movements. Before that, he apparently used to watch without making comment. From around 1977 he started actively participating in the workshops. This opening-up, so to speak, coincided with his coming out of retirement following a lengthy absence from the public arena. Nineteen seventy-seven also saw his stage rebirth, for that was the year in which he first performed *Admiring La Argentina.*

Ohno's talks are by no means just delivered off the cuff. While they might occasionally come across as being somewhat convoluted because of his idiosyncratic manner of speech, his message, for all that, is far from vague. What he has got to say is patently clear, notwithstanding the fact that he sometimes leaves sentences unfinished, frequently omits the subject of a phrase, and on occasion even mixes his own words with citations from other sources. Although he is not at all fluent in English, Ohno does not let that deter him in his attempts to get his point across; he occasionally sprinkles his speech with English and foreign terms, along with their equivalents in Japanese. An interpreter translates his talks into English for the many foreign students. For all their apparent complexity, his talks are comprehensible, even in translation, given the universal nature of his message. Ohno's enigmatic, through ultimately forgivable, way of verbally expressing himself produces a singular effect on his listeners. He not only speaks with great expressiveness but also exudes genuine conviction. In fact, the spellbinding quality of his speech isn't due to the words employed or to striking turns of phrase.

Ohno maintains that when it comes to dancing, he ought, as far as possible, to set aside all he has thought about, spoken of, and written on the subject. Strictly speaking, then, the words he employs at a workshop are in no way related to how he structures his dance. A dancer's verbal utterances are, after all, essentially nothing more than a variation of everyday speech. Their words do not, as such, constitute a dance. Still, if one considers the abiding correlation between the content of Ohno's talks and how he expresses

Introduction

his ideas, one senses a natural connection between his words and dance. Seen from this particular perspective, his words dance; his movements talk. In his case, language and movement unify, evolving as a single syntax. While the mediums ostensibly differ, he is ultimately saying the same thing with movement and with words. In compiling the extracts presented here, we, as editors, had to take into consideration what Kazuo Ohno's dance basically attempts to impart. For the purposes of this book, we decided to restrict our focus on his workshop talks.

Kazuo Ohno has already two other publications to his credit: *Butohfu: Goten, Sora o Tobu* (The Palace Soars through the Sky: Kazuo Ohno on Butoh [Shichosha, 1989]), and *Dessin* (Ryokugeisha, 1992). To date, neither work has been translated into a foreign language. Presenting a vast collection of Ohno's essays and notes, along with minor contributions by other commentators in the field, *Butohfu* is principally devoted to his work notes and written stage directions, compiled in chronological order. *Dessin* is a photographic reproduction of his hand-written notes for *Ishikari no Hana Magari* (The Ishikari River's Hooked-Nosed Salmon), an open-air performance that took place on the banks of Hokkaido's Ishikari River in September 1991. These notes offer the reader an insider's view of the creative process involved in staging that outdoor performance. This present work, however, differs substantially from both previous publications in that here what constitutes our primary source material is Ohno's spoken word at the workshops. Whereas *Butohfu* and *Dessin* focus exclusively on public performances, this collection, as the title suggests, concentrates on another vital aspect of Ohno's creative output, namely, his workshop talks.

Remarkably, it was not until 1980, when he was invited to the Nancy International Theatre Festival, that Kazuo Ohno first attracted international attention. He has since become a celebrated figure in dance circles throughout the world. A series of tours overseas commenced, beginning with *Admiring La Argentina* (1980). Ohno cemented his reputation with his subsequent creations, *My Mother* (1981), *The Dead Sea* (1985), *Water Lilies* (1987), and *Flowers-Birds-Wind-Moon* (1990). Over the last decades, Ohno, together with his son Yoshito, has regularly performed worldwide, in the process earning himself wide acclaim with both the general public and critics. The essays and notes in *Butohfu* offer an overview of the working methods used in creating what could be termed as Ohno's repertory pieces. If those public writings could be considered the corollary of the creative side of his craft, we then hope, by the same token, that *Workshop Words* will be seen as offering a penetrating insight into its noncreative aspects. This collection bears witness to those words and gestures that might initially strike one as nothing other than loose fragments and leftovers from his creative process. Viewed, however, in terms of life's cyclical nature, a fallow period undoubtedly constitutes the spawning ground for regrowth.

I would like to close on a more personal note. During the many long months that the editors at Film Art Sha and I listened to the thirty or so hours of recordings, I was constantly encouraged in this daunting task by recalling how Ohno motivated the workshop participants as they grappled to extricate themselves from self-imposed constraints. He would joyously shout out, "Free style!"

Tokyo
January 1997

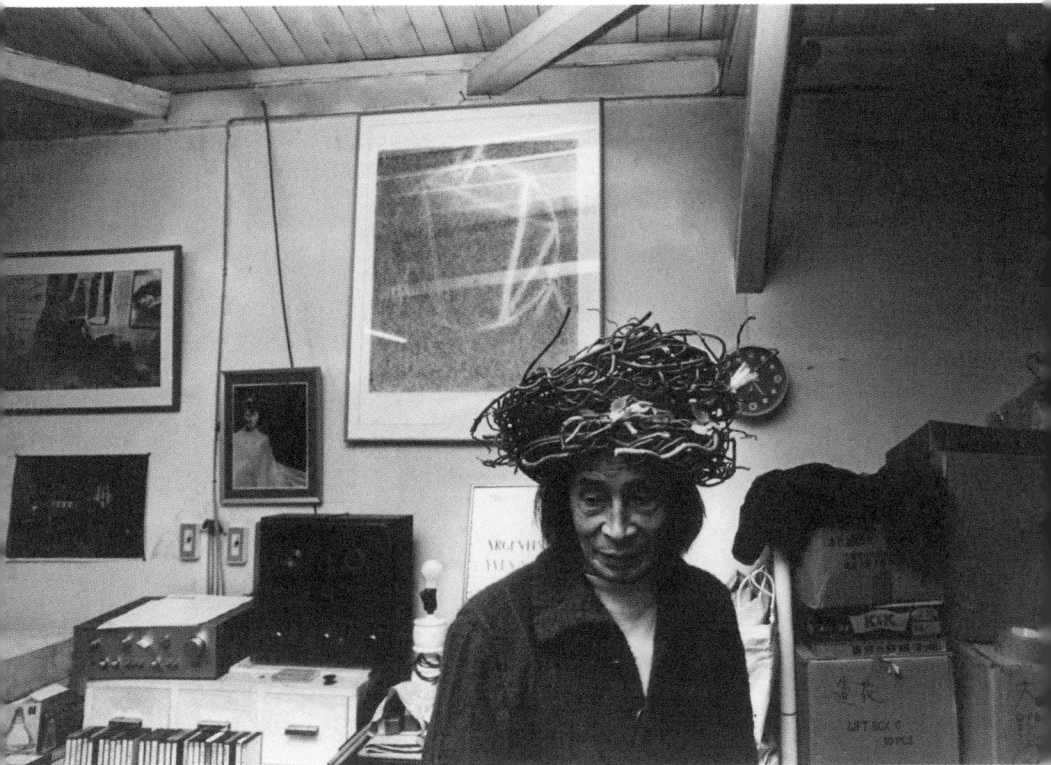

Chapter 1.

What Do You Mean When You Say, "I Understand"?

Outside, a cold rain is falling.

What can we learn from the way in which it falls? Imagine, for a moment, the various kinds of rain: at times, it lashes down upon us; then, at other times it drizzles softly. Here, at the workshops, try moving in an insect-like way. Practicing such precise and delicate movements will be helpful for your dance making. We tend to think that there's nothing to be gained in observing the elements. Perhaps, we just take them for granted. Observe the natural phenomena: rain falls effortlessly; the wind blows without strain. No matter how skillfully you imitate the rain, you'll never succeed.

It's truly inimitable. The question is: Why, then, should we practice?

. . .

I would love to offer you even something as tiny as a grain of sand. If only I could succeed in doing that, then I might fulfill my longing to share a part of my life with you. Isn't it worth risking one's life to offer something as microscopic as that tiny single grain of sand chosen from amongst countless millions? Take great care at all times. Even the most infinitesimal detail of the slightest gesture you make should be executed with loving care.

It's never too late to start.

. . .

(previous spread)
132. Ohno at the entrance to the workshop studio. © Teijiro Kamiyama.

(facing page)
133. Ohno wearing a crown of twigs. © Ohno Dance Studio Archives.

We can see that you intend to execute a particular movement. Even if you try to pretend or conceal what's on your mind, your body language makes it blatantly obvious that you're thinking of what to do next. Face the consequences of your actions; it doesn't matter in the least how off-the-wall, or nonsensical[1] your movements may seem.

I wonder what you mean when you say, "I understand"? When someone tells me that, I really don't how to respond. Why not dance without trying to comprehend everything. The audience can be moved without having to comprehend all that goes into making your performance. Isn't that the very reason we dance—to engage the audience on a visceral level? That's why I'm at a terrible loss to hear people talk of understanding my performance. Of course, you can use your brains to think, but when it comes to dancing, just forget all that.

· · ·

Human beings gradually reach the level where they can verbally articulate their different experiences, and emotions. Didn't you feel a need to express a particular sensation when you looked upward. Haven't you, for instance, been touched by something on looking downward? Perhaps, however, there are times when our experiences go beyond the reach of words. Of course, words do their job in most circumstances, but movement can probably say a lot more.

Movement is indispensable in establishing bonds with others. In our everyday gestures, whether it be facing to the left, or turning to the right, the essential thing is that we connect ourselves with those around us.

What is the driving force behind your movements? Are you peering into your inner life when facing downward? Did you really need to turn around and face to the left, or to the right, so as to share your joys and sorrows? Our bodies and joints have gradually evolved and grown by sharing our inner lives. A living body has no need for logic.

· · ·

Imagine, say, a fish rises to the surface in our midst. What a tremendous impact such a simple act as that fish appearing amongst us will have: your movements become more animated; your relationship with your inner life becomes transparent: It's as though the dead guide the living, and the living guide the dead. Try to dance without any inhibition whatsoever, not only externally, but also amidst the living and the dead who inhabit your soul.

Let's try to get to know ourselves inside out, just as that fish did as it plunged into us. In no time, the fish is trying to grasp what our bodies are saying. It feels as though it's asking, "Those delicate movements that you're making now with your fingers and hands, what are they telling to me?" Mathematics and the sciences can't cast any light on this mystery, for your movements are unlike anything ever seen before.

Oh, but I'm deeply touched by something .

. . .

The roots of my dance can be traced back to the time I spent in my mother's womb. Dance springs from that universal womb where death and life intertwine. Life is teeming with contradictions: others have sacrificed their lives so that we could enter this world. In tracing all the way back to our beginnings, we eventually come to the creation of heaven and earth. Keep in mind that we, as human beings, have existed in this continuum since the genesis of the universe. The very fact we think is living proof of our existence. Yet, while we try our utmost to rationally understand everything that happens around us, the truly important things in life trickle down randomly, drop by drop. Rational analysis only renders it insipid.

(overleaf)
134. Ohno rehearsing in the workshop studio. © Teijiro Kamiyama.

. . .

Suppose we were to give ten points to the soul, that spirit living in the innermost depths of the heart, then the body would receive seven. The soul is the moving force; it leads the way. I keep stressing the significance of their bearing upon each other. If the soul leads, the body will follow. So, let's give ten^2 points to the soul, and

1.

What Do

You Mean?

seven points to the body. Take painstaking care in everything you do. Your movements must at all times be imbued with a spiritual presence. When talking with your mother, for instance, you can understand each other perfectly without having to utter a single word. The essential thing is that you get your feelings across.

. . .

You there, you flower in bloom. We're witnessing a flower unfold before our very eyes. But it vanished as unexpectedly as it appeared. For all we know, it might still be lingering around here somewhere. The very fact that you were all attracted to it in the first place is proof of your sanity. But your dance won't become crazy by moving in such a programmed way. That flower simply vanished into thin air in no time at all.

And yet I can see that flower. While it might have vanished from sight, I can still feel its presence. Where do you suppose it could be? How about looking inside your heart? There's a flower waiting to burst forth and bloom in each and every one of us, in each of our hearts. Our minds are weighted down, however, with preconceived ideas as to what shape or form a flower should have. But, when our dance becomes *crazy*, we're no longer bound by such constraints. On becoming crazy, you won't know what drew forth that flower in the first place. Dance has got to be *crazy*.

There, just as you are about to forget yourself, that flower reappears. You can't explain why, but it's right there. Well then, what's happening now? Aren't you *talking* with the flower? Yes, you're conversing with it. Yet the moment you deliberately set out to talk with it, it suddenly vanishes. In any event, let your dance be *crazy*. Don't figure your movements out in your head. Dance *free style*.

. . .

You seem baffled as to where to start after listening to my talk. There, that "I can't understand!" is as good a starting point as any. Don't allow a lack of comprehension to hold you back; it doesn't matter the slightest if you feel that you *cannot understand* what you're doing. How mistaken we would be to think that we can ra-

Workshop

Words

_____

202

tionally explain everything. If anything, isn't that the very reason we dance—because there are many things we don't understand. It's all right; the truly important thing is that you try to wholeheartedly unburden your worries.

Death and life are inseparable! And while we will all come face to face with death one day, we can't separate ourselves from life. Use whatever movements you like; what's essential is that your heart and soul are in it.

. . .

I've been watching your gaze. Once you open your eyes in such a way that allows your soul to slip out, a birdlike creature, the soul of a birdlike creature will emerge. Will it penetrate the passageway to our souls? Are your eyes open in such a way that your soul can come and go without hindrance? Are they ready to welcome that bird as it tries to enter? Your soul constantly needs to come and go, so keep your eyes wide open as you move at all times. As your soul takes flight, do you share with us your joys and sorrows? What

135. Ohno in the Stuttgart Opera house dressing room, June 1987. © Shin Mikami.

1.

What Do

You Mean?

203

happens as your soul flies in and out? Don't birds flap their wings on taking to, and returning from flight? Are your wings flapping in joy, or in sorrow? How are you responding? Your emotions are in a constant state of flux, ever changing. Your dance should reflect that ever shifting reality. Pay careful attention to the way you gaze about you, for it's possible to create a dance solely with the eyes. They are a world onto themselves. Well, let's focus on how you use your eyes for a while.

. . .

We don't get anywhere by remaining continuously on the move. At some stage along the way we need to stop and rest. Once we do so, a tiny hut unexpectedly appears from out of nowhere, a sanctuary in which we can refresh ourselves and take stock of our lives. There's no need to continue without rest. What's to stop us from just standing still by the side of the road for a while? After being constantly on the move, our hearts utter a sigh of relief to finally come across a resting place. There, we refresh our souls, and avail ourselves of the opportunity to replenish our forces before continuing on our way. And rest again at a later stage. As human beings, we don't grow while on the move, but during those dreams we inhabit as we stop and rest for a while. Isn't it at such times that our souls evolve?

. . .

The human face is said to mirror the soul's true character. Still, we won't open ourselves up to you unless your presence strikes a deep chord in us. It isn't merely enough just to stand there indifferently like that. If you evoke our compassion, we'll identify with your joys, sorrows, and sufferings. I'm roused by that overwhelming joy you're enduring! I can sense that you're telling me: "I'm so unbearably happy that I feel I can't go on any longer." But now, your facial expression differs somewhat from your customary one. I'm afraid that you're about to hang yourself. Now, in reaction to what I've just said about unbearable happiness, your expressions are yet once again changing. The looks on all your faces have

136. Ohno rehearsing in the workshop studio. © Teijiro Kamiyama.

changed radically. But, what about your ribs? Are they expanding, are they stretching themselves, or are they even drooping perhaps? Just as a child doesn't exhibit a programmed reaction to its impulses, so too can our bodies respond to any given situation in an untold number of ways. Your dance won't do anything for us unless we perceive a fluid response to your inner life.

. . .

Basically, "butoh" means to meander, or to move, as it were, in twists and turns between the realms of the living and the dead. The human hand has evolved in such a way that is well able to talk. Its "speech" can finely articulate all that we feel. The foot, by way of contrast, is what anchors the body in life. It is obviously not as expressive as the hand. Doesn't the word "butoh" itself imply this dependence between the hands and feet?[3]

. . .

1.

What Do

You Mean?

We love to look at a flower in bloom, for we ourselves become one in doing so. For the living, to see amounts to the same thing as to eat. Keep in mind, it's no different for the spirits of the dead living in us. They eat in the same way that we do; they nourish themselves through the eyes, through the skin. What we, the living, consider food is also a source of nourishment for the dead.

Your dance must emotionally engage us: remember, your performance has to nourish both the dead and the living. Language springs forth spontaneously when we're deeply touched. Our emotions come to life when we eat of ourselves. But should we really devour so much delicious food?

Keep on eating of yourself copiously, for you yourself are the fountainhead of your emotions and the pleasure you take in life. We've got to sense your passionate affair with life unfold. In asking you to dance *free style,* I'm not merely telling you to use your body as an expressive instrument. Forget everything you've ever practiced here. It doesn't matter in the slightest if you just stood there stock-still.

. . .

Couldn't you delve into a limitless world once you're totally gripped by happiness, say, or any emotion for that matter? You'll feel so overwhelmed that you won't be able to detach yourself from it, so much so that you'll plunge yourself wholeheartedly into it. Regardless of what you do, whether you jump around, leap up and down, roll over on the floor, whatever, it just won't let go of its grip on you. This, however, won't happen with just any passing fancy. But, once you sense that "aah, this is for real," let that be the springboard from which you plunge into that endless depths of emotion, regardless of what it may be. Weave a fabric with that emotion. Why not weave a fabric that reaches the sky?

We can penetrate a boundless world even within the confines of any given emotion. Once we plunge into those depths, we're free as to how we move.

. . .

A butterfly crossing the sea.[4]

Or, simply picture the sea and a butterfly.
What's to stop you from flying through the sea?
How would you fly?
You're already threading your way through the waves.

. . .

We don't dance to gain experience, or to demonstrate our talents. Of course, there are physical limits to what we, as dancers, can do, but the crucial question is how we get beyond those limits.

Our souls, our hearts, our spirits respond spontaneously to beauty; our response isn't merely an intellectual one. Take painstaking care of the way in which you respond to life.

My existence here among the planets revolving around the sun, is embraced by life, nurtured by my mother and the intoxicating cherry blossoms in full bloom. Life, without the slightest reluctance, opens it arms to lovingly embrace me. Don't calculate or mentally work out your movements. Because in doing so, you inhibit yourself from responding spontaneously. Try moving your hands without thinking about it; you've got to go beyond choreographic logic. The human race has survived on this earth and continues doing so without putting any effort into it. We have done so without having to think about it.

Feel the world around us, the sun, your mother, children. . . . How do you stretch your arms out in their midst?

. . .

Once, I had to beg myself, "Please, please leave, please just let go." But of whom did I ask this? Of my body? Of my soul? Of life itself? Anyway, before I realized what was happening, my arms suddenly soared away. These very hands, which embody my soul, had detached themselves from the trunk of my body. They didn't try to bolt into the distance but instead remained hanging around

1.

What Do

You Mean?

within close reach. What I witnessed was nothing other than my soul, *my essence,* leaping out me, as those hands soared into liberty.

Look at those hands [of mine] over there! They're writing melodies of their own making. A vast distance separates my hands from my body.

At that time, I was struck by how my soul, my *essence,* could detach itself without any effort on my part, even though the very "I" who perceived this separation of body and soul, continued to exist. Now I'm able to look upon that *essence* as though I simply were looking at someone else. I was later told by someone watching the performance that I looked like a child having fun.

. . .

Regardless of how technically proficient you become, you'll never touch us with something you don't genuinely feel in the first place. There's no point pretending. We'll see right through you; there's no question about that.

The instant you step out in front of an audience it immediately grasps the state of your inner life; it's impossible to conceal it. As performers, we're faced with several crucial problems: What is the soul? What does it long for? What are these spirits who inhabit our bodies trying to tell us? Inevitably, what these spirits desperately need to tell us reveals itself both in our day-to-day lives, and in our performances. Because those spirits are so desperate to convey their feelings, they do so without the slightest restraint. At times, it's almost as though they're begging us, "Please, please look." Keep in mind though, that unless you visibly tear yourself apart, we won't understand what those spirits in you are trying to say.

. . .

Our souls are continually in motion; they divide, they scatter, they proliferate themselves. Sometimes they grow bigger, at other times smaller and so forth. But, what's happening now? Why are you standing dead still? Are you in pain? Or, perhaps, you're simply being careless?

There's an infinity of ways in which you can move from that spot over there to here. But do your movements allow us to feel your spirit? Have you figured those movements out in your head? Or are we seeing your soul in motion? Even that fleck on the tip of your nail embodies your soul. That's why I'm forever telling you to take great care of every single moment; every single stride you make is carrying your soul. Steel and iron in their natural states, for example, also have a soul. Your dance is worthless unless you succeed in engaging the audience on a spiritual level. It's simply not a case of physically moving from one spot to another; the essential thing is that your movements, even when you're standing still, embody your soul at all times.

Well, what was that you were you trying to work out in your head as you were stuck there motionless just a moment ago? Don't for one moment think that we can't see right through that reflective pose you struck. What if we were to examine that motionless posture under a microscope? Isn't it something devilish, yes, a lit-

1.

What Do

You Mean?

tle demon we'd see. Maybe we'd see a right little demon? Never take the *easy* way out—by just doing things superficially. Don't do that, no matter how easy it seems. Invest your dance with *power*; but your dance will only be *powerful* when you are who you are.

. . .

While your movements might strike us as being totally off-the-wall and far removed from those routine gestures we employ in our daily lives, they perhaps reveal something of the truth of your inner life. Be careful, though. I'm not asking you to mimic senseless movements. If anything, I want you to regain the long-lost freedom you enjoyed in your mothers' wombs.

. . .

I'm aware of the difficulties you face in coping with life. While my lifestyle might appear to protect me from the toils of day-to-day living, I nonetheless feel that my life is centered round that common reality we all share, and that the roots of my dance are firmly grounded in everyday life.

I converse with spirits. You, too, are communing with them here. Though our spiritual concerns might seem unrelated to our daily lives, we nonetheless remain in close contact with our inner selves. Yet we don't commune with our souls in that ordinary, everyday mode of discourse. We speak to them frankly from the depths of our hearts; it's no banal conversation that we simply invent as we go along.

It strikes me now that your soul is trying to tell us something, although I'm not exactly sure what. That spirit in the depths of your heart is reaching out to us, but something seems to be holding you back. How about plumbing that little bit deeper into your heart; then you'll be able to talk with each other, openly. You've stopped right on the brink. How about going that little bit further. Once you reach into the depths of your soul, your every movement, no matter how small, will touch a chord in us.

Ah! I hear you now.

. . .

We can lead our lives in so many different ways: we can be successful and yet die young; we can get by modestly until a ripe old age and so on. On a superficial level, our individual lifestyles are nothing more than a reflection of the variety of ways in which it is possible to live our lives here on earth: richly, poorly, healthily, happily, and so forth. The fact that each of you here exemplifies a distinct lifestyle is in itself just proof that you are alive, and little else. Ultimately, it doesn't really matter how successful or frugal our lives are. What is of importance, though, is how you cherish life. Your every deed creates a connection with others, regardless of how insignificant that relation may appear. Your relationships, irrespective of whether they strike you as being close or distant, do have a direct impact upon your life. Like it or not, we all need to acknowledge that we are interdependent; we are interconnected. We've got to concentrate on improving our relationships with others.

Your movements are not just an expression of your life's superficial facets. Rather, they must clearly indicate how you're connected with your inner life force. So, whether you use a fingernail, raise your small finger, or move any part of the body, harness that energy at all times.

. . .

Imagine a feast.[5] Doesn't a feast, by its very nature, refuse to follow a set pattern? If anything, a feast only erupts when it strays from any predetermined pattern, much in the same way that music starts coming to life once you stop trying to matching your movements to it.

Maybe you're scared that you might lose your balance and fall off your feet by plunging right into the spirit of a feast, straying from the rhythm of the music, and unbridled by any set notions of what dance should be. The true significance of that word "feast" first dawned on me when I came across Rimbaud's poetry collection *A Season in Hell* at a bookstore in Kanda during those chaotic postwar years. There was that one poem, "Feast," which clung to my soul. To this very day I still can't get it out of my head.

Only by forsaking the straight and narrow, and casting off all

1.

What Do

You Mean?

———

the conventions in place, will my dance ever come to bloom. Lately, I keep repeating to myself, "You ought to perform with more care from now on; let your dance step out of your heart."

. . .

Judas hung himself after betraying Jesus for thirty pieces of silver. Though I'm acquainted with the Gospels' version of how Judas informed on Jesus, there is also a completely different take on that story. The common perception is that Jesus felt that Judas had been disloyal to him. Judas, it must be said, felt betrayed as well. Wasn't it Jesus who told him, "I'm your friend"? That's why Judas went and betrayed him for thirty pieces of silver.

But Judas, by taking upon yourself that heavy burden, you risked your life to make me aware of how vulnerable I am!

Jesus, you too made me realize the true meaning of God when you were nailed to the cross.

Judas, you risked your life so that I could realize that I'm no better than you. How miserable, how truly miserable it was for you, Judas. If it's of any consolation Judas, know that there is a Judas in each and every one of us; we are all traitors!

Workshop

Words

_____

212

If we didn't harbor a Judas in us, his suffering would know no end. He took upon himself the burden that I should have carried. Betraying Jesus was the only way that he could make me understand what it means to be unable to worship God. And yet he hanged himself in the end.

. . .

You don't have to look at the setting sun with your everyday matter-of-fact way of seeing the world. There's no need to. What really matters is whether your inner sun is sinking or not. You've no need to identify yourself with that sun out there on the horizon.

Where, then, should we focus our gaze at such times? Keep your eyes wide open, but don't under any circumstances focus on any part of what you see. There's no need to close them; just leave them open, just as though you've been stranded somewhere. Even though the sky is darkening, your inner sun is still ablaze. Yes, keep your eyes wide open. We're quivering at that unfolding beauty.

. . .

I've been watching the way in which you move your eyes. Most of you appear to be thinking of what do next and consequently no longer know where to focus your gaze. The eyes play a crucial role in the way in which you interact with the world: they visually digest and encapsulate all that happens in the universe. In some respects, they are a universe unto themselves; a universe in which one can become completely absorbed.

Your eyes are now wide open. Make your pupils smaller as though you were peering into the distance. Don't focus on any object, nor let anything grab your attention. Let the entire universe slip all the way into there. In doing so, you might be able to dance spontaneously. But you won't become spontaneous by trying to be so. Nothing will come of your efforts to consciously discard your thoughts.

Keep your eyes open, but don't look at anything. Don't react, even if you reach out your hands. Don't question, or seek anything

1.

What Do

You Mean?

———

out with your gaze. If you want to develop an intuitive approach, start by concentrating on the eyes. But what, you ask, of all the techniques you've acquired during years of learning and practice. Get rid of them all! You'll never really do that, however; as all you've learnt will always stand in your stead. I love to see a dance in which the movements aren't only performed on the surface. I'm deeply touched when a performer barely moves, or simply keeps standing stock-still.

. . .

By moving very quietly, it's possible to walk with great care. As soon as we try, however, to codify any of our movements or gestures, the way, let's say, we tumble about, or run, or stop still, and so on, we lose sense of what we're doing. Isn't that what conventional dance in fact revolves around—definable movements?

Couldn't having a meal, for instance, reveal to us the true nature of dance? Don't we sit down for lunch while working on a job? One day, I'm seriously thinking of partaking of a meal onstage during the course of a performance.

. . .

I am so beautiful; you are too! We've never before laid eyes on such beauty. You and I have just returned from an in-depth exploration of the underworld.[6] Music rang out everywhere, though you couldn't hear a sound. Unconsciously, you gave off a fragrance that utterly differs from the way you smell in everyday life. What truly wonderful smells and sounds your habitual movements spontaneously evoke, once you step delicately into the underworld. Perhaps, that was an ultramusic we heard. You look like somebody returning from the hereafter to our everyday reality. You're continuing a journey from the underworld to the here and now. But your former self and the you who have just undergone that experience are not any longer the same person. You may appear exactly the same, but you've completely changed. If possible, I want you to dare to take that risk, the risk of passing through life after death.

. . .

Onstage, it's virtually impossible cut off that internal dialogue. No matter how hard I try, a voice inside my head starts to speak, and before I know what's happening, I'm already talking to myself.

In my everyday life, it's no different. I think from morning till night; I keep racking my brains over how I should do this and that, until I eventually dismiss all that's on my mind and start to trust my instincts. Thinking gets me absolutely nowhere. And yet, over time, I've come to realize that all those seemingly unnecessary ideas that I rack my brains over are the very basis upon which my intuitive approach has been built. Without them, I'd never succeed in creating anything. There's more to spontaneity, as I see it, in any case, than simply dancing any old way. You're searching for a pie in the sky if you think you can step out there and improvise without some preparation on your part.

. . .

The way you walk gives it all away. We can immediately sense whether you're carefree, or burdened with worry. You, for instance —or, all of us, for that matter—have to cope with life's ups and downs. Don't fret, just move naturally. Coping with your problems is as normal an occurrence as walking. So don't hurry, don't hurry. If a wolf suddenly creeps up on you from out of nowhere, just stop and stand still. What's the point of trembling with fear after having come so far in life? Don't be afraid of your fears. Haven't you put your foot forward so as to walk ahead? Let's first of all just walk. In no time your problems will crop up, one after the other. They're constantly increasing. Carry your burdens as you walk forward. Though you're uncertain as to what's going to happen, keep moving!

. . .

1.

What Do

You Mean?

215

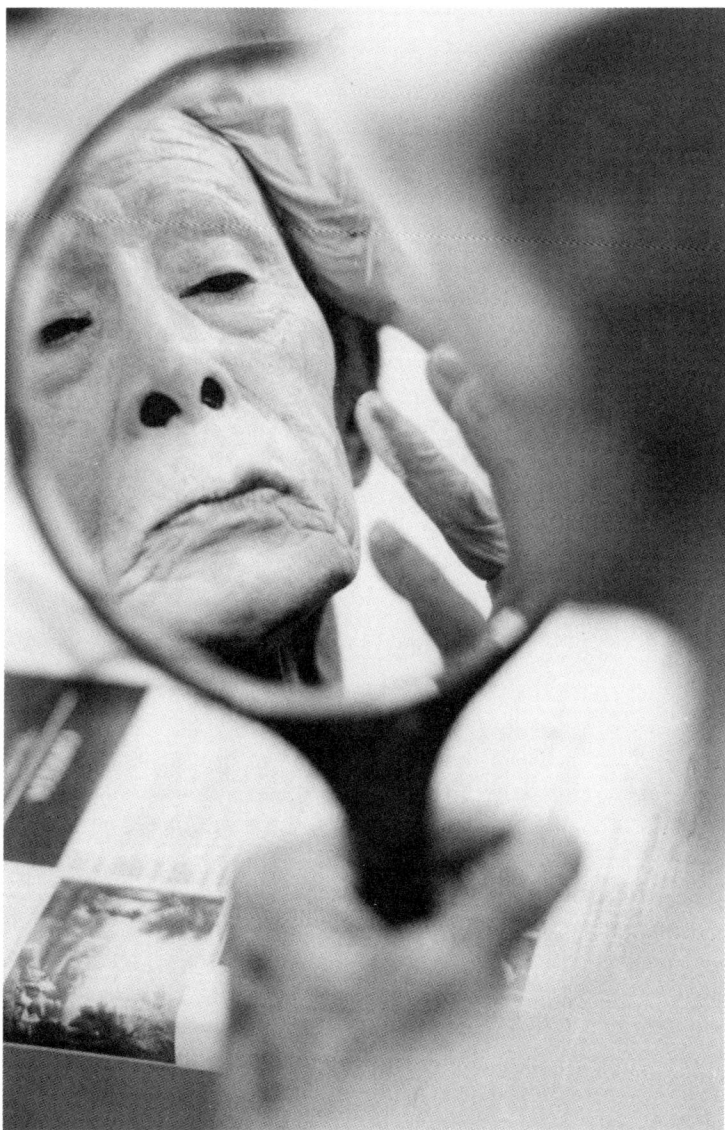

139. Ohno in the
Teatro di Rifredi
dressing room,
Florence, 1990.
© Colomba
d'Apolito.

We don't seem to fully realize that a mysterious creature has been secretly raised and continues to live in each and every one of us. Perhaps, this creature is none other than our soul, that being which has been offered to and dispensed amongst us as a gift from the God, as a gift from the universe. In all likelihood, this was God's way of offering us the possibility of sharing in an awareness of each other. We are all united by our awareness of the universe. Yes, awareness of the universe.

All creatures, be they human, animal, or other, come into this world mentally equipped to confront the various difficulties life will cast in their way. Medically speaking, however, the intestines, stomach, and other vital organs are located in the belly, not in the head. Moreover, we share our bodies with the secret voice that will heal whatever sufferings we endure. The human organism has gradually evolved in this way. If we acknowledge the universal spirit in us, our bodies, in themselves, have the ability to fulfil our mission in life. Thanks to the combined force of our various organs and limbs (the stomach and intestines, where our bones—and the blood flowing through that sanctuary located in the marrow—are formed), thanks to all of these, we possess whatever strength we need to lead a full life. But in this rational world in which we now find ourselves, we've become deranged because we depend too much on our brains. I'm quite something myself; I start pushing others out of my way as greed gets the better of me. In no time, such behavior leads to war. I'm speaking from experience, as I'm no stranger to war. Rather than relying on our brains, we should concentrate on our stomachs and intestines. These are life's primal forces; so cherish them dearly.

. . .

Sliding about or rolling over on the floor doesn't pose you any particular difficulties. Yet these, or any movements for that matter, are not the building blocks with which dance is created. Haven't you ever stumbled upon some extremely perilous situation in performing where you're forced to come face to face with yourself. On reaching that threshold, we all come across emotions that we feel are better kept to ourselves. But we can't lock them away. Should we keep our feelings to ourselves until we depart this world? Or

1.

What Do

You Mean?

should we share them with those around us? The more I perform, the more convinced I've become that we ought to share our inner life with others.

. . .

At one particular performance I felt that both the living and the dead were staring at me. How did that affect me? In some respects, the spirits of the dead come to life during the course of a performance. In the noh theatre, for instance, they speak of *yūgen*[7] a world of profound and delicate beauty in which spirits emerge. The themes of the noh plays tend to touch on the lives of those who formerly existed, or departed spirits. Onstage, the noh player portrays incidents that occurred during the former life of these ghosts.

I, however, don't mimic any person, or spirit, as they were when alive. I'm so grateful to all those who have lived before me, that I want to dance in such a way that I live and walk at their side. What's the point in superficially copying somebody! By means of our imagination, we've got to go beyond mere resemblance so to as to create something more substantial. But don't for one moment think that your imaginative powers are the fruit of your own making; they stem from the guidance we received from all those who have lived before us. There's absolutely no way that my imagination springs from the workings of my brain.

. . .

Just because you admire flowers or find them attractive is no reason to imitate them. What's to stop you from becoming a flower? If those eyes of yours, your soul, your way of looking at the world were to burn as much energy you've so far consumed here at the workshop, you could burst into bloom right here before our very eyes. There's nothing stopping you from becoming a flower. It blossoms for all time by pushing itself to the edge, by offering all it has to give. We're now getting to the heart of the matter of today's workshop. It's absolutely immaterial how you twist or contort your body. That's not going to create a flower. As soon as you offer your eyes, as soon as you offer all that you have to give, I'll see you bloom before me. Offer all you have so as to create a flower.

Chapter 2

Please Just
Do It; There's
Nothing I Can
Teach You

You won't engage our attention unless you demonstrate a willingness to disjoint your entire body.[1] Try to dance in the spirit that every single joint in your body could unhinge itself at any moment. You've never done so before, so how about trying to break new ground today. Please just do it; there's *nothing* I can teach you.

. . .

When asked for a definition of butoh, [Tatsumi] Hijikata replied: "Butoh is a dead body risking its life by planting its feet firmly on the ground." His answer might lead you to conclude that butoh is a dance form that transcends all technique. If we examine the matter closely, it becomes clear that our creative powers are not of our own making. Our imagination not only feeds upon our personal life stories but also our collective subconscious memory. During that incredibly long period spanning from the genesis of heaven and earth right up to the present day, our ancestors, along with all the spirits of the universe, have with each successive generation, embedded themselves in our souls. I am, you are, we all are, nothing but the next layer upon all those things that have already happened in a never ending chain of events. Seen from that perspective, our imaginative force is being constantly consolidated by the gradual accumulation of knowledge we inherit.

But to return to the problems posed by technique: I don't think that technical skills are so easily acquired within the limits of a single lifetime. On questioning myself as to the proper use of technique, I've come to the conclusion that it should endow us with the wherewithal to confront whatever problems we face. The term, however, usually designates the methods we employ to structure

____

219

our work; the underlying assumption being that the more we rationally structure it, the more comprehensible it becomes. But, in reality, the more we shackle ourselves with technical skills, the more difficulties we face, and before we know it, we find ourselves not knowing where to turn with all our techniques.

So, were I to even try to write something on the technical aspects of my work, I simply couldn't. If anything, not being able to do so is a sign of skill.

. . .

Workshop

Words

Let your movements spill out of you; do your utmost to make them spontaneous. If asked to dance a song by, say, Elvis Presley, you couldn't do so unless you went beyond an intellectual appreciation of the music. I'm now going to put on a piece by Presley, so try to move in any way you please while listening to it. That's the starting point for our workshops. Don't figure it out in your head; nobody wants to come to see such a lifeless performance.

. . .

I can see that you're driven to the edge of collapse, so let go of yourself completely; surrender to the flow. Why not ask for help rather than shut yourself off? What does it matter if your posture pleads for help or begs for support? How can life offer you a helping hand if you don't reach out? But are you merely stretching out hands of flesh and bone? You'll make it easier for life to reach out to you if those pleading hands and eyes embody your soul's longing. Who knows, but as soon as life begins to penetrate that enormous universe embracing your eyes, it might take you by the hand and guide you toward the help you need. You're free to do whatever you please, because each and every thing connected to life embraces freedom.

. . .

Discard whatever mental fantasies and ideas you may have. Don't think about where to place your feet. Forget all that, and follow your own impulses. You'll only obstruct your flow of movement by thinking about what a good posture you've got. What's the point of asking yourself what your next gesture should be? Don't look to me. I can't answer your question of whether it's good enough to stand there motionlessly. How could I? There's surely got to be something more than that to dance. Be spontaneous, just like this. How could words ever explain how to move? Just do it. I want dance to spring from an inexplicable source.

. . .

[Spoken while dancing]
    Although I don't clearly understand what I'm doing, nor perhaps do you fully grasp what you're seeing, yet it still comes to life like this, unexpectedly. I want to keep dancing in such a way that deeply touches you for some inexplicable reason.

2.

Please

Just Do It

. . .

When you make a deliberate effort, don't waver. Don't hold your-self back, go all the way. It's important though to realize that you don't need to continuously exert your strength. Making a visible effort isn't what counts; the essential thing is that we perceive the strength of your relationship with God. There's a lot more to dance than the physical energy you invest in your movements. But what a difficult task you're undertaking in trying to move effortlessly!

Picture for a moment the effortless way in which the winds blow through the skies. Think of rain, of clouds, storms. Treat everything with great care. Try to move very delicately; try to move with strength of the young; try to move with delicacy of the aged. Cherish each and every thing as though it were God's precious gifts of life bestowed upon us. Take, for instance, these wooden floorboards underneath us. We relate to them in many different ways: they provide a support for our feet; they offer us seating. Then, there's also the "we" that sits on the floor. Mobilize all those different aspects of life into your dance. Well then, let's try again. All right, let's begin!

. . .

No matter how skillfully you copy a flower's external features, it still does not look right. While it might look similar, it lacks what's really essential. But you'll bloom before our very eyes as soon as the delicacy and inner beauty of your dance engages us. Once you forget yourself, you'll spontaneously burst into flower without hav-ing to give it the slightest thought.

Don't concern yourself with superficial appearances. Does a flower think about how it should bloom? Doesn't it just simply reach out to us and offer all it has to share? I'm all too aware of the difficulties you'll encounter in trying to give of yourself as freely as a flower does. But please try to avoid the temptation to lay it on; there's no need for such exaggerated movements.

Once a flower has passed its peak, you might be tempted to think that it's seen its day. A true flower, however, doesn't fade into oblivion; it remains eternally beautiful. I know a flower can bloom

Workshop

Words

141. A workshop
scene. © Ohno
Dance Studio
Archives.

in many ways, but I can't help feeling that you're laying it on a bit much!

A flower etches itself in our heart for all time; it has done so on countless occasions. No matter which angle you study it from, whether from the front, from behind or wherever, it remains beautiful. How then, can we, as performers, become such an eternally beautiful flower? Try with all your might to physically tear yourself apart, so much so that you tear your heart is torn to shreds. Try wholeheartedly. For the moment, it doesn't matter if your gestures are somewhat too expressive. Please dance *free style;* imbue every single instant with the heart beat of your soul.

. . .

Aren't you being too demonstrative? Aren't your gestures trying a little too hard? In the noh theatre, a player employs nonmovement and nonaction in his quest to create a rapport with the spectators. The ideal is to dance without moving. In fact, such sparseness of expression is an effective means to evoke the world of

2.

Please

Just Do It

223

spirits, for inaction, more than physical movement, affects us on a much deeper level.

Anyway, what's the purpose of our being here? Ultimately, aren't we here to link hearts? It's a difficult challenge. Bear in mind that restraint plays an essential role in creating your onstage presence.

. . .

Petals scatter in no time. Now, as I watch you conversing with the spirits living in you, I'm struck by how you're transforming into a flower in all its glory. A flower soon withers, however, after it blooms, its petals scattered by the winds. For not only does a flower fade away from in front of my eyes, it also slips quietly out of my mind. That's why I bid it *bye-bye*.[2]

Death can be such a terrifying affair. A flower remains eternally beautiful, even though in due course its petals silently wither, lingering there as though nothing were amiss, until one day it is no more. I wave *bye-bye* to those spirits that come and go, just as I bid farewell to those scattering petals. As soon as a flower blossoms in all its glory, its petals begin to slip unawares into my heart. I wave them *bye-bye,* and look forward to meeting them again.

. . .

A clothes rail
In the sunshine.
A breeze
Ruffled through my heart
As I hang
On a clothes rail
In the sunshine.
The winds have risen
I'm free
To flap as I please.
And yet,
I'm barely using the wind.

. . .

Yesterday evening, I performed at Tokyo's Shinjuku Pit Inn for fifty minutes without a break; yes, for a full fifty minutes accompanied by a jazz pianist and drummer. After the performance someone came up and told me that my face looked radiant. Seeing that there are so many possibilities existing within any given dance form, it doesn't really matter what movements we use. I didn't discuss with the musicians beforehand what we were going to do onstage. Had we figured it out, it wouldn't have been a jazz session. Anyway, as I was saying, we performed for a full fifty minutes without any preparation whatsoever. From the outset, we knew the outcome was going to be a risk, so we launched into it, putting our lives on the line. We perform, not because we're able to, but because we have to. Failure or success have got nothing to do with it; what counts is that we give of ourselves, wholeheartedly. In the end, I had to put a stop to our session. Feeling gratitude and thanks, I called it a day. And, on that note, our performance finished.

. . .

Every single phenomenon in the universe manifests itself as a soul.[3] The noh plays reflect this spiritual view of the world. Onstage, the noh player's knowledge and skill must fuse. By means of his artistry, he has to establish an immediate and total rapport with the spectators. This, however, is much easier said than done. Until such time as his craft fully matures, the player faces tremendous difficulty in communing with his audience.

There once was an exceptional case in which an eighty-year-old ballerina continued to perform in public, although, on the whole, dancers' bodies show visible sign of decline by the time they've reached their forties, not to mention what it's like in their fifties or sixties. As physical degeneration sets in, they've little choice but to retire and assume the role of charming elderly ladies.

And what, I wonder, will become of me? At my age, I'm no stranger to pain. And yet, as soon as I step out onstage I make an instant recovery. Once I step out in front of the public I keep on

2.

Please

Just Do It

moving, so much so, in fact, that I wear myself out completely before retiring to the wings. Nevertheless, the longer I perform, the better I feel. Stepping out onstage is like a remedial visit to the doctor; I'm fully cured afterward.

. . .

You let go of yourself ever so briefly. I don't expect you to do so constantly, but if you only could abandon yourself for one second, for just one brief instant. You've got to seize that fleeting moment and ensure that it bears fruit.

To dance onstage is to put one's life on the line. Even I become desperate whenever I step out there: the first, the second, the third step are simply hopeless, and yet that moment will come after the third, the first, the fifth step when I slip into a timeless realm. I know it's impossible that your every moment be imbued with that feeling. As you let go of yourself, you'll carry us all to the sun and the moon; you'll convey to us an eternity with every step you take. And oh, how deeply touching it is to come face to face with the man in the moon. You've got to convey eternity in every second.

. . .

Which, you ask, is the prime mover? The soul? Or the body? Body and soul are inseparable; but unless we feel that your dance steps out of your heart, it won't attract our attention. We won't grasp what your soul is trying to impart to us, if your body remains tense.

Open up; let us see what's going on inside of you. You're now gazing straight ahead. As you shift your center of balance forward, slightly raise your upper eyelid. Hold onto that position. There, you can call out, "Mother." Keep your eyes barely open; just that little bit is fine. That is an ideal posture for your soul to emerge and lead the way. Holding that position, raise your arms. What about your hands? Use them even more freely. Hold them in such a way that they're facing your heart. Your hands are now conversing with each other. Grant them free rein.

. . .

My soul is turning to ashes.
If I breathe out
They spill from my body.
I breathe myself in and out.
My soul floats throughout the sky
As it turns to ashes and falls.

. . .

Have you ever looked at the *Chōjūgiga*,[4] those ancient Japanese illustrated satirical tales? These traditional scrolls depict beasts and
fowl, foxes and frogs, all acting as humans. For some mysterious
reason, whenever I look at one of those scrolls, a ghost-like creature invariably creeps up on me; it suddenly materializes from out
of nowhere, although it's hard to distinguish whether it's a bird or
a human being. What I can't help feeling about its unexpected appearance is that the illustrator has successfully captured on paper
that bird which lives inside all of us.

For today's workshop theme, I thought you could try to reach
out to those creatures living in you. Usually, I talk at length on a
given theme before you begin to practice. You, in turn, then somehow try to adapt your movements to what I've said, or decide to
follow my suggestions. Today, let's try another approach. As far as
I'm concerned, if you're to really bring your dance to life, you've
got to become a spirit. While we obviously can't clearly define
the shape or form a spirit possesses, that is not to say that it does-
n't have one. All of God's creatures, be they birds, beasts, whatever, live in me. I've done enough talking for today. So, how about
a ghost dance? In a word, you're practicing so as to turn into a
specter.

. . .

Shift your center of gravity slightly so that you can move forward. Don't push your rib cage out. Instead, pull your chest in, and stretch upward from the crown of your head. Beginning at the base of the spine stretch as far as possible upward. Hold that position, and then bend slightly forward. Even if you stand squarely, there's nothing to stop you from moving forward. Have your hips, chest, and chin so positioned that you're already in motion as you go to move forward. Step forward a little, bending ever so gently. Release your strength, let go of it, relax. Don't walk with your feet; instead let your torso and shoulders guide you through space. What a beautiful flower you're becoming! Shift your center of balance slightly forward, but don't think about your feet. Look, they're already in motion of their own accord.

. . .

If at all possible, I like to perform in the spirit of a *Kasakurū mai,* a dance performed beneath a halo of madness.[5]

The word "mad" is a fitting description for an infant's cry. Its scream is so saturated with contrasting emotions that it's hard to tell whether the child is feeling wildly happy, enraged, or what's really going on. Leaving behind the comforts of the womb, every newborn has to face a completely different environment. Are their screams an expression of shock on being confronted with an alien planet? Or of joy on discovering a new world? Or even of sorrow on leaving the womb behind? I can't help thinking that their primal screams embody the maddening excitement they feel on coming into contact with life. Didn't the birth of each and every one of us bring madness into this world?

. . .

I notice that your facial and physical expressions are constantly changing. What a bottomless well! You can express yourself in an infinite number of ways. It's not a question of a thousand or two, for we could never count them all. How could we? We carry in us the traces of every conceivable form of human experience since the creation of heaven and earth. So not only does our imagination draw on what we've experienced in our personal trajectories through life; it also feeds on those of the countless generations that preceded us. Our expressive range is not confined only to human dimension. It also embraces those of fishes, plants, and amphibians. Even that gush of freedom we once felt on soaring through the sky is stored in there. We've all experienced such sensations in our mothers' womb.

Your expressions are in a state of flux. That is what I'd like you to explore today: all the many lives you've lead; all the different realms you've known. I'm going to put on a piece of music, so how about experiencing that for yourself? It's a crucial task for any performer.

. . .

Redon's paintings are sometimes considered as commonplace and too orderly, but take a good look at this one here.[6] There's something odd about it; he seems to be deliberately concealing something from us.

During the last workshop you practiced transforming yourselves into a candle that had been set alight. You experienced melting into a complete frenzy. You won't engage us unless you plumb into the deepest recesses of your heart. That will bring you to the brink of a crisis, a crisis where you'll either live or die. [Pointing to Redon's painting of a flower.] Look at all these flowers in bloom. They're slightly unusual; one might even think them a little strange. But, here's a "real" flower. Here's one that isn't hiding anything.

. . .

Are you painstaking in the way you move your knees? And what of your elbows, your joints, your ligaments? Are you careful in how you use them to reach out? Remember, your heart, too, was once supported by ligaments, but they didn't solely depend on rhythm for freedom of movement. Yes, once upon a time, your heart too had joints. Your heartbeat is constantly changing.

2.

Please

Just Do It

_____

· · ·

Try stretching toward the sky using both arms. If you want to soar into the sky, that might be a good a starting point. In the womb, you were free to cast your gaze wherever you pleased; upward, downward, inward, wherever. You were surrounded by sky; it wasn't just above your head, but under your toes as well. In like manner, you are now surrounded by sky. We coexist with the sky. Pay special attention to your feet, for their tactile sense is equally sensitive as those of your hands. You're soaring into the heavens, aren't you? You'd better believe the clouds are below your feet. You'd really better believe it! Aren't clouds supposed to be over-head? Aren't we accustomed to looking at them above our heads? But, playing in your mother's womb, didn't you float inside those clouds above the clouds? Didn't you look upward while playing in the womb? You didn't need to do so, but you still probably ex-perienced the sensation of floating above the clouds. It's possible to feel something without having to look at it directly. So long, of course, that it is imbued with life.

· · ·

The soul is the prime mover in dance. Are we conscious of our feet when walking? No, how could you figure out your steps and walk at the same time? Don't we walk by placing one leg in front of the other? We'd never be able to walk were we to think of which leg to put down first. When a mother beckons her child to come to her, it runs toward her, instinctively. Like life itself, we can never stay still.

· · ·

You're hesitant about what to do with your hands. [But once you forget about them], don't they unexpectedly become as one? You've got to make us feel that your hands and those of the universe have somehow become as one. You won't, however, bring this about consciously; you'll only discover and experience this on becoming the hands of the universe.

Workshop

Words
_____

230

. . .

142. Ohno's
shadow forming
a crane on the
ground. © Hideaki
Ishizaka.

I'm looking up at the sky. Well, then, at what am I looking? Am I facing the sky? No, I'm not; I'm not looking at anything at all. I'm now facing the ground. When I'm looking down in that direction, am I looking at the ground below me? No, I'm not looking at anything at all. What's going on? It seems that my inner life has been completely demolished.

Well, in that case, am I out of my mind? No, I'm no madman. Is madness creeping up on me, then? Though by no means out of my mind, I still want to plunge into an irrational world[7] whenever I gaze around me. Whenever I look upward, face downward, or stare right in front of me I want to be able to plunge into an irrational world.

While it's not inconceivable that human intelligence is an outgrowth of madness, madness could never spring forth from the intellect. If at all possible, I would like you to explore what lies at the root of madness. In gazing up at the sky, look beyond the visible. We should feel that your eyes are embracing the entire universe.

2.

Please

Just Do It

_____

231

. . .

Are you physically prepared to construct a world for a fleeting moment? Are you ready at all times to be carried away to some distant place? It doesn't matter in the least whether that world you create is sweet, or spicy, or even bitter, for that matter. What is important, though, is how the taste, smell, and color of your dance relates to your day-to-day life.

. . .

I'm conveyed at an incredible speed from one realm to another when asleep, or when I lose my bearings. I keep repeating to myself, there's no need to worry, because for all I know, there's the equivalent of a night train to the stars, that intergalactic railway serving the boundless Milky Way, running through my guts.

. . .

Don't reach out only to those directly in front of you: twist your body slightly so as to allow yourself to come in contact with everyone present. This will help you to get all your worries off your chest. While not focusing your gaze on any particular spectator, you should nonetheless establish visual contact with the entire audience. Outwardly, you should appear as if you're looking at us, even though you're not. Although you're avoiding direct eye contact, please open your heart to us. Sharing your inner world is far more important than looking at us directly. Just wriggle your body ever so slightly.

. . .

Repose not only offers us an opportunity to reflect over what lies ahead, but also provides us with an occasion to commune with the spirits of the dead. While I'm grateful to all those people who have helped me throughout the course of my life, I could never forget those who came before me and paved the way. The help given by my family, the help I receive from my contemporaries, doesn't in any way eclipse what I receive from my beloved mother and father and all their elders. The help that we all, as human beings, have obtained down throughout the generations has benefited us immensely; our ancestors' experiences have always stood in our good stead. In our dreams, we can commune with, and receive help from the spirits of the dead. They impart to us not only what they themselves experienced but also what they inherited from pre-. vious generations of the living. When you come across the spirits of the dead in your sleep,—they could be souls from heaven or limbo, or maybe even a wandering soul—they might approach you and ask, "What's the matter?"

You, in turn, will appeal to them for assistance, and they, likewise will ask you for help. Please try to dance as freely as you can, listening attentively to the spirits living inside of you.

. . .

When drunk with joy, or drowned in sorrow, we tend to become blind to what's going on around us. It's as though we tightly close our eyes and shut out the world. But such an approach isn't feasible when performing onstage. We've no choice but to keep our eyes open. But that doesn't mean that you should focus your gaze as you do normally.

You don't need to be theatrical; remain calm. Let go of your strength bit by bit; it's all right. Move delicately, as an insect would. You'll get a taste of eternal life when you reach the point where you can survive like an insect. Insects are alive. Keep at it! Go on, put your life at risk!

. . .

The air in here now reeks of a fox's beast-like smell. What does such a smell suggest? Doesn't it attest to the presence of some vital, life giving energy? Clouds smell of life. The winds are colored. Listen to that baby screaming.[8] Isn't that life itself screaming at us, a life I've given birth to?

Look at me! Why can't I see that I'm turning my life inside out? It may seem incredible, but there's nothing to prevent me from turning my life upside down. If I did so, wouldn't my long-cherished dream come true? Once I'm able to reach out and embrace your hearts, I'll toss myself up into the sky as though I were playing with a ball. I've no need to think about how to do that.

. . .

When you're moved by deep feeling, couldn't you stand there motionlessly like a stone statue perched on top of a rock? Possessed of such conviction, you could walk on water. What or who could prevent you from burying yourself alive under a riverbed? You won't, however, command that degree of self-control with just any passing fancy. Here at the workshops, explore your emotions for what they truly are. That is why you're here. If, say, you feel that a blood-thirsty beast is stalking you, don't dismiss that fear out of hand; instead, experience the anguish of being preyed upon with every single step you take. If a lion bites your foot, live through that horror for all its worth. Even if that beast rips your limbs apart, don't let that stop you from delving into the depths of that excruciating pain. What does being able to endure such an experience mean? Doesn't it suggest that we can transform ourselves radically. What's then to stop you from turning yourself into a dragonfly, a butterfly, a fish, or even an insect?

The important thing is that you live every step, every stride, painstakingly. Perhaps, you doubt your ability to attain such an unwavering degree of emotional focus? But why? There's nothing to stop you.

You're a robot at heart, that's why.

Workshop

Words

. . .

234

Just the other day one of my students happened to vomit during class.[9] She could only bring up a mucus-like substance. There was nothing there but mucus. Something obviously came over her, as she could go no further and collapsed right there on the spot. By going to such an extreme, it was inevitable that she would crack up. That's what caused her to vomit. Mind you, had she not vomited, her experience would have been fruitless.

The same applies to you here at the workshops. It doesn't matter in the least what you do, or how you move. The essential thing is that you've got to reach a crisis point where the mucus clogged up inside of you forces itself out of your system. Be patient. Don't give in! You'll sooner or later confront your demons. They won't reveal themselves willingly unless you discharge that mucus in you. On reaching that threshold, you're free to express yourselves in whatever way you see fit. In saying that, I'm speaking from personal experience.

Strangely, as I scooped up some of that mucus, I was struck by how at once it was both transparently clear and slimy. As such, it was living proof of her vitality. Feel free to go all the way; I won't prevent you from releasing that which is fomenting inside of you.

. . .

Walk as though you were climbing a mountain slope. Maintaining your balance is the least of the problems you'll face. All you have to do is bear in mind the conditions to expect when climbing a mountain.

It doesn't matter that I keep standing on this one spot, motionlessly, without making progress on the slope. How about taking that as our point of departure? I can't fend off the impression that I am not only standing on a slope right this very moment but have been doing so all along.

To walk the mountains is to "fall." When I long to catch sight of the sky, the apparent boundary between the earth and what is beyond it slopes skyward. Turning round to face downhill, there seems to be no end in sight to the downward slope. And then, from out of nowhere, the horizon appears.

. . .

Your world has been transformed into something completely unrecognizable; only your back remains as it once was. Half your body seems to have been torn away, and whatever little flesh remains just dangles there, hanging onto a frame of bones. Still, your back is clutching desperately onto life.

In the midst of this transformation, we can hear the sound of an evening bell ring out. The sound of that bell reaches the deepest the recesses of our hearts. Your dangling flesh quivers; your body trembles as though responding to it. It almost sounds as though you and the bell have become one. Listen! That bell clapper is none other than your soul; even your fingertips are vibrating. While providing you with a living shell, that bell is without interior and exterior. It is none other than your earthly home, that originally came into being when heaven and earth were created. Night after night it rings out, as though handing down stories for the generations to come. It vibrates in every nook and corner of our bodies and lives. It can be heard throughout the here and the hereafter, calling forth to both the living and the dead.

. . .

Even to this very day, you're still a fetus at heart. You're a fetus trying to dance. That's why I say that you are a fetus. Though as yet without eyes to see with, you will soon come to see what so far has been invisible. But what a world awaits you beyond the womb!

Movement is born of life's breath. Don't be shackled by conventions; just let go of yourself. Cry out; even groan if you feel like it. Hear how that fellow over there is groaning. You there, you're over the moon with joy. Don't hesitate, just move simply; after all you're still just a fetus. When listening to a calisthenics program on the radio, there's no need to follow the presenter's instructions. It's up to you, in the end, in what sequence, if any, you do the exercises. You're free to move as you wish. What I want to see, though, is a dance in which you give birth to what's alive inside of you.

. . .

2.

Please

Just Do It

In attempting to elaborate on the ideas I work on here at the workshop studio into a more structured piece for public performance, I invariably run into difficulties. I'd really have accomplished some feat if I even once performed onstage without laying down a structure. Well, in any case, let's try to develop what we're working on now; it doesn't matter for the moment if we put a framework in place.

All of us have specific talents, or affinities for certain kinds of movement. Let's, for example, try to play in the way a child does. Let's take that as a theme. In playing as we normally would, or even when improvising with childlike movements, nothing changes. We remain the same. For some reason or other, our movements don't become dance. What, then, is missing? That brings us to the crucial question: What does movement require before it becomes dance?

Move your feet impulsively at any given moment. As soon as you no longer think about how you move, your whole world abruptly changes. You'll then be able to elaborate on your theme by trying many different postures. In the long run, your dance can only benefit by accumulating those experiences in which you're truly at a loss as to what to do.

You've got to both captivate and engage your audience. Don't ever allow them see through your performance; don't let them figure out what you're next movement is going to be. Don't let them see you setting up the effects in advance, for its arrival will only be all too predictable. But, most important of all, go beyond showing them what you can do.

· · ·

What's the point in imitating a dreamlike phantom? It's nothing more than a caricature of the real thing. You cannot create anything out of nothing.

If, out of sheer frustration, I no longer know where to turn, or what to do, I just let go of myself completely. I start to move on the spur of the moment. In attempting to flee my despair, I give my body free rein. I try over and again, twice, three times, four times, moving spontaneously all the time. While my movements mightn't be as spontaneous as I'd like to think, I still got to lay my life down

Workshop

Words

with that much intensity every time I set foot onstage. And the very instant my mind loosens its grip over me, moonlight floods my world.

. . .

A great many people are constantly coming to life in me. Aren't they reaching out to me in my day-to-day life as their souls permeate my body? That's not inconceivable. Since each and everyone of us is born in and of this universe, we're linked to every single thing in it. There's nothing to stop us from reaching out and touching the entire universe.

. . .

2.

Please

Just Do It

There are times when you think to keep going in a straight line, you've unexpectedly veered off track before you know it. You're free to keep moving ahead or to turn back. Your body houses both your past and future lives. This isn't just some kind of abstract image I've in mind, but rather a realistic description of your posture. That is what a dancer's posture physically conveys to us: the coexistence of the past and future. Maybe that is what you're praying for.

. . .

A symphonic-like music can be heard in my guts. It sounds as though my entrails are performing. Take, say, a rock. It can perform a symphony, for it too has guts. This intestinal symphony, this performance we're now hearing sounds as though it's played by guts that are being torn to shreds.

It doesn't sound as though I'm the music maker. Isn't that a rock I hear performing? Though it seems like it's resonating inside a spacious monastery, it also echoes traces of sound from an extremely confined space. In any case, the stone reverberates beautifully throughout. The audience understands those movements of mine that spring from pure emotion. Yes, our souls readily grasp the source of such music. My past emotions, like my future ones, are about to shimmer. It's not me that's dancing; it's my guts.

. . .

I'm all too familiar with the difficulties we face in trying to perform spontaneously. As I start to walk, I try to move in an insect-like manner. Isn't that why we practice here: to acquire an insect's sensibility? By that, I don't mean just moving in any old way. It's not a case of searching for solutions individually. Your lives have gradually started taking shape as a result of studying together, of walking through life in the company of others. This sense of mutual awareness helps you to share or give birth to what's inside of you. Well then, how about walking from over there? It doesn't matter what way you walk. You could even stop and rest yourself for a while on the way. A little something is missing, however, if you trudge along without getting anywhere.

This segment is a verbatim record of Kazuo Ohno's discourse on 9 September 1989 at his workshop studio in Kamihoshikawa.

William Blake and Emanuel Swedenborg

I suppose you've all heard of the English artist William Blake.[1] He wrote extraordinary prose works, such as *The Marriage of Heaven and Hell*. He also created a unique form of illustrated verse, engraved with images depicting man's relationship with the skies above, or what one might call heaven, hell, and the afterlife. While he always stressed imagination over reason, I don't believe that Blake ever consciously set out to compose romantic or visionary poetry.

Though one sometimes hears speak of a reality more "real" than this transient world, it was the theologian and physicist Swedenborg, however, and not William Blake, who maintained that life after death is more "real" than our day-to-day existence. An unusually gifted man, Swedenborg made significant contributions in many scientific fields; he went so far as to write a treatise on what remedies the then current English economy required to recover.

In Japan, we had writers such as Kumagusu Minakata,[2] who were equally well versed in the sciences. Given that he was a man of science, he would write meticulously on just about everything that interested him, even on astronomy. Among his many works was a lengthy and detailed book about life after death and the conditions in hell. People are inclined to believe that their lives, or what they commonly refer to as reality, are finite and confined strictly to our earthly existence. By that, I suppose they mean that an individual's life begins at conception and ends with death.

Swedenborg was not alone, however, in believing that life in the hereafter was more "real" than that of our everyday existence. This world, as he saw it in any case, is nothing more than a place of passage. In one of his books, I came across an unusual description of a husband and wife who, upon their deaths, went to heaven. Being two autonomous individuals, you'd naturally expect them to have existed as two distinct souls in their future life, but for some inexplicable reason it turns out that they were united as a single angel. Well, considering how they lived together on earth, even they themselves would never for one moment have believed that they'd be united in the afterlife. Their opinions clashed, they constantly argued; in fact, it was totally inconceivable that either of them would ever end up in heaven, let alone as a single angel. If nothing else, they should've been cast into hell. On a personal level, I could relate to this story totally. The interesting thing is that Swedenborg claims to have experienced supernatural visions during which he was spirited away into the afterlife. He apparently passed out—indeed, everybody around took him to be dead—but within three days he came round. He subsequently began work on writing a colossal tome about his experience amongst the dead. To this day, I can still see how thick that book was.[3] Anyway, I couldn't resist the temptation and bought it, though reading it was pretty tough going. What fascinated me most was the section dealing with the human reproductive process and procreation. Conception occurs whenever the sperm fertilizes the ovum. Swedenborg's theological writings examine this subject in great detail, though he does tend to concentrate on the role of the male reproductive cells rather than the female ones. I would read his books over and again, underlining many passages in black ink. Despite all that's said, I don't look upon Swedenborg as having been out of touch with the true nature of reality. His in-depth studies of physics, chemistry, and astronomy led him to a clear understanding of what lies at the heart of life. He consistently speaks of the afterlife as being more substantive than the lives we lead on earth. The afterlife, as he sees it, is the real thing; that's where life begins.

In that book, Swedenborg focused primarily on heaven, but he did also expose the nature of hell. I was particularly struck by that passage where the couple I previously mentioned was reunited, because, here, he wasn't describing heaven, or even the afterlife for that matter, but life on earth. While ostensibly giving a detailed account of heaven and what awaits us beyond this mortal life, it was nothing short of an accurate description of the very world in which we now live.

Anyway, to change the subject completely, I came to know of Swedenborg after reading Tatsuhiko Shibusawa. It was his writ-

Workshop

Words
_____

242

ings that inspired me to go and look for Swedenborg's books. Some years previously, my late aunt, who, were she alive today would be more than a hundred years of age, had given me a copy of a book by Swedenborg called *Heaven and Hell*. That aunt, with whom incidentally I spent the greater part of my youth, suggested that I read it, but the copy she gave me was mislaid after I lent it to someone.

Bedtime Stories

Mothers often read their children stories at bedtime. In the normal course of events, the children won't fall off to sleep after being told just one story. In high spirits, they remain wide awake and insist that they be told another. Eventually a frazzled mother loses her temper, swearing that she doesn't know any more stories, and ends up pleading with them, "Go to sleep now." I'm pretty certain that many a household witnesses such a scene on a nightly basis.

I've often spoken of the time my mother used to tell us Lafcadio Hearne's ghost stories. I must have been about four years old at that time—more than three, in any case. One story in particular has stuck in my mind, not so much for the story in itself, but rather for the way in which my mother would tell it. The story was about a princess in a beautiful kimono wandering down a long corridor, wearing a pair of clogs adorned with tiny bells, known as *suzu*, that jingle-jangled as they brushed against the wooden soles of her footwear. The sound of the jingling bells and clattering clogs were vividly described in the book. Though I haven't as yet actually read that particular story, I distinctly recall the impression my mother made upon us. She would begin by replicating that jingle-jangle and clitter-clatter emanating from the depths of a long corridor. She then went on to evoke how the specter vanished into thin air as the echoes of those tiny bells faded away into the surrounding darkness. Needless to say, my mother could have animated this story a lot better than I ever could. She was obviously fascinated by those ghost stories, for she read a great many of them. I'm unsure when she found the time to do so, but she was very well read and quite familiar with novels by foreign authors.

As soon as my mother started telling that story, it was though she had become bewitched. It was almost as though she herself was living through what Hearne had written. Right from that opening phrase, "Once upon a time, there was a princess," she became very animated and identified herself totally with the heroine of the story. My mother transformed herself into that specter of a

3.

9 September

1989

_____

243

princess, going so far as to embody her. With hindsight, I now realize what came over her: she transformed herself both physically and emotionally into that specter.

Anyway, what has all that got to do with we're doing here at the workshops? There's no point for us to dance in public unless we're willing to put both heart and soul into it. It's not enough to trot out: "Once upon a time there was princess." We've got to live that princess from the inside; we've got to saturate ourselves with her feelings, just as my mother did. She was deeply touched by that story; that's what enabled her to make us feel the princess's plight. That's why I could never forget the emotions my mother shared with us as she transformed herself into a specter right there before our very eyes.

Anyhow, let's move on. What does "taking care" mean? Is it simply a matter of carrying something from over there to here, moving in this and that particular way, doing this, that, and the other until we finish what we're supposed to do. Is that all there is to dance? Is it merely a question of moving correctly and following a predetermined structure? That's not exactly what I have in mind when I speak of "taking care," though. Let me put it this way: what does "cherishing life" mean to you on a personal level? How does your dance and everyday life relate to each other? Do you bring your life with you when you perform? That's where the real problem lies.

Perhaps what I'm doing here at the workshops is an offshoot of my childhood experiences, of listening to my mother telling bedtime stories with all her heart, while we children snuggled up under the bedclothes. She identified herself with that princess, so much so in fact that she almost became physically possessed. That's why at eighty years of age, I've started writing about a bedtime story I heard as a child of four or so. I was so scared that I'd bawl my eyes out. I was so, so scared that I'd cling onto my mother with joy. Listening to those stories scared the living daylights out of me, so much so that even now at eighty years of age, I still remember how terrified I was, though ever so happy at the same time. "Oh mother, how happy I was, so happy that I'd bawl my eyes out!" I wanted my mother to live to a fine old age, but I was so terribly selfish toward her. I now ask myself how I can live each day with loving care. As I've repeatedly said, life itself is my teacher. I believe that all that I've done in life is closely related to the way my mother used to read those bedtime stories. She told them as though her life were at stake. She wouldn't simply dismiss coldly us by saying, "I've read quite enough and don't have any more stories to tell, so go to sleep by yourselves." It didn't matter that she didn't have much time for storytelling; what mattered was that she gave of herself fully. I'm convinced that we cherish life by giving of ourselves, just like my mother did when she told those stories with great expression.

Differences in Time and Space

Nowadays, it strikes me that dance is often structured in such a way that the spectators are meant to comprehend readily what's happening onstage; the structure is meticulously worked out so that they clearly understand the story line. In my way of looking at things, however, such a programmed approach ensures nothing more than an illustration of the ideas that go into the making of a performance. Besides, do I really need to step out onstage to get my ideas across to an audience? Wouldn't they grasp them just as easily by reading a book?

Let me put it this way. There are considerable differences in the way people in East and West [Germany] think on certain issues. While my personal experiences, opinions and ideas might well differ from others, I do nevertheless share something in common with them. For me, certain phenomena are by their very nature beyond human understanding; we could never work them out no matter how much we ponder over them. If, say, we ask ourselves, "What is the meaning of life?" it's not something that can be understood within the confines of an individual lifetime. Despite the contrasting ideological and political systems in place in East and West Germany, their citizens do share a common bond. As they assembled in church that day for a music recital,[4] the individual members of the congregation were free to sit wherever they pleased: in the first, second, third, fourth row, or wherever. At that time, I was forcefully struck by the fact that while every person present had his or her unique perspective on the proceedings, they nonetheless were all deeply united by a mutual concern for their spiritual welfare.

I'm straying somewhat from the topic of dance in speaking about Swedenborg's theological writings, William Blake, and that Tokyo University professor and Japanese literary critic who wrote about differences in time and space. When traveling by plane, say, we cross from one time zone into another. Depending on where the plane lands, local time is different. In such a context, the time difference signifies nothing more than the disparity in clock time between two different time zones. Time and space differences are

3.

9 September
1989

____

245

measurable entities. In our rational, everyday world we can calculate these variances precisely. If it's such-and-such a time in a certain country, then it must be another time somewhere else. By using our brain, we can measure time difference and distances in those worlds that readily lend themselves to comprehension.

Well then, how should we approach the working method required to create a butoh performance? Let me put it this way: I don't want to waste our time together explaining something that I myself don't have a clear answer to. You might ask when it would be a suitable occasion to try to understand the processes involved. To employ that lofty word: art: the function of art is to explain. But, for me, life's crucial problems revolve around our heart and soul. In particular, our relationship with our parents is closely coupled to our spiritual longings. When conversing with our mothers, we've no need to voice our thoughts to discern each other's feelings. The same applies for a child; it doesn't have to utter a single word for its mother to understand what's going on in its mind: "But mother, please understand what I'm saying to you now!" Am I here not confronted with a real time difference? We're separated from each other, both in time and space. Whenever I dance indifferently or carelessly, I end up becoming forgetful of the problems posed by these differences of time and space. While it might seem quite simple, this problem is complex and difficult to resolve in practice.

These days I've been talking to you quite a bit about what we refer to as "Ghost Dances." Incidentally, the subtitle we gave to *The Dead Sea* is *Ghost Dances Set to Viennese Waltzes*. If you saw the piece, the link between the title and the piece would be self-explanatory. Maybe that accounts for why some members of the audience occasionally come up to me after a performance and tell me exuberantly, "*Sensei*, I was able to understand what your dance was all about." What did they understand, I wonder? I must confess that I'm a little disappointed to be told that. I'd much prefer they understood nothing at all. If anything, I'd rather hear them say, "Watching your dance made me feel good to be alive." Or, "I was moved to tears even though I couldn't figure a thing out." But, as soon as someone says to me that they understood my performance, I become instantly discouraged.

Workshop Words

Yukio Mishima and Tatsuhiko Shibusawa

Speaking of how people react to my performances: Yukio Mishima viewed them in his particular way. When alive, he would always attend our performances and happenings and afterward would usually invite us to a lounge in the Ginza neighborhood. Sitting down beside me, he would without fail say, "Ohno-san, you're quite something." Yes, that's how he would put it. Whereupon, I was never sure whether I was being praised or put down. Mishima would constantly advise me, as would Shibusawa and Hijikata, not to concentrate on technique. My son, too, constantly warns me of the pitfalls attached to focusing on style over substance. They all urged me to avoid being deliberately artful and ostentatious. Demonstrating technical skills, as far as they were all concerned, was really beside the point.

For a long time I couldn't get out my head what Mishima would say. It slowly dawned on me that both he and Shibusawa were, even if not directly, doing their utmost to temper my ego. Yes, that was exactly it; they were trying to impart strength and toughness. Hijikata, too, actively participated in their endeavor. Imagine, for a moment, a swordsmith's workshop. The swordsmiths, Shibusawa and Mishima, are beating a steel sword into shape by heating and hammering, alternately pounding out a ton-ton-ton rhythm. Hijikata, standing nearby, marks the time, encouraging them with enthusiastic cries of "Hey, hey, hey" in rhythm to their repeated hammering. Speaking for myself, I believe all three of them to be master craftsmen. Above all else, be it money or whatever, a true craftsman is devoted to his work. He's indifferent to whether the product he creates serves any practical use or not; the essential is that it's well made. Once he starts to create something he just cannot stop. I must admit that I don't really care for that word "artist." For me, Mishima and Shibusawa are craftsmen, not artists. Rather than being referred to as an artist, I want to be called a craftsman. For that matter, I'd like Mishima and Shibusawa, as well as Hijikata, to be considered in a similar vein.

Given that opinions still widely differ as to the significance of Mishima's suicide, it remains a touchy subject in certain quarters.[5] But I, for one, don't really believe that an artist would put an end to his life as a matter of honor. I never want to be set apart from Mishima, Shibusawa, and Hijikata, because we are all craftsmen. As I said, I've never liked being called an artist. I've considered myself a craftsman since many years back.

But to return to my theme, I set out to say that the units, so to speak, we employ to measure the differences in time and distances in space in our everyday material world are not applicable in the timeless world of spirits. What I want to say is that these worlds are fundamentally so different that they simply aren't comparable. Recently, I spoke during two workshops about a poem called "The Ribs and a Butterfly" by a friend of mine, Inui Naoe.[6] Despite the fact that his lungs were only functioning partially and were slowly wasting away, the poet nevertheless continued to write poetry. In that particular poem, he speaks of a butterfly's eyes lighting up in joy as it scaled the ribs of his emaciated body. Step by step, it makes its way up his rib cage, to eventually reach the summit of what he describes as a flight of stairs. Apparently, the butterfly was drawn to the presence of nectar, upon which it loves to feed. Anyway, I took that poem about his wasting lungs as a theme for a dance. Now normally, given the nature of this poem, you might expect or imagine that the movements should be very, very delicate. But something came over me. I didn't take such a conventional approach but instead ended up performing a butterfly scaling ribs with great gusto. I can't explain what came over me. I undoubtedly invested a lot of physical energy into the piece, as I've never before performed a butterfly scaling ribs so heroically. It was an exhilarating experience. The following day, I tackled this theme again, attacking it with great vigor as I had done previously. A butterfly was again climbing ribs, but somehow, I felt something had gone amiss. Had I not changed in the meantime as a result of my experience? Hadn't it become an other world? Wasn't it a different time? There's no such thing as a standard approach to a theme. Besides, when writing that poem, wasn't the poet himself poised at death's door? He composed those lines fully knowing that it was his life that was on the line; he wasn't faced with simply writing on an abstract theme but a head-on encounter with death itself. That poem was written for dear life. It struck a deep chord with me that the poet could write such a poem, fully conscious that his last hour was at hand. Staring death in the eye, the poet plunged right into his fears. We won't succeed in penetrating his sentiments just by putting a lot of physical effort into our dance. It's not a question of technical know-how. The world of spirits isn't our everyday world; no, it's definitely not our everyday world. In facing death, the poet revealed another world: one in which a nectar-loving butterfly scales his ribs. By means of his poem, he penetrated a world in which spirits come forth.

Imbuing Dance with Life

Workshop

Words

_____

Anyway, when writing, we use words to describe what we're doing with ourselves; how others now think and so forth. But are such descriptions true to life? This is a complex matter, for language doesn't necessarily reach into the inner workings of our souls, even if it succeeds in communicating our daily ups and downs in realistic detail. Words, of course, do their job, but I think dance can say a lot more. We enter an entirely different world as soon as we delve into our souls. That's why an identical movement, as performed in a routine way, and as an expression of our inner lives, means something completely different. Differences in time and space exist between these worlds. For me, there is another dimension close by, a timeless dimension inhabited by ghosts.

As I enter that ghostly realm, even the way I walk is no longer the same. I move as though I've been transformed into a spirit who's been released from the nether world. In no time my everyday self vanishes out of sight. With just four paces as I walk like this, yes, in just four paces or so. I don't want to dance in a world in which the only yardstick is a ruler, or where every last detail has to be figured out beforehand. And yet [when working on that theme] I stepped beyond the boundaries of my everyday world into a timeless dimension. Yes, just after about four paces in that direction.

What, you might ask, lies at the root of this longing to cross from one realm into another? I'm driven by an almost unbearable love; I just can't hold myself back. When nursing her child's illness, doesn't a mother almost worry herself sick? She doesn't know where to turn if her child shows no sign of recovery. Even if a mother couldn't save her child's life by sacrificing her own, she would be willing to do so. We've all had occasion to find ourselves feeling so desperate. Confronted with her child's illness, do you think a mother counts her paces one, two, three, four? How could she at such a time! That's what I'm trying to get through to you: I want your dance to step straight out of your heart; to be imbued with your soul. What I don't want to see are movements and gestures that you've figured out in your head. I want your life to unravel itself before my eyes. Even though I do my utmost to avoid that pitfall, I'm still constantly faced with "differences in time and space." And though this term, which I employ quite often, might sound a bit odd, it does have a basis in reality. Your dance has got to be imbued with a spiritual quality. It's only by penetrating the depths of your soul that you will engage us.

I'm getting ready for a forthcoming performance of *The Dead Sea*. Every single day I wrack my brains over it, as I'm unsure as to how to approach it. And yet, I know it's absolutely pointless trying to figure out what to do in such and such a scene, or how to struc-

3.

9 September

1989

———

249

ture the piece and so on. I'm only all too aware of the futility of such a working method, because I've been over that ground before. My past experiences have taught me that when it comes down to it, the truly critical question I have to ask myself is: What are you really trying to do when you step out onstage? Working out movements is a useless endeavor; a dance performed that way won't engage the audience. That's why I'm forever struggling to get beyond such a programmed approach.

Today, I've been speaking about how that poet, who faced with imminent death, wrote a poem about a butterfly making its way up his ribs. This theme will frustrate as you grapple with it; you'll find yourselves at a total loss as to how to endure it. I'm well aware of how difficult it is; I myself find it next to impossible to cope with it. Still, we've got to try, try for all we're worth, even though we might feel that we're not up to the task. Delve wholeheartedly into the poet's world. That's what I want you to see you do. Is that all right? Are there any questions?

What Do We Mean by Reality?

As I was saying, despite the fact that his lungs were only partially functioning, despite being plagued by coughing attacks, the poet continued to write. In the poem I chose as a theme, he describes how a butterfly successfully made it to the top of his emaciated rib cage.

Being unable to attend the poet's funeral, I went to pay my condolences on the following day. When he moved to Tokyo, I had promised him that I would visit during the New Year's holidays, but I couldn't make it in the end. Death took him away before we were able to meet. On speaking with his wife the day after the funeral, I was to learn of things that I had not been aware of. Their married life had been cut short due to the fact that he was dispatched to the war front. As things turned out, they didn't have any children. I was taken aback on hearing this, because I recalled reading a poem he wrote in which he spoke of a boy, who on growing up, was sent to war and died on the battlefield. I could have sworn that that poem had addressed his son's death. What was even more telling was that whenever I visited their home the subject of children would invariably creep into our conversation. On being asked about how my sons were getting on, I would end up chatting away about them, but I later felt on returning home that it must have been heartbreaking for my hosts to revisit their sorrow. Though we'd been friends for almost ten years, I was still under the impression that their son lost his life on the battlefield. All along I had taken it for granted that he perished during the war until his wife told me about their married life. It was only on the day following his funeral that I finally learnt their side of the story: the poet collapsed of an asthma attack on their wedding day, leaving his wife to cope with a pretty tough situation. Though I genuinely believed that they had a son, there were never, in fact, any children. Considering what they lived through, how could there have been? And, you know, for the ten or so years I visited them, I kept warning myself on the way there not to bring up the subject, but since they always inquired about my children, I would inevitably feel compelled to reply. And yet, each time I went to close their gate on my way out I'd say to myself: "You went and opened your big mouth again today."

That belief I've just spoken of, and those differences in time and space I mentioned earlier, are, for me, components of reality. Wasn't that erroneous impression I held for ten or more years part of my reality? We can't fully grasp reality, or realism as some call it, just because we've been around for some time. A true understanding of life isn't reducible to barren facts. For me, reality encompasses such complexities: the fact, say, that I wholeheartedly believed that that couple had a son, even though he never existed. We need to reconsider what the true nature of reality is. Don't our deeply felt emotions also constitute an integral part of our reality? Doesn't the manner in which we perceive something constitute a reality in itself? You won't convey the pulse of that poem by imitating it in a realistic fashion. It's not a case of moving your back in a particular way, or lifting a leg like this just because a stairway happens to be one of the images. Breaking it down into readily understandable segments won't suggest the underlying reality the poet was faced with. To truly grasp a poem's intent, one has got to bear in mind the circumstances under which it was written. Grasping the poet's sentiments is the starting point in fathoming what lies beneath his words; you've got to take into account the emotions he felt on being faced with an imminent death. If you identify with the poet's despair, you will be lead to a true awareness of how precious life is. You're then ready to tackle this poem.

I'd like to try to incorporate this piece into an upcoming performance of *The Dead Sea*. Today, I'd thought to get straight to the point and explain what reality consists of, but I was unable to do so. In fact, this very inability to do so is an integral part of reality. On performing that piece, I completely forgot about that stairway

3.

9 September

1989

_____

251

described in the poem. Dance, for me, has got nothing to do with sequences. It's not a question of the first step follows the second and so on. And yet [when I performed that piece] a butterfly, albeit in my own way, climbed that stairway, lifelike and fluttering.

At eighty years of age, I still vividly remember my mother telling Lafcadio Hearne's ghost stories: Mother, I was so happy. I was terrified. Oh, how happy I was to listen to you tell those bedtime stories. I want you to lead a long life, for we've never been apart. Even in my dreams I scream out your name. I screamed out, "Mother," as you were turned into a caterpillar. Lying there on your deathbed, you told me that a flounder was swimming in your body! Later, in pondering over her farewell words, I realized that what she was trying to teach me that I had to persevere just in the way a flounder perseveres by resisting the surrounding water pressure on the sea floor. Once it comes to dancing, I've got to exhaust all my strength like as though I were lifting the earth itself. Dance isn't a matter of figuring out movements, or structuring steps one, two, three, and so on. My mother's parting words brought home to me the true extent to which I'm indebted to her. Moreover, it became clear that there was little difference between my life and dance; they were deeply bound up with each other.

Anyway, I'm talking all the time. There's an hour and ten minutes left, but what I really wanted to get across to everyone here including myself is that dance is nurtured by our lives, and not by techniques. To participate in these workshops, I want us all to understand that dance springs from care. Anyway, let's take that as a starting point; abandon all your ideas about moving in this and that way; it doesn't matter in the slightest what you do, as long as you dance with your soul. We've an hour and ten minutes or so remaining, so please just do it.

An Encounter in Israel

During our stay in Israel I visited the plateau that looked out over the Dead Sea,[7] though it wasn't of any great altitude. Not a single blade of scorched grass grew there; a few isolated flower-bearing trees were scattered here and there over the hillside. Just as I was remarking to myself that no living creature could ever possibly survive in so a desolate a place, something chanced to move. I was stunned. There was movement about two or three hundred meters away from where I stood. Whatever it was, it kept scampering and bustling about until it drew my attention. And then it would abruptly stop dead still. It occurred to me that this restless scurrying about had something to do with my presence there. The bustling would then suddenly start all over again. I sensed a creature's presence; some type of long-tailed animal. The only way it could possibly survive in such an inhospitable terrain was by digging an underground burrow. But, whatever it was, it wasn't alone, for as soon as I paid closer attention, there were many more of them scurrying here and there all over the hillside, shouting for joy. For some inexplicable reason, I felt a closeness and strong affinity with them.

A blinding sun blazed relentlessly down on that hillside, which offered hardly any shade. Standing there, it dawned on me that those creatures would never expose themselves to such daytime temperatures; naturally, they would remain in their cool burrows by day, to emerge only by night. And yet they had come out of their shelters into that mid-morning sunlight. They can instinctively tell if somebody is related to them; that's why they started to scamper and scurry about on sensing my presence. As a token of their affection, they emerged from their burrows to greet me on my arrival into their world. I felt a natural liking for them, too. Although they mightn't have whiskers and their eyes were spherical, they survived in their mother's womb by digging themselves an underground burrow. My world was turned upside down on coming into close contact with them. There on that barren hillside, where even a fly could barely survive, I once again felt the compassion and warmth that embraced me while being carried in my mother's womb. As that scurrying and bustling started all around me, I was spirited away and carried back to life in the womb. Until the moment I opened myself up, there wasn't a living creature to be seen on that plateau looking out over the Dead Sea. But not only was that hillside home to thousands of creatures; they were also closely connected with me. All this scurrying and scampering about suggested to me that they might be squirrels, as they greeted me in the way that squirrels do. This was far from being a world of ghosts. As I said a moment ago, this was a completely different world from the one I'd taken it to be. Just as I began thinking what an inhospitable place it was, they started to scamper about. It was another world, once I opened myself up to it. And what a different world it was!

We relate to the world around us in many ways. Well then, when it comes to dance, what happens? I've been speaking about how my original impression have on occasion been mistaken. We're going to dance shortly. [Spoken while dancing.] Will we keep

3.

9 September

1989

——

performing as we did before, following set sequences like this, or that, in doubt and bewildered as to what to do? Or alternatively, will we abandon such a rational approach and make a thoroughly fresh start just as though we were discovering a new world. It doesn't matter, if initially we go astray and can't find our bearings. Whatever your expectations, don't concern yourself with creating something new; it will emerge of itself, despite the despair you might be subjected to at times. I've been through that experience countless times. A hitherto unknown world unexpectedly emerges just like this, just as it did during my visit to that plateau looking out over the Dead Sea, where not even a blade of growth was in sight. You'll reach the point where you forget yourself. Remember, the visible world is only one of many.

Gifts from the Dead.

Anyway, to continue, the poet Yasuo Irisawa once wrote:[8] "As the sun was about to set by the lake, I put on my glasses to admire the evening glow. On putting them on, I suddenly felt that someone else was watching the sunset together with me. While supposedly alone, I was looking at that scene through the eyes of someone else." In writing of looking at the world together with the dead, the poet alludes to the fact that our ancestors live with and in us. Alive, in each and every one of us, are countless individuals whose lifetime experiences, joys, sorrows, angers, doubts, and so forth have been successively passed down from one generation to the next. The physical form I now assume is but the fruit of what I've inherited from those who have existed before me. What, you might ask, has become of our ancestors' ideas and emotions? Where do you suppose our creativity springs from? There's no way that it springs forth from our finite and limited knowledge of life. I'm not the only one who has ever existed; our ancestors haven't just died and vanished into oblivion. We're not the fountainhead of our creative powers. Down through the ages our ancestors' emotions and ideas have accrued and ingrained themselves in the imaginations of each successive generation.

That's why whenever we start to unravel the threads of life's tapestry, we ultimately reach the creation of heaven and earth. Each thread leads us deeper into the past. Don't we dream? We certainly do so. Do our dreams only explore our finite experiences? And what about children, whose dreams do they dream? Our dreams not only unveil the world we've known from birth, but also the long period stretching back to the genesis of the earth. Our

Workshop

Words
_____

progenitors densely inhabit our souls. To put it even more radically, it's as though the spirits of the dead are alive and breathing inside of us. But, is creativity something we can summon as we please; is it on tap, so to speak? If we cherish life, our creativity unfolds, and spurs us on to live life to the full. That's why we're so obligated to our ancestors for the gifts they've bequeathed us. We should cherish the souls of the dead. What empty lives we'd lead were we to think that we'd survive on our own steam, forgetting how much we owe to those who've preceded us and ignoring the true source of our creative imagination.

We're not alone; we share our bodies with many, many others. That's what the poet experienced while watching the evening glow over the lake. Though I didn't partake in his experience, I'm convinced that the dead remain constantly at our side. My world expands as a result of this shared awareness. We've evolved as human beings by the grace of those who have gone before. We've grown in all respects as a result of the help they've given us. Our ancestors haven't vanished off the face of the earth; how could they, when they continue to live and grow within us? I'm convinced that our creative force springs from their guidance. My way of looking at life changes as a result of their presence. If I hesitate and am unsure as what to do, they help me find my way. In daring to reach out to them, just like I'm doing now, I discover that, even on stretching out to them, my hand is reaching into my self.

Do your hands touch the shoulders' of those dead spirits who inhabit your body as tenderly as you touch those of your parents? Your dance has got to generate that intensity. It's not a case of your father or mother being absent; if you reach out to them, they'll make their presence felt. You don't cherish them just because you suppose they're in some far, faraway place. They're right here in our very midst. That's why I want your dance to embody the love you feel for them. And what a different world it becomes as soon as you open yourself up and accept their help. You've got to cherish the souls of the dead; without their help we would be bereft of our living force. It's sheer vanity to regard our lives as something of our own making. We coinhabit this world with our ancestors.

Whenever I prepare a piece I've got to take into consideration so many different things: those "Ghost Dances" I just spoke about, those differences in time and space between our everyday material world and that timeless spiritual realm, the way my world changes as soon as I open myself up, all these things need to be taken into consideration. The realm where I long to dance is one in which I

3.

9 September

1989

____

255

merge with the spirits of the dead. Aside from that, I have no other role to play. Please continue; try to reach out to those with whom you share your body.

Feelings and Reality

We have so many different kinds of emotions, feelings, ideas, and so on. Indeed, our emotions are the basis of our individual realities. While on that subject, his wife [Allen Ginsberg's] springs to mind.[9] He genuinely strove to do whatever he could do for her. Wouldn't we, as human beings, become completely unbalanced were we to consider that our deeds alone, and not our feelings, are what constitute reality? What would become of the human race, had we no longer had to capacity to feel? Our feelings are what constitute the reality of our lives, and our individual realities are underpinned by what we feel.

I spoke to you recently about being invited to give a short performance at the book-launching party of the well-known American poet Allen Ginsberg. On learning that I wasn't familiar with his works, the Shichosha publishing house immediately sent me an anthology of his poems. I was struck by a passage in one of them ["Kaddish"] in which he laments his wife's [sic] passing away.[10] She had gone away somewhere, leaving behind her corsets and the glasses she usually wore. These observations indicated her demise. In this poem, Ginsberg's addresses the despair he felt. Though the subject wasn't his mother, but his wife, I could nonetheless feel the pain of his loss while at the same time revisiting the grief I suffered at my mother's death. As I began to feel sorry for Ginsberg's sorrowful plight, I desperately wanted to do something to help him. Before I knew what was going on, I found myself giving my mother a piggyback. If only, I thought to myself, I could somehow give expression to how badly I wanted to help; if only I were able to transmute one of my bones [Ohno points to his hipbone], I'd instantly transform it into a horse carriage. And here it is. Let me check to see that its hood is properly attached; I'd prepare everything—I'd even go so far as to provide a coachman, dressed in jet-black attire. Ginsberg's mother could then board the carriage, along with my mother and their companions.

But it's just not enough to cater for their needs before boarding the carriage. It's not just enough to go through the outward forms; I must also assume all responsibility for whatever happens to them thereafter. I must remain by their side at all times. Once they're on board, how am I to nourish them? What do the spirits of the dead like to eat? In carefully and lovingly preparing their food, I show them how much I cherish them. In fact, I believe that not only are these my individual sentiments, but those of each and every one of us. It's not good enough just to think about it, or have them board the carriage without taking into consideration what's going to happen afterward. Our deeds speak for themselves; they do have consequences given that they ground our feelings in reality.

Anyway, I performed at the party following the book launching, on a floor space about the size of a single tatami.[11] For about ten minutes or so, I improvised, accompanied by a saxophonist.[12] During that short time, during those ten or so minutes I tried to somehow embody what I felt on reading his poem. Performing in such a tiny space, I was able to link hearts with all those present. But what if I didn't genuinely feel such concern or love for the dead? What then? Is reality merely a matter of purchasing something and then giving it to somebody? Can we reduce it to a series of verifiable events? Is it only about material things? For me, what I feel is part and parcel of my day-to-day reality. That's why I'm forever stressing the fact that our emotions inform our lives on every level. A world in which our feelings didn't permeate our lives wouldn't even be worth thinking about.

Well, what on earth does all this mean? Preparing a horse carriage, inviting the spirits of the dead to climb on board, providing the coach driver, rigging out the carriage-horse, and so on. Aren't these gestures the very embodiment of my love for the dead? Yes, these are our human feelings. I transform myself into the coach driver and the carriage horse all at once; I make sure that hood for the carriage is in place and provide nourishment for the passengers. And then, we're all ready to set off on a jaunt. Ginsberg's poem brought it home to me to what an extent our personal feelings color reality. Ginsberg was overjoyed with my improvisation as he could relate to it fully; it really spoke to him.

But if our feelings weren't the basis for reality, what then would dance be? Would it be just a matter of measurable movements? Would that be the sum of it? As I've said time and time again, our personal feelings color everything for us. Our feelings and the reality of our lives are bound up in such way as to be inseparable: our feelings are what ultimately constitute reality as we perceive it. Likewise, reality is made up of that which we feel. Movement, in that respect, becomes a kind of metareality. I spoke a short while ago about how our deeds externalize our feelings. You might feel that your ideas and intentions in themselves are worthless, but that's not the case. The essential thing is that we give of ourselves, to the point that we're willing to suffer. Pain and suffering quicken our sense of reality. When, say, I take a schematic approach to a particular scene, nothing comes of it. If I thought that I'd somehow profit by allowing those spirits ride in the carriage, or flatter myself that they'd be delighted to ride on board, then something is wanting. Regardless of what happens, I've got to stick by them through thick and thin. It's not only a matter of calculating sufficient provisions. I've got to remain by their side at all times, regardless of whatever ups and downs we encounter. I've got to give of myself entirely. That's what I believe love to be: a willingness to suffer for others. Merely thinking that one is doing enough is of absolutely no use to anybody. Of what use are our thoughts or feelings when not backed up by deeds? Whenever we think to do something for somebody, we've got to be willing to help in whatever way possible, with as much as affection as a mother offers a sick child. Wouldn't a mother forego anything for her child, wouldn't she go so far as to sacrifice her own life? Given that we all know what it means to suffer, we can share in her distress.

We've got to explore the reality of our feelings. Well then, we've almost come to the close of today's workshop. For the remaining five minutes dance *free style*, yes, *free style*, all the while bearing in mind that our personal feelings color our reality.

Chapter 4

Don't Reveal
Your Love

Do you really need to look us in the eyes to say: *I love you?* If anything, not looking at us directly is a better way of expressing what you feel. Faced with such uncertainty, our souls become desperate and listen all the more attentively. A good case in point is when I perform with my son: I can always sense his presence, at times here, at other times way over there, while all along we keep brushing past each other as though we weren't there.

Just because you feel detached from us is no reason to perform in any old way you please. That's nothing more than shirking your responsibility. We will be responsive to your call if your soul reaches out to us. If you incorporate such tension into your movements, you will make us feel that you're standing on the threshold of a crisis. You won't, however, engage us emotionally if you fail to give of yourself. Let's practice such movements, movements in which your spirit moves.

. . .

Yes, I feel it; it's love. While not expressing it openly, that's what it is: love. Don't be taken aback when she suddenly appears. Argentina is here at my side, though she passed away many years ago. When approaching each other, we not only do so on earth—we also find ourselves suddenly strolling through the wide expanses of the universe, through the heavens, through the skies. Yet, we're not counting our paces one, two, three, four as we dance through the heavens.

Picture a stalking cat, lying in wait, about to pounce upon a fish. Who knows, but that it might be quietly eyeing its victim before pouncing into action. Yet I'm pretty sure that the cat itself is

259

caught off guard when it grabs its prey. Before it realizes what's happening, that fish is already clenched between its teeth. What do you expect? It's a cat, after all.

. . .

We weren't conscious of what we were doing as we devoured each other. On eating our fill, we both ceased to exist, leaving only love in our wake. Did I sacrifice myself as we tore into each other? He allowed me eat my fill. For my part, I ate as much I wanted. He offered me everything, and I likewise offered him all I had to give.

We can take each other's life, just as we can allow each other to live. Knowing that we can't extricate ourselves from the life cycle, we didn't suffer as a result of following our instincts. We took great pleasure in being devoured. It was just as though we were frolicking about like children. We found gratification in eating our fill, by devouring each other.

And now, I live in a world where I strum this wooden floor beneath my feet. I live in a world where there are no boundaries between the here and the hereafter.

I recall when I felt trapped and unable to decide what to do, I went to pieces. I was at once victim and perpetrator: I had a hunch that I was going to be attacked, and at the same time it was I who tore myself apart. Yes, but what happened to me as my mind went to pieces? Didn't I turn into a fox? Isn't that a fox you're seeing right over there? What will become of it? Will it to survive? Don't worry. A fox doesn't need to learn how to survive. Let it fend for itself, because it instinctively knows how to cope with danger.

. . .

Don't write a *love letter* with your brains. Write it with your every limb; write it straight from the heart. Your loved one is right there beside you, conversing with you as you write each stroke. It doesn't matter what you write it with, so why not write a *love letter* with your foot. What a letter that would be! I want to see you dance like as though you were writing to your lover. Even though we mightn't

145. Ohno at the studio window, holding a paper flower. © Ohno Dance Studio Archives.

grasp everything you say, reading such a letter will engulf us with a sense of gratitude and thanks for the help you've offered us. A *love letter* written with body and soul—that's the dance I long to see.

. . .

Your eyes are wide open. While not focusing on anything in particular, it still strikes me that you're forever seeking after something. I can sense that something is not quite right with you. While you're not looking at anything, I still can't fend off the impression that your soul is quivering. Don't use your eyeballs. Instead, look at us with your entire body, let your whole body and soul become your eyes.

The stage was bare, just like the Garden of Eden. But yet, wasn't that garden of paradise, in spite of its apparent emptiness, the very place where God laid everything on?

. . .

"Mary [Magdalene] come," an angel cried out. "Mary, come and see for yourself if you don't believe me." And so the angel proclaimed that Jesus had risen from the dead. Jesus stood there. But, Jesus was now a woman [sic]. Mary then let his grieving apostles know that Jesus had been resurrected.

Hadn't an angel told Mary [of Nazareth]: "You are blessed amongst women. You'll give birth to the Son of God." To which she replied: "Why should a humble maidservant like me be chosen to conceive the Son of God. I cannot possibly fulfil such a role." Though considering herself unworthy, Mary accepted the angel's message as having been sent by the grace of God. Joseph, too, accepted the angel's revelation as the word of God. But Joseph and Mary feared for what would their neighbors would say about a virgin being with child. They would doubt Joseph's faith in his wife. Mary too had to question herself why it was that Joseph could accept that she conceived the Son of God, while she herself couldn't? In due course the infant Jesus was born. The Lord informed Joseph that the newborn's life would be in grave danger unless they fled into exile. Taking the infant Jesus in their arms, Mary and Joseph set out on their journey to Egypt, and out of harm's way.

Mary Magdalene[1] beheld the resurrected Jesus standing there in front of her. On seeing her, Jesus immediately stretched out his arms, whereupon his life began anew. In doing so, he made good on God's promise to mankind many thousands of years ago, and thereby gave humanity hope of a life after death.

. . .

Aren't there occasions, say, while walking along the street, or while carrying out our daily chores that we're unexpectedly filled with a yearning to stop dead-still. Onstage, however, I rarely stop moving. I'm forever itching to move, although I realize that I ought to stop sometimes. Mind you, even in my daily life, I often continue working at those times that I ought to stop in my tracks for a while. It's important to pause for a few moments every now and then. Why do we need to do so? Because our mothers are calling out, that's why!

In my everyday life, I can't prevent myself from stopping now and then. My souls stops to listen. How would I hear my mother beckon me otherwise? And, in doing so, we can reach out to each other like this. . . .

146. Ohno in a stony terrain close to the shore of the Dead Sea, 1983. © Nourit Masson-Sekine.

. . .

When performing onstage with my son, we both feel as though we're "talking" with each other on some level. Ideally, however, it should appear to the audience as though he and I were both completely oblivious to each other's presence. Sometimes, I have to ask myself whether he has vanished into the wings? I wonder where he's gone? I haven't a clue really, for our eyes don't meet. Our bodies, though, are constantly on the watch out for each other. Though it might appear that we're looking at each other straight in the face, we're not, in fact. The audience should feel that our gaze is fixed on something. And yet we're looking straight through each other, just as though we weren't there. That's the kind of dance I aspire to.

. . .

Consciousness of the universe. At some point or other, haven't we all pondered over the origins of the universe? The sky, the earth, the sun, the winds. What causes the winds to blow? Where's that sun located? Over time, humans have given names to all these diverse phenomena. We even refer to ourselves as "people of the earth." The human species has a unique capability to immediately adapt to its environment. It might be better that we call ourselves "children of the universe." Well, on second thoughts, you might argue that it's inconceivable that such creatures could exist.

Nowadays, I can't get the universe off my mind. I've come to the conclusion that we'll never become people of the earth until we experience becoming one with the universe. Domesticating ourselves into people of the earth isn't what really matters. Above all else, we've got to realize that we belong to, and are part of this entire universe. That's what I've got to say to you. Something existed before the advent of the human race. When and how, you might ask, did the universe begin? We merely confuse ourselves by trying to fathom the mystery of creation, and the origins of this world.

. . .

Whenever using chopsticks to eat your food,[2] let them reach out to touch the ridges of the universe; let them become living proof of your existence. Let your way of holding chopsticks embody your every joy, your every sorrow. And yet, partake of that meal as though nothing were happening. You don't have to hold them that way just right now, but if you haven't done so within the next ten thousand years or more, your way of holding chopsticks is useless.

. . .

In that duet I performed with my son, it seemed as though we were inhabiting an abandoned garden, or a derelict public park that had been long neglected. Even the grass had withered away due to the bitter cold. There was nothing there; the stage was completely bare. But at the same time, here we were in a world where we were free to move as we pleased. While on the surface there seemed to be *nothing*, it was in a fact a paradise. It was just like *Eden's Garden*. There, in the midst of pure nothingness, we performed this piece together [*The Dead Sea*]. We had no need to establish a rapport with each other, for it existed already, irrespective of how we moved. We allowed each other the freedom to be as we are. Of all our performances together, this particular duet with my son was the most moving. And, you know, we didn't even discuss the piece beforehand, let alone work out any of our movements or gestures.

. . .

La Argentina and I are *together*, at all times. We've never parted though it's been some fifty years since I last laid eyes on her. If I die through illness, in an accident, or however, I still want to remain by her side. I don't care if one day my flesh is cremated and reduced to ashes, for my ashes will continue to walk at her side. Yes, ashes. That's what I said. And what of your soul, your heart? Never forget, you are a *spiritual* being. There are ashes everywhere; no matter where you stretch out your hands, you'll encounter them. I myself am composed of ashes, ashes that merge as one with my soul. Ashes are the sole clue we have to help us fathom

4.

Don't Reveal

Your Love

———

who we truly are. Yet rather than imagining ourselves as purely ashes, we'd better believe that we consist of nothing at all. We're *no-bodies* composed of ashes.

I was sent small pamphlet from New York containing a photo of La Argentina. On coming home [from the gallery] that evening, I was delighted to discover that package they [Eiko and Koma] had sent containing a few articles and other written materials about her. "Ah, La Argentina" I thought to myself on looking at the photo. She spoke to me: "Ohno-san, please dance, please dance for me." I couldn't take my eyes off her. I didn't know what to do as my soul, my heart, the photograph were pleading with me to dance. I was in a terrible state because I hadn't neither the strength to reply, nor the resolve to perform. La Argentina then addressed me, smiling warmly: "Ohno-san, I'm going to dance, so please let's dance together."

I was so overwhelmed with gratitude on hearing her utter those words that I was performing in public again within a year of that auspicious day.

. . .

It's my feet that are forcing the rest of my body to go on an outing. On coming to a *stop*, the upper half of my body tries to separate itself from the rest, as though it were venturing out into the world,[3] all the while leaving my legs and feet behind.

Try moving your torso outward while standing rock-steady on your feet. Thrust it as far as you possibly can. My torso can do anything; it can reach anywhere; it could even stretch out and embrace the whole world. Unless you release your arms from captivity, you'll never succeed in breaking out of yourself.

But, what happened just now? Something or somebody prevented you as you stretched out your arm to open the front door. Somebody bid you to stop. It reminded me of that moment in which God warned Adam and Eve to consider the consequences of human error. On banishing them from the Garden of Eden, God warned them that they should not let their hands fall prey to temptation. He told them that suffering would ensue, and that the earth would be cursed because of their selfish deeds. "You shall," he said, "eat in sorrow for the remaining days of your life. I told you that if you didn't heed my warning my world would be shattered,

Workshop

Words

_____

266

and the heavenly life here in this garden of paradise would no longer be. You shall suffer eternally, doomed to work the earth." Whereupon, God was once again laden with a heavy burden.

. . .

A mother nurtures her developing infant in the womb. The souls of those sperm who perished during fertilization also find repose in life's cradle. But, do not mistake the uterus for the world after death.

A woman doesn't care if she shortens her life by nourishing the unborn child she carries. She is filled with a natural desire to share; she looks after the fetus's every need. Look. The eyes of a dead soul. It looks on with ease, because all its yearnings have been taken care of.

. . .

I was anxious because I didn't know how I was going to join La Argentina. How could we possibly unite again, given that I had to keep treading over pile upon pile of dead bodies? When, in the end, I couldn't take another single step, La Argentina stretched out her hand to me. Words such as "sorry" or "thanks" come nowhere near expressing my gratitude for her kindness. Because the love she embodied wasn't merely that of a solitary human being but that of the whole world, of an endlessly expanding universe of love and care.

. . .

The spirits of the departed have taken refuge in my body. Leaving aside the little knowledge I've acquired over this lifetime, I am who I am thanks to all those who paved the way for me. If I'm to evolve, it will be largely thanks to the help I receive from all those manifold spirits living in me. Their constant companionship, along with that of all the other souls in the universe, nurtures my growth as a

4.

Don't Reveal

Your Love

_____

147. Ohno with
workshop students
in the studio, circa
1977. © Teijiro
Kamiyama.

human being. On slipping into the sleep of the dead, I penetrate their dreams of the past and the future. It's at such times that I grow. My knowledge of life has been enhanced, and rendered effective thanks to the guidance they've offered me. They've provided me with all the necessary material for growth. My creative powers, my knowledge of life, my soul feeds upon their guidance.

. . .

You breathed as one with your mother in the uterus. Along with oxygen, she delivered all your other nutritional requirements to your stomach by way of the umbilical chord attached to the placenta. You had a taste of unconditional freedom in there, for you could move in any way you pleased. There was no such thing such as a correct or bad way to move. When listening, say, to a radio broadcast of a calisthenics program, what's to stop you from following the presenter's instructions in any order you like? In like manner, the womb was a haven where you were at liberty to do as you pleased. If only we could plunge in there and observe how the unborn child plays about in that gravitationless atmosphere, we'd see a restriction-free world. The womb of the universe is not unlike the world you're constantly yearning for. In some respects though, it's the very epitome of "madness." Seen, however, from an everyday perspective, it might strike us as being a totally inconceivable time and place.

Dance is likewise a domain where madness reigns. After our forced severance from the womb, a part of us longs to regain that long lost freedom. Increasingly though, we find ourselves facing a dilemma. Blindly following the dictates of reason, we sooner or later end up as prisoners to our own selfishness. We're surrounded everywhere by like-minded sorts. Yet, you standing over there, or you here stretched prostrate out on the floor, you're awakening memories of that "madness" we experienced in the womb. You're manifesting the freedom that each and every one of us so longs to regain. By rendering such "madness" visible, you might help that part of us fettered by reason.

. . .

The Bible says: "Judge not, that you not be judged." It's not for me to judge how you dance. God alone can do that. God isn't concerned whether you've performed your movements correctly or not. That doesn't mean, however, that it's a case of anything goes. Even the slightest movement is potentially of great significance.

If you judge others, you're simply behaving in a merchant-like fashion. Let others judge you, if they will. But remember, God alone is our true judge.

. . .

I've lived through a lot in this lifetime: I've planted flowers in the garden, played baseball, and at times even been fortunate enough to have known real happiness. For me, dance isn't simply a means of saying thanks. Naturally enough, I'm truly grateful for all the opportunities that life has afforded me. Indeed, at times, I feel I could go right out of my head with gratitude. I could wail with joy at the beauty of water lilies; I could give away all that I own because everything is so beautiful. As for the hardships and sorrows others have to bear, allow me to carry their burdens. Still, I know deep down that I could never relieve them of their sufferings. . . .

. . .

By comparing myself to God, I've gradually come to know who I am. I've now come to the point where I ask myself: Why have I become like this? We all mature as a result of the gratitude we feel for being granted the gift of life.

Through self-reflection, we come to realize how obligated we are to God. Initially, we compare ourselves to flowers, with others, or to whatever else we come into contact with. We thus come to know who we are by noting our respective similarities and differences. But it's highly unlikely that we'd ever come to a true understanding of ourselves were we to remain aloof—it's only through contact with others that we will truly grasp who we are. In like manner, as performers, we come to know of our strengths and weaknesses by how we engage an audience.

Didn't I first catch a glimpse of myself on coming into contact with others? "To know myself," that has been my destiny all along.

. . .

Is it possible to dance, and at the same time to think of where we should place our feet? This remains a fundamental question for anyone who steps out on to the stage. Is it really possible to perform in that way? Let me say this: a dance built solely upon a rational structure lacks something.

That warmth and sense of relief I feel on holding a baby in my arms is, for me, an essential element in dance. That's not something I need to figure out in my head, is it? I grew up in my mother's womb, albeit on a smaller scale. To this very day, I'm still remorseful about all that I left unsaid, all that I didn't express clearly enough in the first place, all that I overlooked, all that I didn't listen to carefully. All those scars remain faintly ingrained in my soul. That's why I'm of a mind to tell you not to figure your steps out in your head.

. . .

That night train to the stars not only interconnects the distant galaxies, it also happens to serve the stations of your inner life. Its network doesn't solely cover, as one might expect, the outer universe, but extends deeply into the bowels of the earth as well. Do your movements whisper to us the conversations you overheard on a station platform while traveling on the night train through the bowels of the earth? Your emotions are closely linked to conversations taking place in the sky above, and the earth below.

. . .

When trying to express something specific, you can do so by repeating a gesture or a movement in the same way that a songwriter makes use of a refrain as a compositional device. You've got to plunge all the way into our hearts and continue doing so until you succeed in jolting our emotions. But, to be quite honest with you, I myself am being constantly admonished that I should concentrate on a single image rather than constantly jumping from one thing to the next. Of course, I'm disgruntled by my shiftless

4.

Don't Reveal

Your Love

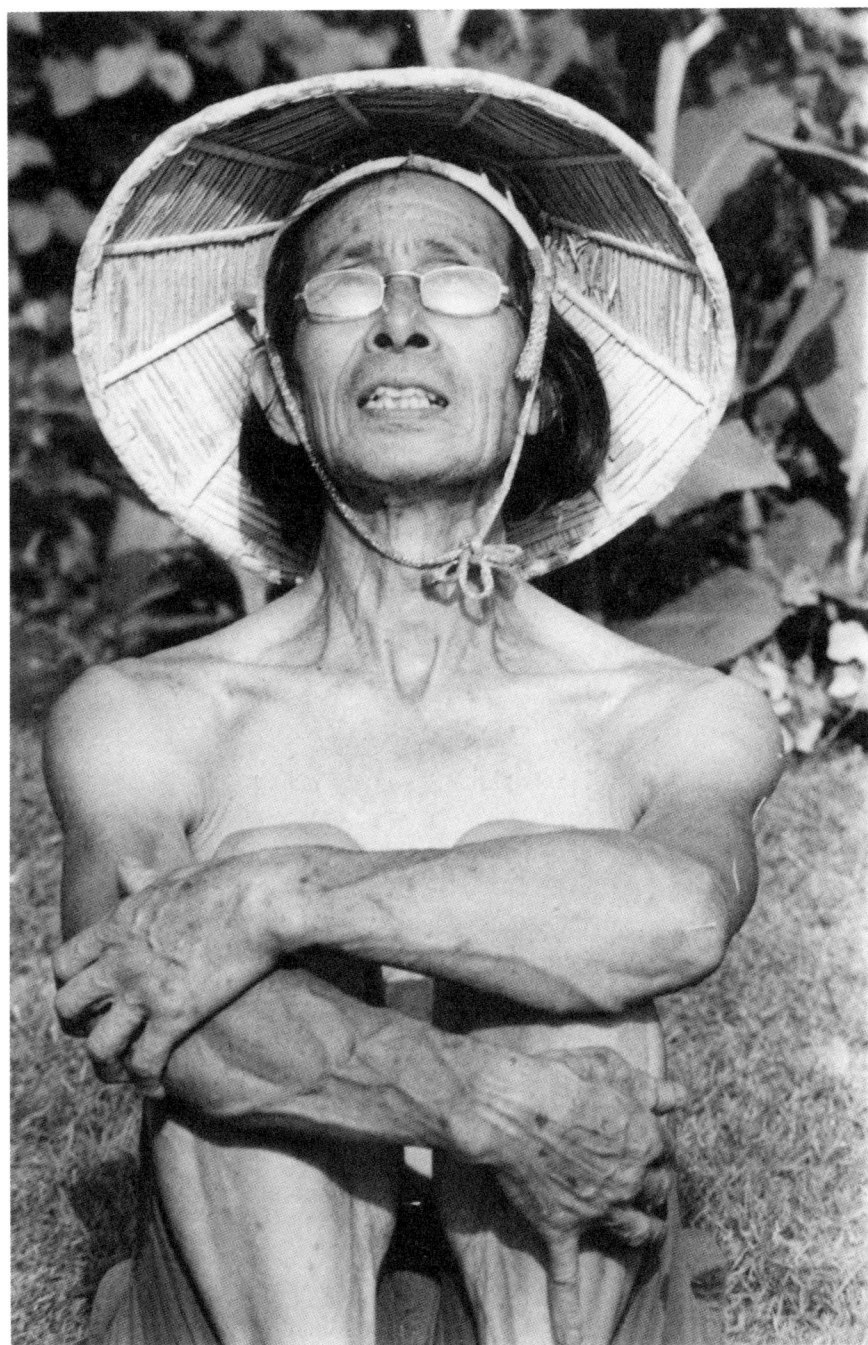

ways. Nonetheless, I fluctuate between sorrow and joy. One minute, I'm told, my hands are soaring through the air, while the next my feet are stomping.

. . .

There's no need to memorize movements and gestures, because no matter what I do, I'll forget them any way. The essential thing is that the experience remains perfectly ingrained in my mind, and in my soul. That's what comes with repeated practice. It's of little consequence that I forget what I've practiced, because, despite myself, I'm constantly absorbing the fruits of my endeavors.

Imagine a candle melting slowly when suddenly wax starts dripping earthward. In like manner, my soul begins to drip whenever it's set alight. I feel as though I'm in a state of *ecstasy*. When *together* with Argentina—*together* we are flower-like. We become ecstatic.

On becoming ecstatic, doesn't saliva dribble from our mouths? Be careful, as you would when holding a lighted candle in your hand. Enraptured, your soul permeates Mother Earth like melting wax. And then, it rises all the way up through your body from the earth to enter your mouth. As it continues to soil your mouth, you're driven over the moon. It sounds as though your soul is trying to surge forth. While unable to clearly grasp what it's saying, we nonetheless hear the echo of something comfortingly familiar. Your soul's cry carries all the way into the deepest recesses of our hearts.

. . .

Their child was dead when born. But, as far as its father and mother could see, their baby had a pair of hands, it had two feet, nails, in fact everything it required to live life to the full. They were so besieged by wave upon wave of pain that they wanted to cling to the walls for support. Heartbroken, they just kept on looking at their loved one lying there motionlessly while the others present decided to step outside for a cup of tea.

The human lot strikes us as being all the more pitiful when we

4.

Don't Reveal

Your Love

_____

come face to face with the joints, or whatever part of the body for that matter, of those approaching death. We're left feeling completely powerless. The joints play a crucial role in dance. In creating a performance, don't concern yourself about whether it's entertaining or not to watch. The essential thing is to evoke happiness and sadness. You've got to leave us feeling helpless. Don't, however, only aim at stirring our emotions; your performance should also leave us with an enforced awareness of our vulnerability. Today, let's try to become a lighted candle.

. . .

While I don't really know a lot about Creation, scientists assert that the human race originally emerged from the sea. Look at how the earth's water cycle functions. Water erodes rock. Water evaporates and turns into moisture. This, in turn, triggers off an inconceivable number of processes that continually repeat themselves. Collisions occur, fires erupt, moisture is created, which in turn becomes the rain, which falls from the clouds. These patterns repeat themselves over and over again, creating an unending series of activities in perpetual motion. The ocean tides are to the earth as the blood circulating through our veins and arteries is to the body. Your heart throbs whenever you're in love.

. . .

They clung to me in droves as I climbed those stairs—some were old acquaintances, others I'd never even lain eyes on before. Had they not stood behind me, I don't think I could have ever stepped out onstage again.[4] I climbed each one of those steps at the Dai-chi Seimei Theatre, feeling at once anxious and relieved. On finally reaching the dressing room, I started to put on makeup—not, as such, with the intention of highlighting my features, but rather to shroud my soul in pure white. I was so ashamed of myself that I felt that I had to paint my face and body as white as that wall there. Otherwise, I could never have exposed myself to the public. By means of that white makeup, I stripped myself of everything. So

Workshop

Words

---

many [spirits] followed me as I walked out onstage. They ran ahead, stepping on feet, climbing backs, all the while saying, "Thanks," "Sorry," and "Excuse me." In contrast to me, however, they were almost carefree. Why was it that only I remained so tense? Was it because I knew in my hearts of hearts that I had not come there to apologize, or to ask for forgiveness, or even to express gratitude? My feelings were ambivalent due to that immense lightness and heaviness of spirit that reigned simultaneously inside of me. That's why I ultimately decided to refrain only from saying thank you. You might ask why? Was it due to some hardship, sadness, or joy I've known? Perhaps, but it's better that that remain a mystery.

. . .

The sun emerges, shining down on the earth. It creates warmth, the warmth to enable life to evolve. In due course, a child is born. The earth warmly embraced the newborn. I too, along with the earth, want to wrap that child lovingly in my arms.

> Ah, the sun has risen !
> Hey, a child has been born
> Come eat, the food is ready.

Everyday life revolves around such simple matters. When your mother nurtured you in her womb, she gave of her own flesh and blood so as to allow you to develop and grow. What nutrition do we require to survive? Ideally, we should peel the fruits of our own individual experience and eat of life itself. But, it's no easy thing to eat one's own body.

. . .

Didn't you experience moving your toes as you played inside the womb? At that time, you were one with your toes. You and your toes weren't in any way separate, nor were you in the least bit self-conscious as to how wonderful it was to be as one with your body.

4.

Don't Reveal Your Love

275

Try to move freely once again; forget all you've learnt in the meantime. If you're still feeling dissatisfied, it's because you're harking back to that time you "were" your toes.

Is that person over there crying? Maybe, he's laughing. Is he happy, or, then again, unbearably sad? For me, happiness and sadness are essentially alike. So as to satisfy our longing to see a dance full to the brim with life, try becoming once again one with your toes; let each one of them move in a way that touches us. By stomping your feet, the flames rising from your body seem to climb even higher. There's no need to laugh loudly; a subtle smile will do. If your movements are to give birth to another life, they must at all times come from inside of you. Let each and every moment bear witness to life's flow.

. . .

During a visit to southern Argentina,[5] we went on a sightseeing trip to a glacier that has probably been in existence for some thousands and millions of years. As the glacier melts into the Antarctic Ocean, its snout collapses, breaking into larger and smaller fragments that crash into the water to create a deafening roar. On hearing that noise, I had the impression that the glacier's wake was taking place. A wake is one of the noisiest occasions here on earth. Despite the fact that the remains of the deceased are laid out to rest, a great uproar erupts as friends and relations flood into the room, gathering around to bid farewell, all the while creating a terrible din, telling stories, smoking, and what not. It's the noisiest silence imaginable. And yet, mysteriously calm. Not only is it a sorrowful occasion, but also a celebration in which we can thoroughly refresh ourselves.

. . .

Your funeral arrangements have already been made. Inevitably, our lives evolve in such a way that our instincts lead us to that parting moment. Stop being so self-conscious! Look at that hand over there spontaneously soaring upward. I felt that life itself was in motion as soon as that hand sprung up in front of us; I felt it reaching out to touch us as it moved away from the front of the face and out of your hair. Human behavior isn't only a matter of instinct, however; some of our responses have been learnt over the course of a lifetime

How is it that when we appear happy, we're actually sad; and when we seem sad, we're happy? This contradictory nature is a characteristic of our instincts. I wouldn't go so far as to say that to follow one's instincts is a simple matter of child's play, yet as I watched those hands soar joyously into the air, I couldn't fend off the impression that a child was at play. Your eyes lit up with joy as your hands became free to keep on playing for ever and ever. Your instincts are at play at all times.

Look, isn't that a Chagall figure floating through the sky?[6] Your hands are like those freely floating forms in a Chagall mural; they hold every conceivable form of human experience in their embrace. Unlike our bodies, our instincts have no final resting ground. While our flesh will one day or other be reduced to ashes, our instincts will never come to a standstill; they will transform themselves and continue on their way to the next world—in the depths of Mother Earth.

. . .

For a big tree to grow to its full potential, it requires that smaller trees be planted around its base. Unless smaller trees are planted in close vicinity, the tree won't grow to its full height and will remain stunted as a result. In other words, smaller tress are indispensable for a great tree to grow. So, whenever you feel a tree growing inside of you, you can be certain that several smaller ones have been planted around it.

. . .

So many birds are flocking about that it's impossible to count them all. They keep stabbing and jabbing you with their beaks. If left to their own devices, they'll leave nothing on you but bone. You'd love to turn into raw bone, wouldn't you? All you birds up there, come, come, peck at my flesh!

When we pass away, the many different feelings we've experienced over the course of a lifetime ought to linger in this world; our bitterness, our sadness, our joy, the entire gamut of emotions we've known ought to be passed on to the living. Take painstaking care; make sure that you overlook nothing, for each and every one of us harbor many feelings in us that remain locked up in our souls. These will shape your character and the subsequent course your life takes. Hush! Listen carefully, for the dead are whispering something. Can't you feel that they're inhabiting your fingertips? Or how about down there in your left foot? Can't you feel their raging nails digging into you? You've inherited that anger. Their feelings have been handed down to you, becoming one with your own. In like manner, as your turn comes to depart this world one day, you too will transmit your "heirlooms" for future generations. Tears rained down my cheeks as the dead's feelings started to permeate my body's every pore. I was swept away by the close rapport that emerged between us.

. . .

I suppose you've all heard of that brilliant actress Gloria Swanson.[7] She eventually passed her prime and grew old in comfort. And what of Jesus Christ? Fate was not so kind to him. Didn't the rabble cry out, "Let him die, let him die" as he hung there nailed to the cross. They both attracted public attention, but for very different reasons. Swanson was greeted with joy and adulation. Jesus, on the other hand, was a butt of contempt: think of how his face drowned in sorrow as that rabble glared at him with murderous intent.

Difficult and all as it might seem, I believe dance to be a form of response to my life's manifold experiences. What matters most is that my performances unfailingly embody all the many conflicting emotions I've known. My joys, sorrows, remorse, my encounter with La Argentina, these are the foundations upon which my work is built. My dance has got to embrace both that rousing passion I felt on seeing Gloria Swanson raise her hat, and my sorrow for the pain inflicted upon Jesus as those soldiers guarding him yelled, "Kill him, kill the Christ." Granted, love and hate are not the only emotions that we harbor in us; there are so many layers to our emotional makeup. You're free to move in any way you please amidst all those of emotions. The essential thing is, don't lose sight of your soul. Once, La Argentina[8] appeared in the sky to ask me: "Ohno-san, shall we dance together?" My dance is born from the midst of all this.

. . .

Each and every one of you has become a flower; a beautiful flower. Please delve deeply into yourselves; go all the way, with both body and soul—that's all you need to do. We're all familiar with how a flower opens and blossoms; yet it inevitably droops and withers away. Strangely, why is it that on reaching that particular stage of its life cycle, it's no longer considered beautiful? Why do we ignore it while yet another form of beauty unfolds as soon as it starts to fade and vanish into thin air? A flower's beauty is unconditional; it's not only beautiful at its peak. Of what interest would a flower be were we to regard it as beautiful for only a very limited period of its entire life cycle? Not only do I rejoice as it bursts open with an emotional upsurge, but I'm also deeply moved by its beauty as it withers.

You've got to reveal a kind of beauty never seen before—an endlessly withering beauty. Were we to consider a flower's withering phase as the pinnacle of its beauty, we could then perhaps look upon its leave-taking without anxiety. Losing one's vigor is only but one aspect of death.

. . .

You can linger there alone in the midst of dead silence, if you wish. But outside, life continues around you as though nothing were happening. We're all accustomed to watching our lives unfold in the same unassuming manner in which spring turns to summer. As such, we're able to get on with our everyday lives without having to give it too much thought. But why is it that as soon as you try to lift your foot without thinking about it, you find yourself in a fix. It's not simply a question that you're lacking in technique.

4.

Don't Reveal

Your Love

Focus on life's primal forces. Before you know it, your movements will come to life. Your soul, not your brain, is the moving force; so let your movements gush forth. Watch how a wolf follows its instincts; smell how spring responds to springtime.

. . .

Imagine a purification ritual at a swordsmith's forge. The participants begin by thoroughly cleansing their bodies, performing ablutions so as to wash away all impurities. By my side are [Tatsuhiko] Shibusawa, along with [Yukio] Mishima. After completing their ablutions, they commence the ritualistic hammering, continually beating the sword with a constant rhythm. [Tatsumi] Hijikata stands close by, encouraging them with a vocal rhythm corresponding to their physical motions.

Granted, this is nothing but sheer fantasy, as I've no recollection of such an event ever having taken place. Yet I do feel an affinity for all three of them. If anything, that "memory," so to speak, has been forged by my respect toward them.

They coaxed me into participating in this ritual not only to forge a sword from my flesh and bones, but to temper my ego as well. And, look what an excellent blade they beat into shape! They're master craftsmen. Long ago the term "artist" didn't even exist. I've never really cared for being called an artist; for some reason or other I've always disliked being called so. I can't put my finger on exactly why, but somehow it's disagreeable. I'm delighted, however, if someone refers to me as a craftsman because a craftsman gives of himself fully. In like manner, a dancer trains his body, tempers his character, creates—he creates life itself. What's the point in being merely skillful?

. . .

Treat everything with painstaking care: whether it be a cigarette butt, an object, those near and dear to you, strangers.

A ray of light somehow found its way into my soul, a ray of light nurtured by the spirits of the dead. Streaming into my soul,

149. Ohno on the shore of the Dead Sea, 1983. © Nourit Masson-Sekine.

it invited both the dead and the living to take each other's hand and dance together. . . .

And, what about that conversation we overheard on the platform, while on the train? Wasn't that some lively conversation! As to what they were saying, I haven't the faintest idea.

. . .

Thanks to a lifetime's experience, I now feel as though I'm making some progress, however small. My talks here at the workshops, like my performances, are not solely based on suppositions and abstract ideas: they are firmly rooted in my individual experience of life.

While I obviously speak with those closely related to me on a daily basis, I also have occasion to commune with the dead. At such times, I'm not only speaking with a single spirit. Picture, say, the way in which houses, or even mushrooms, lie scattered about

4.

Don't Reveal

Your Love

281

here and there. Each of those dwellings is a home for a group of individuals. And each and every one of those homes has its own particular lifestyle.

Take a look at my own household, for instance. Insofar as can be seen, it appears modest and unassuming, having a decent and regular income, and neither lacking for anything, nor indulging itself in what it doesn't need. In broad terms, this is what is meant by one's "standing" in the community. Neighbors work hand in hand so as to help each other out. In doing so, they communicate in a manner that doesn't require language. Words, in fact, are not the only way we can help one another. Down through the ages our collective survival has been ensured by standing shoulder to shoulder with those around us. This became clear to me as I observed how my own family has functioned and survived over generations. Needless to say, the individual members of each household cope with life in their own particular manner.

Bearing the current situation in mind, I wonder how it was in former times? Customarily, the family unit consisted of a grandfather and grandmother along with their immediate offspring all living under the one roof. The great-grandparents might have lived within the family group as well.[9] However, such living arrangements are much less common nowadays, due to the changes in the fabric of society. We all eventually die, and with us will go our customs and habits. Yet it's important that we realize that our elders, our grandfathers, grandmothers, all those close to us are constantly at our side. The family circle is composed of both the living and the dead.

· · ·

As we reach a certain point [in our lives], death and life become as one. By examining the cyclical nature of human existence, it becomes clear that life precedes death. As I'm constantly telling you, a flower's beauty is eye-catching. It entices me to follow it down that stairway into the afterlife, for the world of flowers and the world of the dead are but one.

I'm looking at a flower right here. As my body becomes one with my soul, it shares with you its joys and tribulations. No longer fettered by my everyday self, I'm dancing freely amongst the spirits of the dead. One moment I'm in the afterlife, the next I'm back amongst the living. I'm standing here, where we all stand, in the midst of life and death, coming and going. Death, life; death, life . . . they become as one.

. . .

Dreams play an essential role in our lives. But you can't go to sleep deliberately setting out to dream.

Continue dancing in that sleeplike way. Don't think about where to place your foot. While your eyes remain wide open, they are sleeping eyes. If you admire someone, you don't need to lock your gaze on them. You can have a conversation in your dreams without looking directly at the person with whom you're speaking. Yes, you can engage in a conversation even if your gaze is cast elsewhere. There's no need to scream out, "I love you" for us to be able to grasp how you feel. Words aren't necessary, but do make sure that we catch what you're trying to say.

. . .

Don't treat dance as some kind of abstract game. Take each and every step as though you were putting your life on the line. Mastering technique has never interested me for the simple reason that if I were to focus on skill I'd instantly lose touch with the natural phenomena. If I were to concentrate on acquiring technical skills, I'd probably turn into nothing more than a technician, and thereby unwittingly lose sight of what I'm aiming for. Technique could never provide me with the wherewithal to achieve what I've set out to do. I don't care whether you're skillful or not. What I do care about, though, is that your performance makes me walk away afterward feeling grateful for being alive.

Does your dance ask for forgiveness?

Why do we, as human beings, exist? What are we looking for in life? What nurtures us? How do we cherish both our own lives and those of others around us with painstaking care—these are the fundamentals. Treat suffering, both your own and those of others, with care. In doing so, you'll in no time become desperate and break out of yourself. If a child becomes ill, its mother would do anything—she would even go so far as to surrender her own life for that of her child. But in real life she can't switch places with her child. We've got to feel such heartache emanating from your dance—that's the kind of dance I want to see.

Don't remain aloof and perform as though you were unconnected to us. At the same time, don't treat it as though it were a sacrifice. Instead, offer us something; offer us whatever help you can. That feeling, that deep longing to help others won't in itself, however, hold enough appeal. Your dance will engage us all the more decisively as soon as we can sense that you're driving yourself toward the brink of sanity. Such determination doesn't express itself with a [physical] language, but through madness. Don't dwell on your thoughts; instead let your movements surge forth spontaneously. This is what we truly long to see. Anybody can figure out which movements to use, but I want your dance to go far beyond that.

Chapter 5

The Wind Sweeping through My Soul

That inextricable link between death and life becomes clear whenever the spirits of the dead rise to the surface and make their presence felt. Dance is not a language, but the radiance of your expression. It strikes me as though you're playing hopscotch throughout the length and breadth of the universe.

. . .

Why refuse the flowers Jesus offers you? Rather than giving Jesus flowers, wouldn't it be better to accept them from him. I've nothing to offer him; not one solitary petal. Petals are floating in the air; floating throughout the sky. They were soaring skyward because I've given all I had to give.

. . .

Inside the chrysalis a caterpillar prepares to undergo a radical change in body form before it escapes its confinement. On completing its metamorphosis, it turns into a fully developed butterfly. I must admit that I'm unfamiliar with the internal changes occurring during that combustion-like process. But as I watch you here, I can see how you're inclined to say to yourself, "I can't go any further; I can't take another step." Yet remember, we evolve constantly. By surmounting self-imposed constraints, we can transform ourselves. Just in the same way that a butterfly finally breaks out of its cocoon and transforms itself into a free spirit, so too, can you traverse that pupal-like phase in which you are now confined. In performance, our capacity to transform ourselves is truly critical. Note how a butterfly's compressed wings are extremely brittle on first emerging from the chrysalis. Moreover, nature has created a butterfly in such a way that it's physically impossible for it to take to the air immediately; it must wait some time before it is capable of flight. I wonder how it feels on its first contact with the external world, during those agonizing moments in which it finds itself unable to expand its wings to their full breadth and fly away? How does it physically respond? Does it ponder over how it should open its wings? No, how could it? There's no way I can explain what's going on inside its body. Yet those precarious moments, that short period in which a butterfly is completely helpless, is pure dance. It's an extremely moving moment. A master craftsman could never create a work of such intensity, no matter how much skill he invested in the endeavor. What can we learn from this?

. . .

Start from scratch; discard all you've worked out so far. Once you abandon a rational approach, your dance will leap to life. And while the shapes that rise to the surface might be amorphous, they will truly reek of you. Dance doesn't need a structure, but it must be as detailed and lifelike as a miniature portrait. Performing inevitably involves the use of intentional and nonintentional elements. We won't get a clear glimpse of your inner life unless you let go of yourself. Your dance now embodies that formless yet distinct presence surging forth from the depths of your soul. Look. What's happening with the sky? Accept with good grace all that spontaneously emerges from inside of you. What on earth is happening to those clouds? Spread your limbs freely. Your hands and feet will move of their own accord as soon as they are no longer fettered by conscious control. Your limbs must move in unison with your heartbeat.

. . .

Watching how you grappled with that theme brought it home to me that you all share something in common with insects. Given that insects inhabit our bodies, we've all had occasion to examine them thoroughly. An author couldn't possibly write if he or she didn't become acquainted with the insect living in them. An understanding of insect life grants us another perspective on how we human beings respond to sensory stimuli. That's why I want to study them, especially those ones who genuinely incarnate their insectness.

Don't let us see that you're putting your life on the line. You might be confronting a serious danger, but don't force it upon us. What's the point in shoving your feelings down our throats: "Look at me, look at how I'm putting my life at risk?" Such a dance is simply intolerable to watch. You'll evoke our compassion, however, if you perform as though everything was fine.

. . .

To perform in front of an audience requires that we examine ourselves thoroughly. We've got to take a good hard look at who we really are. Being a Christian, I attend church on a regular basis. I must confess that in the beginning I didn't truly understand what brought me there. Yet over time, I've gradually come to recognize the forces that have made me into the person I am. While I can't in all honesty say that I've fully come to terms with my shortcomings, I nonetheless continue examining myself. Had I not taken the time to self-reflect, I'd never have recognized my failings. I'd never have realized that I was always bragging and so forth. I simply couldn't have continued performing had I not taken the time out to take a good look at myself. Can't we observe in a detached manner the thickness and height of those clouds? We can grasp without any difficulty how the sky and the clouds remain in a constant state of flux. Consider yourself as though you were those clouds in that sky overhead. If I one day succeed in looking at myself impartially, it will only be because I've taken a good hard look at who I am. I couldn't dance otherwise.

. . .

Regardless of how insignificant your relationship with the world might seem to you, it still has the inherent capacity to utterly destroy it. Even the way you handle something as ostensibly harmless as a pebble could generate great destruction, so take care with how you use it.

(facing page)
150. Ohno in Madrid, 1987.
© Sachiko Takeda.

. . .

I'm afraid that we're continually being confronted with worsening levels of violence; we're constantly faced with that destructive impulse to wreak devastation upon one another. As I see it, there's little difference between physically destroying someone and harboring hatred in one's heart. I still recall seeing those dismembered bodies. It felt as though my own body had been ripped apart. I longed to reach out to those scraps of flesh with my bare hands; I yearned to wrap their hearts in my arms. In the midst of such carnage, there was absolutely no way that I could refuse to offer a helping hand.

As performers, it's our duty to ask ourselves how we can help to overcome the rampant hatred afflicting the human race. Our hands must embody life itself, as this will allow us to reach out and touch the audience. That is our sole responsibility, and yet I can't help feeling that there's something more we could do. Hatred and love know no frontiers, as does man-made culture. Like all dynamic forces in nature, culture expands in every direction. But let me finish by saying this: I am no stranger to hate and destruction. That's what I must impart to you.

. . .

What's truly essential is that my work will someday mean something to somebody. It's of little consequence that no one accepts what I have to offer right now; it's immaterial if I've to wait a thousand, or even ten thousand years before somebody can relate to it. Yet if my dance will never have anything to offer, I'd better take a good hard look at it.

5.

The Wind

Sweeping

through My

Soul

· · ·

The role of raising children isn't confined exclusively to fathers and mothers. Given that we coexist with millions of others on this planet, it's not only mothers and fathers, it's not just our immediate parents who are responsible for bringing us up. I suppose what I'm really trying to say is that are we beholden not only to our parents and ancestors, but also to many, many others, both living and dead. Lately, I've been thinking quite a bit about the origins of my dance. While it sometimes strikes me that there are certain sequences I can create by myself, the fact of the matter is that I can't really work out anything on my own. I'm continually being aided by others. To ensure the continuing survival of the human race, we receive what is to be received from all those who've gone before, and we, in turn, pass on what is to be given. We live through life's hardships together. Obviously, we're not always on the giving end. Greed, unfortunately, sometimes gets the better of us and we end up robbing one another. On reflection, I've got to admit that I've probably never worked anything out for myself. I've inherited all my supposedly original ideas. I'm inextricably linked to all those past generations. How can we talk of learning about life in the here and now; our repository of knowledge doesn't merely derive from what we've experienced during our short time here on earth. The combined experiences of all those countless past generations are ingrained in our subconscious memories. We are deeply bound to those who have paved the way for us. In fact, we've inherited all our physical and psychological attributes.

· · ·

Once, I had a daydream while at the school office about these incredibly huge boulders pounding down like hailstones from the sky. In the course of the dream I sat down on a stool in the garrison office, thinking to myself that no matter how quickly I tried to flee the deluge, I'd never succeed in saving myself. It was as though my time was up, and that my final hour was at hand. It was so intensely real that I took it for reality. At times, dreams confront us with such truly overwhelming situations, situations from which we feel there's no escape, no matter how quickly we run. I'll never

Workshop

Words

_____

forget that terrifying realm, even when I pass away. But on reflection, there was no need for panic when faced with what seemed like life's closing moments. Despite the despair we feel on being confronted with the irrevocability of death, we still have time on our hands. If it feels pointless to run, or if we, as sometimes occurs in dreams, find ourselves cornered into situation from which there's no possible escape, don't forget that there's something working in us that enables us to survive. My future lay ahead of me even though it seemed that my time had come. Though it seemed futile to run for cover, life awaited me beyond that dream.

. . .

The question we all need to ask ourselves is: Are we genuinely free when crammed into a sack? You there, your eyes are filled with longing. What are you seeking after? And yet, the freedom you enjoy while crammed into a sack is by far greater than that you'd have without one. For all you know, my body could be a sack.

. . .

Rather than analyzing your movements, why not try to feel them in as simple a manner as possible. Talking of "doing one's best" or "trying one's utmost" is neither here nor there; that's not going to help you. Just do it. Just let go of yourself and dance spontaneously. I want you to push yourself right to the very edge of sanity. We've only about fifty minutes left, so please do something wholeheartedly outrageous, something truly unbelievable. Our dance becomes godlike once the ghosts of the universe surge forth from the depths of our consciousness.

. . .

Over the course of a lifetime, I've come to learn many different things. Our sun and moon are but residual matter from a galaxy where they no longer served any purpose. On learning that the sun

**151. Ohno on the
street in New York.
© Haruhisa
Yamaguchi.**

won't shine forever, I started wondering about my destiny after I vanish from the face of this planet. Our sun is just expendable matter in a corner of the solar system, matter that one day will crumble into pieces after continuous use. Seen in that light, its disintegration is comparable to death. Yet wasn't our solar system born of that continual process in which death engenders life. Our galaxy exploded only to subsequently regenerate itself, albeit in a different form. The sun and earth are just cosmic debris from a universe perpetually falling apart only to come together again. And, as for the satellites of the sun . . . .

. . .

As my time to bid farewell came, I was carried away by the wind. Yes, lifted by the wind; it was the wind that carried me there. As the skies calmed, I discovered myself interred in a gray cloud. Why did I linger up there? What could I see? I could see something, couldn't I? What am I peering at inside that gray cloud? Is my gaze locked upon myself? Or have I completely transformed myself into that gray cloud? Who knows what shape I'll grow into, if any. Everything I touch becomes part of me. Let me rouse the sky; why shouldn't I boldly thrust my thundercloud-like head deeply into the clouds? I'm beside myself with joy as those clouds carry my body hither and yon. Ahhh, the wind has risen. I am that wind. I am the wind sweeping through my soul.

. . .

From now on, just continue until such point that you can no longer breathe. Don't let yourself be distracted; keep at it until you're fit to faint. Take yourself to the very edge. By going to such extremes, won't your appearance change? You'll never undergo a radical transformation unless you plunge wholeheartedly into yourself. For the next twenty-five minutes or so, try in whatever way you can to keep delving into yourself, thrust as deeply as you can.

What do I mean by saying "to thrust as deeply as one can?" Basically, what I want to say is: How does your dance relate to the

5.

The Wind

Sweeping

through My

Soul

____

293

"you" existing in the here and now? Does it connect with those lives you harbor in your soul? If you never challenge yourself, you'll simply end up sticking to set of tired patterns. Have your shoulders carried all they possibly could? Have your eyes seen all that's to be seen? What about your fingertips? And, your neck? How about your tempo? Can you move within immobility? Can you thrust into the depths of yourself at your routine pace all the while knowing that the pace of your emotions remain in a constant state of flux. This is not a question of time. Don't be shackled by inertia; delve as deeply as you can.

I'm now making a blind leap into that universe, a universe in which my back plays an essential part. Something mysterious is looming in front of me, but I'm not scared. Because no matter what I encounter, it will belong to the universe.

. . .

One step leads to the next and then to next, and so on. What have gradually rising steps got to do with the way we lead our lives? Imagine a helical form for a moment. When climbing a spiral staircase, what difference does it make whether we move sinuously or not? There's nothing to stop us from occasionally moving counterclockwise. The truly important thing is that we gradually evolve. In order to evolve, we need to follow a spiral path, albeit in our own way. With each step we take, we slowly come within reach of the sky.

. . .

Unexpectedly, I sensed a spirit; a deity or some godlike presence assume visible form right before my very eyes. I was struck by how birdlike my body was; I was simply present. I was extremely calm and composed; even my face didn't betray any tension. That dance was very powerful. In fact, in reflecting over all my performances, that particular solo dance I performed to the bandoneon accompaniment[1] was by far the most fulfilling. That was the only occasion I danced as though I were a bird. To this very day, I still consider it to be the most outstanding piece I've ever performed.

. . .

Approaching my mother with open arms like this, I feel as though she's warmly embracing me. My performance must at all times embody that loving bond between us. I'm now eighty-eight; next October I'll turn eighty-nine.[2] In another year, I'll see ninety. Thereafter, I'll take another step, followed by a shorter one until eventually my days here on earth will come to an end. With death at hand, I'm finally about to meet my mother again. My body and soul will travel to the ends of the world to rejoin her.

My soul will lead the way. With every step I take, my flesh is slowly withering away. I'll soon leave this world behind. How does one dance without a body? Don't be afraid, in the hereafter we can continue to dance as a spirit, as a ghost. A ghost dance is so truly beautiful, so beautiful, in fact, that one completely ignores that it lacks a material form. Even on taking leave of my flesh and bones, I want to continue dancing as a ghost.

. . .

Listen, the moon has risen. So? You might wonder what bearing does the moon have on the way we dance? Sadly, we've fallen out of touch with the moon because our human lives down here on earth have evolved at a different pace to life up there. *Everyday life* and the moon. That voice from the mountain ridge whispers to us, "Look, I've risen." It keeps beaming down into the depths of the valley where smoke rises from the humdrum of our day-to-day lives under that enormous sky. In calling out to us, the moon reminds us that it hasn't gone away. After all, how could the moon and its shadow lose sight of each other; how on earth could they exist apart from one another?

If you take a single pace forward, feeling as though it were spanning a hundred years, then you'll come to know the true meaning of the moon. Even those around will ask, "And how did you manage to reach the moon?" You'll be able to roam freely on the moon surface once your steps travel across time and space. Try to dance *free style*, throughout the length and breadth of the universe. Lifelike and breathing.

5.

The Wind

Sweeping

through My

Soul

—

152. Ohno on the
shore of the Dead
Sea, 1983. Ohno is
on the left; Yoshito
Ohno on the far
right. © Nourit
Masson-Sekine.

. . .

You're smiling. Yes, I see that smile playing across your face. Yet a fierce rage is ablaze behind that mask. Don't count yourself amongst the lucky if you're able to camouflage your inner frenzy. That devious smile concealing your true face is nothing other than the personification of an evil spirit. A demon wouldn't dare to step out onstage with a sinister air. No, you can be sure it appears at all times smiling deviously, revealing a form of beauty seldom, if ever, seen. Embodying diametrically opposing qualities, its countenance is as sweet as its ego is tough as steel. While a demon would never dare expose its scars or scabs, you can be sure that its insides are completely disfigured. If it developed a boil, you would never see a trace of that on its polished skin, though all the while its insides are utterly rank, and festering with pus and excretion. Even if wounded and covered in scabs, a demon would never allow such impurities to blemish its appearance. We, as dancers, need to bear this in mind.

. . .

Your every movement, regardless of how small, carries huge consequences.

No matter how fiercely the wind roars, remain calm.

. . .

Don't we presume that heaven and hell actually exist? Isn't heaven supposed to be located somewhere "way up there on high," and hell "far below"? In my travels through life, I've stumbled upon different domains: the worlds of the dead, heaven, limbo, and so forth. After reading a lot about heaven and hell, I've come to the conclusion that what's been written on the subject is nothing less than an accurate description of our everyday reality.

Haven't we all had divine or hellish experiences at some point or other? Granted, since I have neither seen nor experienced

5.

The Wind

Sweeping

through My

Soul

———

heaven or hell at first hand, I'm not in a position to say what, or where they are. But let me tell you one thing, when it comes to my own mind, I've come to know of one living hell.

. . .

Put your heart and soul into it. "I'm being spontaneous," you say. But it strikes me that you've figured out everything out beforehand. While you might think that it's mere child's play to spontaneously make up things as you go along, don't fool yourself, for such a sham is a far cry from the real thing.

. . .

Some time ago when breaking up the ground to make a tennis court with my students,[3] I accidentally happened to fall off my feet as I went to strike the ground with a pickaxe. It felt exactly as though a judo master had floored me. Though pretty accomplished in judo myself, I've never been the victim of such a knockout blow. Anyway, I got back on my feet and went to strike the ground again when what should happen—I fell over yet once again, hitting the ground with an almighty thump.

In light of this and other experiences, I've come to believe that such unintended happenings don't only occur but once. What's to prevent them from occurring a hundred or even two hundred times? Whenever you start something, stick with it right through to the end. Chance might visit you just that once, but then again it might come your way countless times. You might even encounter it endlessly—that, too, is a possibility.

. . .

Workshop

Words

_____

Please begin each workshop by telling yourself that dance isn't something remote from your day-to-day lives—let that be your starting point. As you start moving, I can't fend off the impression that you're already wavering and in doubt about where to place your feet, or what to do with your hands. But in your normal daily intercourse, you speak without faltering when you create and conclude relationships with others. Unlike everyday speech, dance has the potential to release us from the chains of language and its specific meanings. And yet, at the same time, it's as volatile as ether. The essential thing in dance is that it haunts and cling to your body in the same way that your lifelong experience has. Does that gesture tell us something about a wound you once suffered? Or is it perhaps a spontaneous outburst of pain surging forth? The human organism rejects poisonous or foreign matter by first attacking and then excreting it in the form of pus. The sufferings of others have, without our ever fully realizing it, been engraved in us. Let me put it this way. We survived only because others died in our place. We owe our existence to the sacrifices made on our behalf. Don't rest on your laurels; it's utter nonsense to believe that you are life's be-all and end-all. Each and every one of us has gradually evolved through the good grace of the dead: yes, each and every one of you, novelists, dancers, whatever you are: you're alive thanks to the sacrifices others made on your behalf.

. . .

Our galaxy isn't the only one in the universe; there are countless other galaxies out there. Within reach, there's even a galaxy among the countless millions that will respond to your yearnings.

Perhaps you now feel that your yearnings will never be fulfilled. Or, then again, you mightn't understand the true nature of what you're longing for in the first place. Trust yourself; your instincts will change your posture accordingly. Dance can embrace your longings.

. . .

Though I can see that you're all trying your utmost, I would like to ask you whether you think there's room for improvement. By its very nature, doesn't perfection suggest imperfection? We have to treat every last detail with painstaking care when deciding how to assemble a piece. Even if the result is far from perfect, the experience nonetheless will indicate what improvements could be made. Don't concern yourself with moving skillfully. Don't abandon hope if a perfect solution isn't found. Failure is a powerful stimulant; it only makes you all the more determined to take be more painstaking. Yes, take greater care. There's no standard approach; find your own way. That lesson not only applies to you, but to me as well.

. . .

I don't mind whether I come across as an enthusiastic beginner, or just as plain inexperienced. Nonetheless, there is something that I do care about and deeply long to change. That is that I can't remain still onstage; I'm always itching to move.

If you grasp where your strengths lie, you'll blossom like an everlasting flower. But if, on the other hand, you stretch beyond your true capacity, or indulge in vanity by trying to perform skillfully, the flower that once sprung forth so naturally will soon wither and fade away.

And, as to what a true beginner is—isn't it somebody who remains as open as on the day he or she started performing? When young, we've all got to thoroughly experience living life to the full. And, even now at my age, I've got to remain watchful that I never loose my initial enthusiasm.

. . .

Nowadays, people no longer refer to it as the avant-garde movement; instead, the word "performance" has become fashionable. The other day I happened to hear Kenji Nakagami lecture on the subject. When he touched upon the current state of the Japanese avant-garde movement, he didn't mince his words on to how intolerable and embarrassing he found it. Not being someone to hold himself back, he launched into a tirade.

Personally, I don't feel that avant-garde and performance artists of our time help us to confront life's basic problems; they have failed to command either our affection or our attention. Aren't we somehow missing the point if we describe a craftsman's technique as simply "skillful"? Skillful? A craftsman won't stop at what he's

doing until he's thoroughly assured that he's given all he's got to give. That is his primary concern. A craftsman, by definition, sets out to tackle the fundamental problems confronting us as human beings.

153. Ohno in the workshop studio. © Teijiro Kamiyama.

. . .

The next time you stand in front of a steel door why don't you try convincing yourself that you could pass through it, rather than simply dismissing the idea as far-fetched. One thing is for sure: those who doubt themselves won't be able to pull it off. Yet if you firmly believe that you'll succeed as you go to put your foot forward, who knows but that you might've already passed clean through that door. I'm convinced that we can overcome our in-built fears. It's force of habit that makes us cling so tenaciously to our self-doubts. Obviously, if considered from a conventional viewpoint, how could anybody conceivably pass through a steel-faced door? You'll never escape the prison of the self if you continue looking at life in that way. Once you feel your mind holding your feet back, you should already be on the move.

5.

The Wind

Sweeping

through My

Soul

. . .

At some time or other we've all been through the mill. We're constantly undergoing trials and tribulations; we've known the pleasures and pains of life, the hardships, joys and sorrows. I see somebody clutching onto to their problems, making their way over there. Your body language is crying out: "Look, look at the problems I've to cope with, see how I'm suffering." There's no point resorting to such a caricature of yourself ; your movements and gestures don't need to be ostentatious to elicit our sympathy. Why not walk naturally, without pretense, employing simple movements that don't force your feelings upon us. Let us infer for ourselves the hardships you're going through.

Let's begin with simple movements, like this. Look, there's a wolf. You didn't loose your nerve—even though that wolf unexpectedly pounced upon you. Listen, a moneylender is hammering on the door. Times are hard and you're constantly being caught off your guard. Ahhh, there he is again, that moneylender. But, you don't need to run and hide when he turns up at your doorstep. Don't panic and run away when confronted with your problems. Just move ever so gently. Take an insect as a model—think of how delicately it moves. Beginning with its entrails, its entire body then begins to move. Every last nerve, every last muscle, every limb moves. Watch out! There's that wolf! Remember how an insect responds. Move ever so gently.

. . .

Take your time; your each and every instant has got to convey us a true-to-life image. Let all those distinctive moments merge so as to create a unique world. Whether you're sliding the sole of your foot along the floor, stretching your back into space, standing still or whatever, you and your body have got to come across as one. Slowly, gently does it. And let that world you create penetrate our souls.

Endnotes

Chapter 1 What Do You Mean When You Say, "I Understand"? pp. 189–218

1. *Nonsensical:* Ohno frequently uses the term *detarame* when asking the participants to let go of rational control. Literally, it means nonsense, or an irresponsible action. At times, it even carries a pejorative connotation of rubbish or gibberish.

2. *Ten:* Ohno uses the English word "ten" here. Though not a fluent English speaker, Kazuo frequently sprinkles his talks with foreign words to help the many overseas participants attending the workshops. The words printed in italics are those he spoke in English, unless otherwise indicated.

3. The kanji, or Chinese characters, for butoh 舞踏 is comprised of *mau* 舞 (denoting a refined dance with the hands), and *fumu* 踏 (signifying a pounding of the feet.) The original form of the character *mau* was *mu* 無. Nowadays, this character means "nothing," but it originally signified a ritual dance performed in a costume with decorated sleeves. Its meaning later changed when the particle indicating the shape of the legs and feet in motion was added to form the character *mau* as it is employed today. The second kanji, 踏 (*fumu*), also has magical connotations. Composed of the pictorial elements for a foot, 足 and water 水 placed above an instrument 日 used in rituals, it signifies the pouring of water on a ritualistic instrument to reduce its power. Pounding the feet also played an important part in these ritual dances.

4. Ohno here loosely quotes Anzai Fuyue's poem "Spring," taken from the anthology *Gunkan Mari* (The Battleship *Mari*). Here, the butterfly represents the harbinger of spring.

5. Ohno uses the Japanese word (*matsuri*) meaning festival, or celebration. Basically, a *matsuri* is a symbolic act whereby the participants enter a state of communion with the gods. In a social context, it is also an occasion in which the strictures of daily live are somewhat relaxed. Though not specifically mentioned, the Rimbaud poem to which Ohno refers is "Festin."

Jadis si je me souviens bien,
Ma vie était un festin où s'ouvraient tous les cœurs,
où tous les vins coulaient.
(Once, if I remember rightly,
my life was a feast at which all hearts opened
and all wines flowed.)

6. Ohno uses the term *meifu* in speaking of the afterlife. In Buddhist scripture, *meifu* designates the location where the souls of the departed go to repose in the afterlife.

7. *Yūgen*: The word broadly designates an ambiance of mystery, darkness, depth, elegance, transience, and melancholy. Literally, it means an object too deep to comprehend. In a Buddhist context, it refers to the ultimate truth that cannot be grasped through the intellect. *Yūgen* later developed into a poetic principle, and became one of the principal tenets in the noh aesthetic.

Chapter 2 Please Just Do It; There's Nothing I Can Teach You, pp. 219–40

1. This is one of those rare occasions in which Kazuo Ohno emphasizes the physical aspect of dance. He is speaking in the context of his Ausdruckstanz training. Before the outbreak of the World War II, Ohno took lessons in German expressionist dance under Misako Miya, who had been a student of Mary Wigman. Initially regarded as both inelegant and lacking the grace of classical ballet, this dance form pioneered the idea of completely unhinging the different body parts.

2. *Bye-bye:* This term, borrowed from English, is a common way of saying good-bye in Japanese.

3. Ohno very loosely quotes Zeami (also known as Motokiyo Kanze), the noh dramatist, whose genius brought the noh theater to the level of great art in the fourteenth century. Zeami's view of the world, whereby the ultimate reality is entirely composed of one substance, resembles that of the followers of monism. He wrote several outstanding critical studies, notably the *Kadensho,* which to this day is still considered the final authority on the subject. He writes of the necessity to make separate things into one. A noh player's craft had to unite music and movement, even though they were two different phenomena. Zeami speaks of making two hearts into one. The aesthetic principles central to his critical writings are *hana* (flower), a quality that distinguishes the fine player, and *yūgen*, which distinguishes a good performance.

Workshop

Words

———

4. *Chōjūgiga* (Scrolls of Frolicking Humans and Animals): Dating from the Heian (794–1185) and Kamakura (1185–1333) periods, these satirical scrolls consist of animals burlesquing the activities of monks and laymen.
5. *Kasakurū mai, a dance performed under a halo of madness:* Ohno borrows this expression from the poet Minoru Yoshioka.
6. Odilon Redon (1840–1916): French lithographer and painter, who is considered a precursor of the surrealists. Through his work, he strove to give graphic form to his emotions and dreams.
7. *Irrational world:* Ohno uses the phrase *kyōki no sekai,* which means "a world of madness."
8. *That baby screaming:* Ohno is alluding to the birth of his great-grandchild.
9. Ohno was still employed as physical education teacher at the Soshin Girls Baptist High School at the time this workshop took place. He retired in 1980.

Chapter 3 9 September 1989, pp. 241–58

1. William Blake (1758–1827): English poet, painter, and engraver. He created a unique form of illustrated verse largely inspired by mystical visions. Ohno here refers to *The Marriage of Heaven and Hell,* written around 1793, whose central theme was "without contraries is no progression."
2. Kumagusu Minakata (1867–1941): Biologist, ethnologist, and folklorist. An independent scholar, he spent fifteen years in America and Europe. His studies encompassed both the humanities and natural sciences.
3. Here, Ohno refers to one of the eight volumes of *Heavenly Secrets: Arcana Coelestia* (1749–56), in which Swedenborg advocated a theological system founded on an allegorical interpretation of the scriptures.
4. Ohno was invited to perform by the Dresden Contemporary Music Festival in 1988. He also gave a lecture demonstration at the former Mary Wigman school.
5. Ohno alludes to the polemic concerning Yukio Mishima's ritual suicide. In 1970 Mishima committed seppuku by first ripping open his abdomen and then being beheaded by an assistant, at the Defense Ministry headquarters in Tokyo. In some quarters his death was seen as his ultimate protest against the Westernization and weakening of Japan. Extreme

right-wing factions subsequently took up his cause, provoking a lot of virulent debate in the wake of his suicide.

6. Naoe Inui (1901–58): During his long illness Inui composed *Kaigansen* (The Coastal Track) and *Rokkotso to Chō* (Ribs and Butterflies). A personal friend of Ohno's.

7. Ohno visited the Dead Sea during the 1983 Israel tour.

8. Yasuo Irisawa (1931–): Japanese poet known for his anthology *Shishatachi no muragaru fūkei* (Haunted Lands). He has also translated Gerard de Nerval's writings into Japanese.

9. Ohno refers to the American poet Allen Ginsberg (1926–97). Ohno confuses Ginsberg's mother for his wife.

10. *Kaddish and Other Poems* (Unwin and Allen 1957). Ginsberg dedicated this poem to his mother, Naomi Ginsberg, on her death. The opening lines of "Kaddish" read: "Strange now to think of you, gone without corsets&eyes, while I walk on the sunny pavement of Greenwich Village." The medieval association of the Kaddish with mourners is based on a folk belief that this prayer for the deceased is efficacious in releasing the souls of the dead from Purgatory.

11. Tatami: Traditional Japanese thick-woven straw mat, measuring approximately 200 by 75 centimeters. The term is also widely used to determine the dimensions of an interior space.

12. The musician who accompanied him was the avant-garde jazz saxophonist Kazutoki Umezu.

Chapter 4 Don't Reveal Your Love, pp. 259–84

1. "Now when Jesus was risen early the first day of the week, he appeared first to Mary Magdalene, out of whom he had cast seven devils" (Mark 16:9).

2. Traditionally, it was customary in a Japanese household for each person to have a pair of *hashi* (chopsticks) reserved for his or her exclusive use.

3. Ohno uses the colloquial Japanese phrase *itte mairimasu*. Customarily, people use this form of farewell on leaving their homes to go outdoors. Literally, it means "I'll go and come back."

4. Ohno refers to his comeback performance on 1 November 1977, when the première of *Admiring La Argentina* was staged in Tokyo.

5. Ohno visited Tierra del Fuego during his South American tour in 1986.

Workshop

Words

6. Marc Chagall (1887–1985): Russian-born painter and designer. His works combine recollections of his childhood in the Jewish community with folklore and fantasy.

7. Ohno had read a press article about Gloria Swanson at this time.

8. Ohno refers to a dream he had while in New York, in which La Argentina's face appeared above the Manhattan skyline, inviting him to dance with her.

9. While Ohno is not specifically referring to his individual circumstances, he does, in fact, live with four generations of his family. His own parents migrated from northern Japan to come and live with him in the postwar years.

Chapter 5 The Wind Sweeping through My Soul, pp. 285–302

1. Ohno here refers to his experience on watching a video recording of his performance in *Bird*. It was apparently filmed during the première of *Admiring La Argentina* in Tokyo, 1977.

2. This workshop took place in 1994 or 1995.

3. Ohno refers to the time he was a physical education teacher at the Soshin Baptist Girls High School in Yokohama.

1906 Born in Hakodate, Hokkaido, Japan on 27 October, the eldest
boy and second child in a family of ten children.

1925 Graduated from Ohdate High School, Akita prefecture.
Taught for one year at Izumizawa Elementary School,
Hakodate, Hokkaido.

1926 Entered the Japan Athletic College (Nihon Taiku Daigaku) in
Tokyo where he studied Denmark and Rudolf Bode corporal
expression exercises.

1929 Saw the Spanish dancer, La Argentina (Antonia Mercé), at the
Imperial Theatre, Tokyo.
Graduated from the Japan Athletic College.
Began his teaching career as a physical education instructor
at the Kantō Gakuin, a private Christian high school in
Yokohama.

1930 Baptised a Christian. His conversion was encouraged by
Tasuke Sakata, the Kantō Gakuin principal.

1933 Married Chie Nakagawa.
Attended the Baku Ishii Dance school for one year.

1934 Saw Mary Wigman's student, Harold Kreutzberg, perform.
Took up a teaching post at the Soshin Baptist Girls' High
School in Yokohama.

1936 Started dance lessons under Takaya Eguchi and Misako Miya,
both of whom had studied Ausdruckstanz at the Mary Wigman
Institute in Dresden, Germany.

1938 His second son, Yoshito, born in July.
Called up for military service in August.

Drafted as a second lieutenant and spent the following nine years in active service in western China and New Guinea. Rising to the rank of captain, he was eventually to take charge of provisions.

1945 Spent a year in detention in Menakawari, New Guinea.

1946 Discharged from the military on his return to Japan.
Resumed dance classes and becomes a substitute teacher at the Eguchi Dance School.
Reinstated as a physical education teacher at the Soshin High School, Yokohama.

1949 Participated in Mitsuko Andō's group performance *Ennui for the City.*
November: Debut solo and group dance recital in Kanda, Tokyo. The program included *The Devil's Cry, Tango, First Flower of the Linden Tree, Statue of Ernst Family, Good Morning,* and *Praying Mantis.*

1950 Second recital, Kanda, Tokyo. The program included *Spring Offering, Festival, Beyond the Field, Harp of Zion, The Tropics,* and *The Lotus Wandering Child.*

1951 Third recital, Kanda, Tokyo. The program included *Fate Seller, The Honeybee's Song, Tango, Downtown Rain,* and *Spring Tide.*

1953 Fourth recital, Dai-ichi Seimei Hall, Tokyo. The program included *Fruit from Heaven, Unfinished Thoughts,* and *Fox and Stone Figure.*
Appeared on a NHK (Japanese Public Broadcasting) television program in which he performed *Dansō* (Random Thoughts).

1954 Participated in *Crow,* a Mitsuko Andō group recital.
Ohno made acquaintance with Tatsumi Hijikata at the Andō Dance Institute.

1956 Participated in *Ballet Pantomime,* along with Tatsumi Hijikata and Mamako Yoneyama at the Haiya-za Theatre, Roppongi, Tokyo.

1959 April: Fifth recital, Dai-ichi Seimei Hall, Tokyo. Performed *The Old Man and the Sea,* featuring Yoshito Ohno in an adaptation of Ernest Hemingway's novel. The program also included *Shoes, Dove, Oh Kind God,* and *A Hat.*
May: At the Japanese Art Dance Association, Tatsumi Hijikata

presented *Kinjiki* (Forbidden Colours), featuring Yoshito Ohno in the role of a young boy.

1960 July: Participated in the first Tatsumi Hijikata "Dance Experience" at the Dai-ichi Seimei Hall, Tokyo. Ohno performed a solo *Divinariane* and also participated in *Disposal Place*, an adaptation of Lautréamont's *The Songs of Maldoror*.

1961 September: Participated in the second Tatsumi Hijikata Dance Experience at the Dai-ichi Seimei Hall, Yurakucho, Tokyo: *Secret Ceremony of a Hermaphrodite in the Early Afternoon* and *Sugar Candy*.

1963 November: Participated in Tatsumi's Hijikata "Dance Experience" *Masseur: A Story That Supports Passion*.

1965 November: Participated in *A Rose-Colored Dance: A la Maison de M. Civeçawa*, directed and choreographed by Hijikata; also featuring Yoshito Ohno, Mitsutaka Ishii, Kōichi Tamano, and Akira Kasai. Natsuyuki Nakanishi, the painter, and Tadanori Yoko, the graphic artist, also collaborated on this performance.

1966 July: Participated in the final performance of the Hijikata's Ankoku butoh-ha group at Tokyo's Kinokuniya Hall, *Instructional Illustrations for the Study of Divine Favour in Sexual Love: Tomato*.

1967 Guest appearance in Tomiko Takai's dance recital *Keijijô-gaku* (Metaphysical Emotion), based on the poet Ikuya Kato's collection of the same title. Directed and choreographed by Hijikata, it also featured Yoshito Ohno, Kōichi Tamano, and Akira Kasai, with artwork by Akira Shimizu.
Performed in *House of Artaud* with Yoshito Ohno.
Guest appearance in Mitsutaka Ishii's performance *Butoh Genet* at the Dai-ichi Seimei Hall, Tokyo.

1968 Guest appearance in Mitsutaka Ishii *O-Genet Shō* at Tokyo's Ginza Gas Hall.
Guest appearance in Tomiko Takai's second recital *Mandala Mansion* inspired by Ikuya Kato's poetry at the Dai-ichi Seimei Hall, Tokyo.

1969 Collaborated with the film director Chiaki Nagano in the making of *Portrait of Mr O*.

1971 Featured in Nagano's second film, *Mandala of Mr O*

1973 Featured in Nagano's third film of the trilogy, *Mr O's Book of the Dead*

1975 Guest appearance in Yasuhiko Takeuchi's dance recital *Song of Narcissus* at the Shinjuku Kosei Nenkin Hall, Tokyo.

1977 November: Stage comeback. Première of *Admiring La Argentina*, directed by Tatsumi Hijikata at the Dai-ichi Sei Mei Hall.
Received the Dance Critics' Circle Award for *Admiring La Argentina*

1980 May: first ever overseas appearance when he presented *Admiring La Argentina* and *Ozen* at the fourteenth Nancy International Theatre Festival.
Gave lecture demonstration at the Montreal's 'Symposium 80' at the University of Quebec.

1981 January: Première of *My Mother* in Tokyo, directed by Hijikata.
July: Lecture demonstration at the University of Caracas, Venezuela.

1983 March: Visited the Dead Sea during his performance tour to Israel.

1985 July: Première of *The Dead Sea* at the Tokyo Butoh Festival, directed by Hijikata.

1986 Tatsumi Hijikata died 21 January of liver cancer, at the age of fifty-seven.

1987 June: Première of *Water Lilies,* a duo with Yoshito Ohno, at the Staatstheater, Stuttgart.
August: Performed *Water Lilies* at the Butoh Dance Festival at Tokyo's Ginza Saison Theatre as a tribute to Hijikata.

1988 October: Participated in the Dresden Contemporary Music Festival.
Gave a lecture demonstration at Mary Wigman's old school.

1989 November: Gave a workshop in West Berlin.
Visited Cremona, home of Antonio Stradivari, the violinmaker. This visit inspired him to create a piece that was later performed at the Municipal Theater in Cremona in 1990.
Kazuo Ohno's first book, *The Palace Soars through the Sky: Kazuo Ohno on Butoh* published by Shichosha, Tokyo.

1990 May: Première of *Flowers-Birds-Wind-Moon* in Cremona.
November: Workshop at the Isle de Danse Festival in Paris.

1991 Appeared in Katsumi Hirano's film *The Scene of the Soul.*

1992 Second book, *Dessin*, published by Ryokugeisha, Kushiro.
November: Première of *A White Lotus Bloom, Oguri Hangan,*
and *Terute Hime.* Also featured Yoshito Ohno, Tsuchitori (per-
cussionist), and the singer Harue Momoyama.

1993 March: Appeared in *Kurozuka,* based on a noh play, on the
NHK (Japanese Public Broadcasting) TV program *Music
Fantasy.*
November: Received a cultural award from the Kanagawa
prefecture.

1995 Featured in the fourteen-minute film *Kazuo Ohno,* by Daniel
Schmid.
October: Participated in the Art Summit in Indonesia, 1995.

1996 Guest appearance in Daniel Schmid's film *The Written Face.*

1997 Third book, *Workshop Words,* published by Film Art Sha and
the Kazuo Ohno Dance Studio.
His wife, Chie, dies in June.

1998 Designated "Messenger of the Year" by the International Dance
Theatre Studio on International Dance Day.
June: Performed *Mu* (Nothingness) with the noh actor Hideo
Kanze in Tokyo.

1999 March: Started presenting a series of intimate recitals at his
workshop studio in Kamihoshikawa.
October: Performs *Celebration* at the Teatro Goldini, Venice, on
the occasion of his receiving the Antonioni award.

2001 The Kazuo Ohno Dance Studio in partnership with NHK
coproduced the DVD *Beauty and Strength.*

2002 Completion of dance documentary DVD *Oh, Kind God,*
directed by Gianni Di Capua.
Received Asahi Performing Arts Award.
The Kazuo Ohno Archives opened at Bologna University.

1949 November	Kanda Kyoritsu Kodo hall, Tokyo	Ohno's first modern dance recital
1950 October	Kanda Kyoritsu Kodo hall, Tokyo	Ohno's second modern dance recital
1951 November	Kanda Kyoritsu Kodo hall, Tokyo	Ohno's third modern dance recital
1953 November	Dai-ichi Seimei Hall, Tokyo	Ohno's fourth modern dance recital
1959 April	Dai-ichi Seimei Hall, Tokyo	Ohno's fifth modern dance recital
1960 July	Dai-ichi Seimei Hall, Tokyo	*Divinariane* solo in first recital of Tatsumi Hijikata's "Dance Experience"
1961 June	Sōgetsu Hall, Tokyo	In *A Rose to Emily*, Akiko Motofuji dance recital.
1961 September	Dai-ichi Seimei Hall, Tokyo	In performance of Tatsumi Hijikata's *Secret Ceremony of a Hermaphrodite in the Early Afternoon*
1962 June	Asbestos-kan, Meguro, Tokyo	In performance of Tatsumi Hijikata's *Three Phases of Leda*
1965 November	Sennichidani Kokaido, Tokyo	In performance with Hijikata in *A Rose-Colored Dance: A la Maison de Monsieur Civeçawa*
1966 March	Sōgetsu Hall, Tokyo	*Room,* with Yoshito Ohno

1966 July	Kinokuniya Hall, Tokyo	In performance of Hijikata's *Instructional Illustrations for the Study of Divine Favour in Sexual Love: Tomato*
1967 April	Sōgetsu Hall, Tokyo	*House of Artaud* featuring Hijikata
1967 July	Kinokuniya Hall, Tokyo	Guest appearance in Tomiko Takai's *Metaphysical Emotion*
1967 August	Ginza Gas Hall, Tokyo	Guest appearance in Mitsutaka Ishii's *Butoh Genet*
1969 September	Shinjuku Kosei Nenkin Hall, Tokyo	Screening: *Portrait of Mr O*
1971 June	Meguro Meijinkai Gekijo, Tokyo	Screening: *Mandala of Mr O*
1976 May	Yasuda Seimei Hall, Tokyo	Screening: *Mr O's Book of the Dead*
1977 November.	Dai-ichi Seimei Hall, Tokyo	*Admiring La Argentina* (première)
1979 February	Yubin Chokin Hall, Tokyo	*A Canoe Passes under the Cherry Blossoms*
1980 March	Sound House City, Seibu Ikebukuro, Tokyo	*Poetry, Butoh, and Jazz*
1980 May	Salle Poirel, Nancy, France	*Admiring La Argentina Ozen*
1980 May	Église Saint Fiacre, Nancy	*An Invitation to Jesus*
1980 May	The Place Theatre, London	*Admiring La Argentina Ozen*
1980 June	Église Saint Jacques Du Haut Pas, Paris	*An Invitation to Jesus*
1980 June	Des Quatre Temps, La Défence, Paris	*Admiring La Argentina Ozen*
1980 June	Kulturfuset-Horsalem, Stockholm	*Admiring La Argentina Ozen*
1981 January	Dai-ichi Seimei Hall, Tokyo	*My Mother* (première)

1981 July	Teatro Cantv, Caracas	*Admiring La Argentina*
1981 July	La Mama ETC, New York	*Admiring La Argentina* *My Mother*
1982 May	Grosses Zelt, Munich	*Admiring La Argentina* *My Mother*
1982 June	Grammont, Montpellier	*Admiring La Argentina*
1982 June	Théâtre de la Comédie, Geneva	*Admiring La Argentina*
1982 June	Saltlageret, Copenhagen	*Admiring La Argentina* *My Mother*
1982 June	Casa de la Caritat, Barcelona	*Admiring La Argentina* *My Mother*
1982 July	Eglise des Célestins, Avignon	*Admiring La Argentina* *My Mother*
1983 February	Teatro del Elfo, Milan	*Admiring La Argentina* *My Mother*
1983 March	Kh'an Theatre, Jerusalem	*Admiring La Argentina*
1983 May	Kushiro, Hokkaido	*Universal Restaurant*
1984 April	Studio 200, Ikebukuro, Tokyo	*A Journey to Mr. Kazuo Ohno's World*
1985 February	Asahi Hall, Tokyo	*Admiring La Argentina* *The Dead Sea* (première)
1985 August	La Chiesa di Santa Maria delle Grazie, Rimini	*The Dead Sea* *Admiring La Argentina*
1985 August	Teatro Zandonai, Rovereto	*Admiring La Argentina*
1985 August	Cologne Academy of Music Auditorium	*Admiring La Argentina*
1985 November	Joyce Theater, New York	*The Dead Sea* *Admiring La Argentina*
1986 March	The Arts Theater, Adelaide	*The Dead Sea* *Admiring La Argentina*
1986 April	Teatro do SESC Anchietta, Sao Paolo	*The Dead Sea* *Admiring La Argentina*
1986 April	Teatro Municipal General San Martin,	*The Dead Sea* *Admiring La Argentina*

Buenos Aires

1986 June	Ordway Studio Theater, Minneapolis	*The Dead Sea* *Admiring La Argentina*
1986 June	New England Life Hall, Boston	*The Dead Sea* *Admiring La Argentina*
1986 September	Théâtre de la Ville, Paris	*Admiring La Argentina*
1986 September	The Place Theatre, London	*The Dead Sea*
1986 September	Théâtre des Célestins, Lyons	*The Dead Sea* *Admiring La Argentina*
1986 September	Théâtre de la Bastille, Paris	*The Dead Sea* *Admiring La Argentina*
1986 October	Théâtre 140, Brussels	*The Dead Sea* *Admiring La Argentina*
1986 October	Maison de la Culture, Grenoble	*The Dead Sea* *Admiring La Argentina*
1986 October	Laboratorio Teatrale, Universitario Eduardo de Filippo, Rome	*The Dead Sea*
1986 December	Shimin Kokaido, Fukushima	*The Dead Sea* *Admiring La Argentina*
1987 March	Centro Cultural de la Villa de Madrid	*The Dead Sea* *Admiring La Argentina*
1987 April	El Pa-ku, Sendai	*Admiring La Argentina* *My Mother*
1987 June	Theater an der Wien, Vienna	*The Dead Sea*
1987 June	Staatstheater, Stuttgart	*Water Lilies* (première)
1987 June	Staatsschauburg, Bremen	*Admiring La Argentina*
1987 July	Okura village, Yamagata prefecture	*Mushi-biraki*
1987 August	Ginza Saison Theatre, Tokyo	*Water Lilies*
1988 June	Asia Society, New York	*Water Lilies*
1988 August	Studio 200, Ikebekuro, Tokyo	*Mushi-biraki*

1988 October	Staatsschauspiel, Dresden	*Admiring La Argentina*
1988 November	Outdoor performance Ushimado, Okayama	*The Dead Sea*
1989 September	Théâtre Maisonneuve de la Place des Arts, Montreal	*Admiring La Argentina*
1989 October	Tornaterem, Budapest	*The Dead Sea*
1989 October	Teatro Juarez, Guanajuato, Mexico	*The Dead Sea* *Water Lilies*
1989 November	Spazio Zero, Rome	*Water Lilies*
1989 November	Akademie der Künste, Berlin	*The Dead Sea* *Water Lilies* *Admiring La Argentina*
1990 January	AI Hall, Itami, Hyogo	*The Dead Sea* *Admiring La Argentina*
1990 February	Nanatsu Dera Kyodo Studio, Nagoya	*Mushi-biraki*
1990 May	Teatro Ponchielli, Cremona	*Water Lilies* *Flowers-Birds-Wind-Moon*
1990 May	Teatro di Rifredi, Florence	*Water Lilies* *Flowers-Birds-Wind-Moon*
1990 August	Seibu Akarenga Studio, Sapporo, Hokkaido	*The Dead Sea* *Water Lilies*
1990 August	Tsurui Psychiatric Hospital Garden	*A Crane Coming down the Stairs*
1990 September	Premiere Dance Theater, Toronto	*Water Lilies*
1990 October	Junges Theatre, Göttingen	*Water Lilies* *Flowers-Birds-Wind-Moon*
1990 November	Théâtre du Lierre, Paris	*Water Lilies* *Flowers-Birds-Wind-Moon* *Admiring La Argentina*
1990 November	Divadlo Disk, Prague	*Water Lilies* *Flowers-Birds-Wind-Moon*
1991 August	Ginza Saison Theatre, Tokyo	*Flowers-Birds-Wind-Moon*
1991 August	Savoy Theater, Helsinki	*Admiring La Argentina* *Water Lilies*

Chronology of Public Performances

1991 September	Outdoor performance at the Ishikari River, Hokkaido	*Hooked-Nose Salmon of Ishikari*
1991 September	Chofuku Temple Precincts, Nanao	*The Dead Sea*
1992 January	Schauspielhaus, Wuppertal	*Admiring La Argentina*
1992 February	Terpsichore, Tokyo	*Dream of 10 Nights*
1992 March	Tokyo FM Hall	*White Lotus Bloom*
1992 April	Akademie der Künste, Berlin	*Flowers-Birds-Wind-Moon*
1992 June	Cine Teatro Universitario, Ouro Verde, Londrina	*Flowers-Birds-Wind-Moon Water Lilies*
1992 August	Astor Plaza Hall, Hiroshima	*Water Lilies*
1992 November	Cultural Hall, Ogaki	*Oguri Hangan and Terute Hime* (première)
1993 February	HKAPA Drama Theatre, Hong Kong	*Admiring La Argentina Water Lilies*
1993 April	Yokohama Red Brick Warehouse	*The Palace Soars through the Sky*
1993 August	Tokyo Cultural Hall	*Strength of the Ageing*
1993 August	Ohdate Cultural Hall	*White Lotus in Bloom*
1993 August	Akita Cultural Hall	*The Dead Sea*
1993 August	The Post, Seoul	*Admiring La Argentina Water Lilies*
1993 October	Japan-America Theater, Los Angeles	*Admiring La Argentina*
1993 October	Moore Theater, Seattle	*Water Lilies*
1993 October	Chamizal National Memorial Theater, El Paso, Texas	*Water Lilies*
1993 November	Japan Society, New York	*Flowers-Birds-Wind-Moon*
1993 December	Shonandai Cultural Center, Fujisawa	*Oguri Hangan and Terute Hime*

1994 April	Teatro Fonte, Yokohama	First retrospective of Kazuo Ohno's works: *Water Lilies*
1994 May	Jubilee Hall, Singapore	*The Dead Sea* *Water Lilies*
1994 June	National Arts Institute, Taipei	*The Dead Sea* *Water Lilies*
1994 July	Centro Cultural de Belem, Lisbon	*Flowers-Birds-Wind-Moon* *Water Lilies*
1994 July	Jardins du Palais Royal, Paris	*Water Lilies*
1994 July	Cloître des Célestins, Avignon	*Flowers-Birds-Wind-Moon* *Water Lilies*
1994 September	Teatro Fonte, Yokohama	Second retrospective: *Admiring La Argentina*
1994 October	Theatre Dramatyczny, Warsaw	*Water Lilies*
1994 December	International Forum, Akasaka, Tokyo	*Oguri Hangan and Terute Hime*
1995 February	Teatro Fonte, Yokohama	Third retrospective: *The Dead Sea*
1995 May	Prefectural Museum Hall, Kōchi, Shikoku	*Water Lilies*
1995 October	Padangpanjang, West Sumatra	*The Road in Heaven, the Road on Earth*
1995 October	Gedung Kesenian, Jakarta	*Water Lilies*
1995 October	Chōnenji Temple, Hyogo	*Dance with Crazy Halo*
1995 November	Teatro Fonte, Yokohama	Fourth retrospective: *My Mother*
1996 February	The Japan Society, New York	*My Mother*
1996 March	Torii Hall, Osaka	*The Road in Heaven, the Road on Earth*
1996 May	Teatro Fonte, Yokohama	Fifth retrospective: *Flowers-Birds-Wind-Moon*
1996 May	Joseph Lavergne Auditorium, Quebec	*Water Lilies* *Flowers-Birds-Wind-Moon*

Chronology of Public Performances

1996 September	Theatre X, Tokyo	*At the Entrance to a Firework's Home*
1996 October	Kanagawa Kenmin Hall, Yokohama	*Kazuo Ohno's Butoh World: Excerpts from Divinarianes*
1996 November	Manabotto Nusamai-dai Hall, Kushiro	*My Mother*
1997 March	Teatro Communale di Ferrara, Ferrara	*The Road in Heaven, the Road on Earth*
1997 May	Teatro SESC Anchietta, Sao Paolo	*The Road in Heaven, the Road on Earth* *Water Lilies*
1997 October	Kanamori Hall, Hakodate	*Water Lilies*
1997 November	Teatro Fonte, Yokohama	Sixth retrospective: *The Road in Heaven, the Road on Earth*
1998 March	Event Hall, Miyazaki	*The Road in Heaven, the Road on Earth*
1998 April	Chiba City Museum Hall	*Kazuo Ohno: Dance with Shohaku*
1998 June	Cocoon Theatre, Tokyo	*Mu* (Nothingness)
1998 November	Setagaya Public Theatre, Tokyo	*The Road in Heaven, the Road on Earth* *An evening with Kazuo Ohno*
1999 March	Kamihoshikawa workshop studio	*An Evening with Kazuo Ohno*
1999 April	Keio University Campus Hall, Yokohama	*Kazuo Ohno's Universe at 92*
1999 May	Kamihoshikawa workshop studio	*An Evening with Kazuo Ohno*
1999 May	Hasedera temple, Nagano	*Kazuo Ohno at the Hasedera Temple at 92*
1999 June	Kamihoshikawa workshop studio	*An Evening with Kazuo Ohno*
1999 June	Outdoor performance, Juksan, Korea	*Requiem for the 20th Century*
1999 October	Teatro Goldoni, Venice	*Celebration*
1999 December	Japan Society, New York	*Requiem for the 20th Century*

2000 February	Kamihoshikawa workshop studio	*An Evening with Kazuo Ohno*
2000 June	Teatro Fonte, Yokohama	*Flower of the Universe*
2000 October	Rene Kodaira, Tokyo	*Flower of the Universe*
2001 February	Kamihoshikawa workshop studio	*An Evening with Kazuo Ohno*
2001 March	Kamihoshikawa workshop studio	*An Evening with Kazuo Ohno*
2001 April	Kamihoshikawa workshop studio	*An Evening with Kazuo Ohno*
2001 May	Kamihoshikawa workshop studio	*An Evening with Kazuo Ohno*
2001 June	Kamihoshikawa workshop-studio,	*An Evening with Kazuo Ohno*
2001 July	Kamihoshikawa workshop studio	*An Evening with Kazuo Ohno*
2001 October	Park Tower Hall, Tokyo	*Hana*
2002 May	Tsumari, Niigata	*Hana-gurui,* performance with the ikebana artist Yukio Nakagawa
2002 June	Kushiro, Hokkaido	*An Evening with Kazuo Ohno*
2002 September	Theatre X, Tokyo	*Life: Form and Soul*
2002 November	Isamu Noguchi Room, Keio University, Tokyo	Performance
2003 February	Kinmori Hall, Ohdate	*Our Mothers' Songs*
2003 April	Yokohama Red Brick Warehouse	Performance and screening of *The Palace Soars through the Sky*
2003 August	Aichi Geijutsu Bunka Center, Nagoya	Performance and screening of videos from the Ohno Studio Archives
2003 September	Yôrô, Gifu prefecture	Open-air performance of *Death's Connection*
2003 October	Tarô Okumoto Museum, Kawasaki	Performance in honor of Tatsumi Hijikata
2003 November	Kiryu, Gunma prefecture	Duet with Yoshito Ohno *An Important Person*

About the Authors

Kazuo Ohno was born in Hokkaido, Japan's most northerly island, in 1906. On graduating from the Japan Athletic College he began studying contemporary dance in Tokyo during the mid-1930s. His first public dance recital took place in Tokyo in 1949, but it was not until 1980 that he came to the attention of an international audience after his performance of *Admiring La Argentina* at the Nancy International Theatre Festival. With a career spanning almost six decades, Ohno is currently one of the oldest performers— if not the oldest—to grace the stage. In the early 1960s he started giving workshops in the studio he constructed at the rear of his home in the suburbs of Yokohama. Ohno's fame is not solely due to his charismatic stage performances; he has equally inspired many throughout the world with the incisive nature of his workshops. A prolific writer, Ohno's previous Japanese publications include *The Palace Soars through the Sky: Kazuo Ohno on Butoh* (Tokyo: Shichosha, 1990) and *Dessin* (Kushiro: Ryokugeisha, 1992).

Yoshito Ohno was born in Yokohama in 1938. His first stage appearance was in 1959, when he appeared in his father's stage adaptation of Ernest Hemingway's *An Old Man and the Sea*. In the same year he danced in the role of a young boy in Tatsumi Hijikata's controversial adaptation of Yukio Mishima's *Forbidden Colours*. During the 1960s he was a prominent participant in Hijikata's experimental performances and happenings. He retired from public performance in 1968 and was not to reappear onstage until he co-performed with his father in *The Dead Sea* in 1985. Following Hijikata's death in 1986, Yoshito Ohno was to take charge of directing his father's creations, notably *Water Lilies* (1987) and *Flower-Birds-Wind-Moon* (1990). In the mid-1990s, he embarked on a solo career; his most recent performance, *The Last Picture of Dorian Gray*, was inspired by Oscar Wilde's novel. In parallel with his stage career, Yoshito Ohno is an established teacher and regularly gives master classes throughout the world.

Toshio Mizohata was born in Tokyo in 1956. He started attending Kazuo Ohno's workshops in 1983. Later, he was to assume the role of tour manager and lighting artist for the Ohnos on their many international tours during the 1980s and 1990s. A gifted linguist, Mizohata was responsible for founding the Ohno Dance Studio Archives in 1995. With the help of Hiroshi Tsuda, editor at Tokyo's Film Art Sha publishing house, he was the driving force behind the publications of *Workshop Words*, a collection of Kazuo Ohno's aphorisms (Tokyo: Film Art Sha, 1997), and Yoshito Ohno's edited commentaries on his father in *Kazuo Ohno: Food for the Soul* (Tokyo: Film Art Sha, 1999). In cooperation with NHK, the Japanese Public Broadcasting service, he produced the DVD *Kazuo Ohno: Beauty and Strength* (2001). In 2002 he set up Canta management agency. Its first DVD was the critically acclaimed *Oh, Kind God!* (2002). He was also instrumental in setting up the Kazuo Ohno Archives at Bologna University in 2002.

About the Translator

John Barrett was born in Ireland in 1958. He holds a B.A. in mental and moral science from Trinity College, Dublin, where he specialized in aesthetics. As well as being a regular participant in Kazuo Ohno's workshops between 1985 and 1900, he also worked as a sound technician with the Ohnos during their 1989 tour of Japan. He translated the texts by Tatsumi Hijikata and Kazuo Ohno in *Shades of Darkness*, the first significant publication in English on butoh (Tokyo: Shufunomoto, 1985), and excerpts from Ohno's book *The Palace Soars through the Sky* (the excerpts were published in *Ballet International*, 1990). Currently, he works as a freelance translator.